ARCHAEOLOGY
AND THE EARLY CHURCH
IN SOUTHERN GREECE

Elizabeth Rees

OXBOW | books

Oxford & Philadelphia

Published in the United Kingdom in 2020 by
OXBOW BOOKS
The Old Music Hall, 106–108 Cowley Road, Oxford, OX4 1JE

and in the United States by
OXBOW BOOKS
1950 Lawrence Road, Havertown, PA 19083

Paperback Edition: ISBN 978-1-78925-575-1
Digital Edition: ISBN 978-1-78925-576-8 (epub)

A CIP record for this book is available from the British Library

Library of Congress Control Number: 2020944063

Printed in the United Kingdom by Short Run Press
Text layout by Frabjous Books, UK

For a complete list of Oxbow titles, please contact:

UNITED KINGDOM
Oxbow Books
Telephone (01865) 241249
Email: oxbow@oxbowbooks.com
www.oxbowbooks.com

UNITED STATES OF AMERICA
Oxbow Books
Telephone (610) 853-9131, Fax (610) 853-9146
Email: queries@casemateacademic.com
www.casemateacademic.com/oxbow

Oxbow Books is part of the Casemate Group

Cover photos: Nemea's basilica, baptistery and Christian artefacts
(photographs by Stephen Miller).

CONTENTS

LIST OF COLOUR PLATES

LIST OF FIGURES

PREFACE

In the past, the primary focus of Greek archaeology has been upon its magnificent heritage of pre-Christian sites, with their fine sculptures and temples. However, Greeks were also attending the international congresses of Christian archaeology in the late 1800s; they published articles in Greek about Christian sites, and excavated numerous basilicas in the twentieth century. As soon as systematic excavations began, foreign schools became interested in the archaeology of early Christianity in Greece. The presence of St Paul in various Greek regions was the motivation behind fundraising for the earliest excavations in such locations as Corinth: Oscar Broneer wrote articles about the archaeology of sites associated with St Paul as early as the 1950s.

There is now a shift of interest to later Christian periods among American, British, and European scholars. A generation ago, few classical archaeologists or classical historians trained in Europe, America, or the UK studied late antique archaeology; now this has become a vital field of research. Meanwhile, New Testament scholars have become increasingly interested in archaeology. Situated between Israel and Italy, Greece is now yielding significant evidence of the development of early Christianity.

Mainland Greece with its surrounding islands is a vast region, and I have therefore chosen to examine an area rich in early Christian remains, namely the region stretching from Athens southwards. We shall focus on the material dimensions of Christianity in the north-east Peloponnese, Attica, and central Greece from New Testament times until about the twelfth century, although the majority of sites examined date from the seventh century or earlier. The seventh century saw the start of a break in material evidence (Greece's so-called 'dark ages'), and the ninth century is generally considered to mark the end of the early Byzantine period. We shall take into account contemporary theological research and discoveries made in the course of recent archaeological excavations. Where relevant, we shall consider parallel sites in other parts of the Roman empire.

As the title of this book indicates, I have chosen a dual focus – both 'archaeology' and 'the early Church'. The archaeology can be understood only within the context of the early Church, and therefore there will be frequent references to early texts that enable us to reconstruct the Christian world on which archaeology sheds its own light. Where possible, I examine the texts before the archaeology, so that material details can be placed within a larger framework. Thus Chapter 1 will focus on Phoebe, an outstanding Christian woman who lived in Kenchreai, and will decipher what we can glean about her world from early Christian writings, before we explore the archaeological sites themselves. Using this approach, I draw on the work of scripture scholars and archaeologists in equal measure.

This book could not have been written without Rev. Eve Wiseman who made it possible for me to visit the Peloponnese for many years: she offered me generous hospitality at her villa in Kenchreai, and drove me to the sites that I describe in the book. I am grateful to Professor Guy Sanders, for many years the Director of Excavations at the American School of Classical Studies, Athens, for his generous help and advice. He also kindly gave me access to the American School's extensive library in Ancient Corinth – a unique resource of excavators' reports, journals, books, and monographs – and allowed me to use a number of their excellent plans.

I thank Professor David Pettegrew, Professor of History and Archaeology at Messiah College, Pennsylvania, Cavan Concannon, Professor of Religion at the University of Southern California, Stephen G. Miller, Professor Emeritus of Classical Archaeology at the University of California, Berkeley, and Yannis Lolos, Professor of Archaeology at the University of Thessaly. I also thank Dr Patricia Rumsey, Abbess of the Poor Clare monastery at Arkley, to the north of London, and Canon Loveday Alexander, Emeritus Professor of Biblical Studies at Sheffield University, for their helpful suggestions, which have greatly improved my text. Sr Christine Owen has also read my text and made valuable comments.

I'm grateful to Professor Stephen Miller for his photographs of early Christian Nemea, where he was Director of Excavations for over forty years. The remaining photographs are my own, except where indicated otherwise. I thank my sister, Dr Frances Jones, for scanning and preparing the photographs and I'm grateful to Annette Wells for her painstaking work on many of the plans. Any errors are my own. For information about current excavations and new conclusions, one can visit the American School of Classical Studies in Ancient Corinth, an unpretentious building opposite the entrance to the Archaeological Museum.

Elizabeth Rees, August 2020

FIGURE 1. Map of southern Greece, indicating sites described in the text.

Chapter 1

PHOEBE OF KENCHREAI:
A GENEROUS WOMAN

We shall begin this exploration of early Christian sites in southern Greece by focusing on first-century Kenchreai, the busy eastern port of ancient Corinth, where textual evidence from the mid-first century hints at the evolution of Christianity when it was still a relatively small sect, partly Jewish and partly gentile. Here, a woman named Phoebe was a leader in the early Christian community; she was also a close friend of St Paul. By exploring the language that he uses to describe Phoebe, we can learn more about this remarkable woman and her role in the Church. Later texts explain the meaning of the words that Paul chose to describe her ministry. These authors also shed light upon the unexpected role of women in the Church and in wider society at this time.

A series of excavations, largely around the seashore, tell us a considerable amount about life in first-century Kenchreai, much of which lies beneath the modern village of Kenchries. No evidence of early house churches has been discovered but, as we shall see, early texts suggest that Phoebe was moderately wealthy, and we can to some extent envisage her way of life. Early tombs re-used by Christians in the fourth century, and a sixth-century basilica at Kenchreai, now largely submerged, provide information about the life and worship of Christians in the port during succeeding centuries, when the region became thoroughly Christianised. These later sites will be examined in Chapter 2.

St Paul's relationship with Phoebe is a fascinating one. He speaks of her at the end of his Letter to the Romans, which he wrote when he was living in Corinth, around AD 56/7:

> *I commend to you our sister, Phoebe, who is a deacon* (diákonon) *of the church at Kenchreai, in order that you might receive her in the Lord, as is appropriate to the saints. Help her in whatever she might need, for she has been a patron* (prostátis) *of many, including myself* (Rom. 16. 1–2).[1]

A letter of introduction

Chapter 16 of Paul's Letter to the Romans appears to be a letter of introduction which would enable Phoebe to be welcomed by another Christian community. It is often assumed that this was the community in Rome, but this may not be the case. Internal evidence suggests that Romans 16 may be a short letter written to a different group of Christians, apart from its final doxology, or closing words of praise to God. This doxology may constitute the last paragraph of the entire Letter to the Romans:

> *Glory to him who is able to give you the strength to live according to the Good News I preach ... He alone is wisdom; give glory therefore to him through Jesus Christ for ever and ever. Amen* (Rom. 16. 25–7).

The oldest surviving manuscript of Paul's Letter to the Romans, a papyrus from the early third century, places the great doxology of Romans 16. 25–7 at the end of chapter 15; this suggests that some early Christians believed that Paul's Letter to the Romans ended at this point. Of the later manuscripts, some place the doxology at the end of chapter 14; chapter 15 then becomes an epilogue. Most of the later texts place the doxology at the end of chapter 16, where we find it today.[2]

Scholars have reached differing conclusions about the origin of Romans 16, but this short letter of commendation may have been intended for Phoebe to take with her to the Christians in Ephesus (Fig. 2).[3] It consists of a recommendation of Phoebe (vv. 1–2), followed by greetings to specific families and individuals (vv. 3–16). A short exhortation to stay faithful to the gospel follows (vv. 17–20), and the letter of introduction ends with some final greetings from Paul, from Gaius who was his Corinthian host, from a scribe named Tertius who wrote the letter, and from a few more of Paul's friends in Corinth (vv. 21–3).

Paul's words, 'Greet my dear friend Epaenetus, who was the first convert to Christ in the province of Asia' (v. 5) would make less sense in a Roman context than in an Asian one; such a reference would have little meaning in a letter to Roman Christians.[4] If Phoebe was a businesswoman – a possibility that will be explored later in the chapter – she would be more likely to have traded with cities in Asia Minor, such as Ephesus, than with clients in Rome. Kenchreai was Corinth's point of departure for Asia Minor; we would expect Phoebe to live in

FIGURE 2. Paul gives Phoebe her letter of introduction, before she departs from Kenchreai harbour. Drawing by a modern Greek monk.

Lechaion, Corinth's northern port, if she travelled to and from Rome. Perhaps Phoebe already knew the Christians of Ephesus before Paul entrusted her to them with his letter of commendation. It is important to remember, however, that many scholars find the traditional Roman destination of Phoebe's journey to be equally convincing.[5]

Paul greets his friends

Paul identifies Phoebe as 'our sister' (Rom. 16. 1) to underline that as a disciple of Jesus, she is one of them. Mark recalls Jesus saying 'Whoever does the will of God is my brother, and sister, and mother' (Mk. 3. 35). Even if the Christians of Ephesus met her for the first time when she arrived with her letter of introduction, she was already their sister because she belonged to the Christian family.[6]

The first couple to be greeted are Priscilla and Aquila (vv. 3–5), who appear to have been living in Ephesus at this point, according to the author of the Acts of the Apostles:

> *After staying on [in Corinth] for some time, Paul took leave of the brothers and sailed for Syria [i.e. to Antioch], accompanied by Priscilla and Aquila. At Kenchreai he had his hair cut off, because of a vow he had made. When they reached Ephesus, he left them, but first went alone to the synagogue to debate with the Jews. They asked him to stay longer but he declined, though when he left he said, 'I will come back another time, God willing'. Then he sailed from Ephesus* (Acts 18. 18–21).

As we have seen, the next person that Paul names in his letter of commendation is Epaenetus (v. 5), the first person whom he converted at Ephesus. Then there are brief messages to other Christians in the church to which Phoebe is travelling:

> *Greetings to Mary who worked so hard for you; to those outstanding apostles, Andronicus and Junia, my compatriots and fellow prisoners who became Christians before me; to Ampliatus, my friend in the Lord; to Urban, my fellow worker in Christ; to my friend Stachys; to Apelles who has gone through so much for Christ; to everyone who belongs to the household of Aristobulus; to my compatriot Herodion; to those in the household of Narcissus who belong to the Lord; to Tryphaena and Tryphosa who work hard for the Lord; to my friend Persis who has done so much for the Lord; to Rufus, a chosen servant of the Lord, and to his mother who has been a mother to me too...* (Rom. 16. 7–16).

The list of friends to whom Paul sends his greetings demonstrates an intimate knowledge of family groupings, domestic arrangements and descriptions of individuals' work. This is what one might expect of the Christian community in Ephesus, among whom Paul has just been working for almost three years, in contrast to the Christian community in Rome, which Paul is unlikely to have visited. Phoebe's letter of introduction appears to end at verse 20, with a characteristic Pauline closing formula, 'The grace of our Lord Jesus Christ be with you,' just as Romans 15. 33 appears to be a similar ending for his Letter to the Romans.[7]

Why does chapter 16 include so many names? Nowhere else does Paul greet so many individuals at the end of an epistle. However, if this is a letter introducing Phoebe to a community unfamiliar to her, the list is quite appropriate. Where was she to stay? It was difficult for a Christian woman to travel alone in the ancient world; it was unsafe for single women to stay at inns. Phoebe needed more than a church in which to worship: she needed to be introduced personally to different Christian families, if she was to be safe and comfortable in Ephesus. These are Christians, particularly women, to whom she can turn for help and hospitality.

Perhaps Priscilla and Aquila will take her in: they did so much for Paul. Perhaps the mother of Rufus will look after her: she acted as a mother to Paul.[8]

Phoebe needs an invitation into more than one Christian home in Ephesus, and so Paul introduces her to twenty-eight people or groups of people. We do not know if Phoebe went to Ephesus for business reasons or at Paul's request to minister in the church, or for both purposes. Women could be traders: in the Acts of the Apostles, Luke tells us that Lydia was in the purple dye trade (16. 14), while women might sometimes even be ship-owners.[9]

Letters of commendation

Romans 16 is a fairly typical Graeco-Roman letter of recommendation or introduction; it is one of at least seven such letters that feature in Paul's writings. Some are brief, while others are longer: other examples include 1 Corinthians 16. 10–11; 15–18; Philippians 2. 29–30; 4. 2–3 and 1 Thessalonians 5. 12–13, while the entire Letter to Philemon is also a letter of recommendation, in which Paul commends to his friend one of his own slaves who had been baptized by Paul.[10] In a graphic passage in his second Letter to the Corinthians, Paul describes the Christian community as his personal letter of commendation:

> *Unlike other people, we need no letters of recommendation either to you or from you, because you are yourselves our letter, written in our hearts, that anybody can see and read, and it is plain that you are a letter from Christ, drawn up by us, and written not with ink but with the Spirit of the living God, not on stone tablets but on the tablets of your living hearts (2 Cor. 3. 1–3).*

Paul's commendations resemble other Graeco-Roman examples: they follow the same pattern of naming the person, giving their credentials and making a request, and they use similar vocabulary – the words 'receive', 'recognise' and 'honour' appear in similar letters to those of Paul. As in other Greek and Roman examples, Paul highlights the importance of 'character' – the letter writer's, the recipient's and that of the person commended. The qualities of love, loyalty and persistence in the face of hardship are often described.[11]

The phrasing of Romans 16. 1–3 indicates that Phoebe was the carrier of the letter from Paul. We do not know who would have read out the letter, but Phoebe could answer questions and ensure that the letter was understood correctly. She would have been its authoritative interpreter, since she knew Paul and understood the letter's context. She may have advised the reader on its meaning, since such texts provided few hints to their readers, such as spaces between words and paragraphs.[12]

Phoebe the deacon

The two words that Paul uses to describe Phoebe, *deacon* and *patron*, are rich in meaning. While Paul functioned as *diakonos* in service to the entire Church, Phoebe's *diakonia* appears to have been tied to the church of Kenchreae. This is the only occasion in the New Testament when such service is linked to a local church. Paul uses the Greek word *ousa* (being) together with the noun *diakonos*; this reference to *being* a deacon suggests that Phoebe had a recognised ministry or held a position of responsibility within her local house church. She is probably the first recorded local church deacon in the history of Christianity.[13]

The first verse of Romans 16 also contains the earliest reference to a female deacon, and so it is a significant marker in the unfolding ministry of women in the Church. At this point in Christian history there was no distinction between male and female deacons, but by the third century women's ministry had been curtailed, and female deacons had developed a particular, more limited, office of ministry to other women. They remained popular in the east, but declined rapidly in the west.[14]

Male deacons are first mentioned in Philippians 1. 1, while the earliest description of the qualifications for deacons and their role in the community appears in the First Letter to Timothy, which probably dates from the late first century. It was written by an anonymous author within the Pauline tradition, a generation or two after Paul's death, as was the Letter to Titus, and perhaps 2 Timothy. Candidates are examined in some way, for deacons must be approved before performing their ministry. The author writes:

> *In the same way, deacons are to be serious, not given to double talk, not with a tendency to much wine, not eager for dishonest profit, holding to the mystery of faith with a clear conscience. And let them first be approved, then let them perform their diaconal ministry blamelessly. In the same way, women are to be serious, not irresponsible talkers, sober, faithful in all things* (1 Tim. 3. 8–11).

The women referred to are likely to be women deacons, since the structure of verse 8 about men and of verse 11 about women, ('In the same way... in the same way') is identical, except for gender changes.[15] Furthermore, the author continues his description of deacons in the following verses.

It is unclear what a deacon did at this time, but the earliest commentary on Romans 16, written by Origen (AD 185–253), and surviving in a Latin translation by the monk Rufinus (345–410), provides us with some clues. Origen writes:

> *'I commend to you Phoebe'... This passage teaches by apostolic authority that women are also appointed [constitui] in the ministry of the church [in ministerio ecclesiae], in which office Phoebe was placed at the church that is in Kenchreai. Paul with great praise and recommendation even enumerates her splendid deeds*

6

... And therefore this passage teaches two things equally and is to be interpreted, as we have said, to mean that women are to have ministry [haberi ... femini ministras] in the church, and that such ought to be received into the ministry who have assisted many; they have earned the right through their good deeds to receive apostolic praise.[16]

Origen here describes a formal ministry in the church for deacons, which is a more developed concept than simply helpful service. However, we know little about what such ministry entailed, for Phoebe is the only deacon of a first-century church whose name we know, since the seven men appointed by the Twelve in Acts 6. 1–6 are called to *diakonía* of the table, a service of giving out food, but they are not called deacons.[17] Furthermore, Luke wrote the Acts of the Apostles towards the end of the first century, and much of his textual detail derives from a period later than Paul.[18]

FIGURE 3. Mural of Phoebe in the modern church at Examilia.

Phoebe as patron

The second term that Paul uses to describe Phoebe is *prostátis*, meaning benefactor or patron: Phoebe is a patron of many, and of Paul himself. This term had a specific meaning in the Graeco-Roman world, and was accorded to women as well as men. Under Roman law, women enjoyed great freedom and privileges: by this time, wives had the same rights as their husbands over owning and disposal of property. They could apply to write their own wills, while freeborn women with three children or freed women with four children no longer required a tutor to transact their business. Women could now acquire wealth and freely dispose of it, which meant that financially and legally they could become patrons of voluntary associations – these included philosophical schools, and both pagan and Christian religious groups.[19]

A text dating from the second century BC describes a woman named

Agdistas who was a patron and member of a cult group dedicated to Zeus. A woman named Nikippe became a priestess and chief officer of an association of worshippers of the god Serapis, who was the Egyptian equivalent of Asclepius, the Greek god of healing. Thus wealthy women not only became patrons of religious groups, but gained positions of leadership within them. This benefited both the patron and the group which she patronised.[20]

When Paul tells the church at Ephesus that Phoebe is a patron of many, including himself, he implies that she is likely to become a benefactor of them also. She is already a patron of Paul, although equally, given his unique position in the Christian community, Paul is her patron, which is why he can introduce her to the Christians of Ephesus. Phoebe and Paul were benefactors to each other: Phoebe could introduce Paul, who was, after all, only a tent maker or leather worker, to her friends who might be reasonably well off, and together the two of them could talk about their faith. As a patron saint of the region, Phoebe is depicted in murals on the north wall of Kenchreai church and that of Examilia, four miles to the west (Fig. 3).

Junia Theodora of Corinth

A contemporary of Phoebe named Junia Theodora is also described as a patron; she lived in nearby Corinth.[21] Her activities may throw light on those of Phoebe. Junia Theodora was not a patron of a religious group, but a number of inscriptions refer to her patronage of the town; they suggest that a 'patron' was someone with a high profile in the community, who might not only donate money but also offer social care. One inscription runs:

> [T]he council and people of Telemessos decreed … [that] since Iunia Theodora, a Roman, a benefactress of the greatest loyalty to the Lycian federation and our city, has accomplished numerous benefits for the federation and our city … displaying her patronage [prostasian] of those who are present … it is decreed that our city give honour and praise for all the above reasons to … Iunia Theodora.[22]

The inscription describes a wide range of activities that Junia Theodora carried out as a patron of her city; these include financial support for building projects, hospitality to travellers, especially foreign dignitaries, and negotiations with the Roman authorities on behalf of her region. It is possible that Phoebe undertook 'hospitality to travellers' and similar activities in Kenchreai, though perhaps on a smaller scale. She appears to have done so in a significant way both for Paul and for 'many others'. As a patron, she may have had the financial resources to provide for Christian churches, established by Paul and perhaps by others.[23]

Patrons and clients

We do not know precisely what the term *prostátis* meant for early Christians, since it appears only once in the New Testament, in Paul's description of Phoebe. However, one of the Apostolic Fathers uses it three times: it features in the late first-century Letter from Clement of Rome to the Corinthians, where the masculine form of the term is used to describe Christ. The context makes it clear that Clement understands the term to mean 'protector' or 'guardian'. Christ is 'the protector by whom our feebleness is aided' (36. 1), 'guardian of our souls' (61. 3), 'our high priest and protector' (64. 3).[24] For Clement, Jesus is the patron of the entire human family.

In the first-century Graeco-Roman world, the patron-client relationship was at the heart of all economic, social and political transactions. Paul thinks of his churches as clients; in his Letters he often reminds them of all they owe him. He recalls how he has done a great deal for them, and therefore they owe him allegiance. He sees himself as a client of no one except of God and Christ.[25]

Nevertheless, Paul describes Phoebe as 'a patron of many, and of myself as well'. She was not merely a financial benefactor of Paul, because in the ancient world, giving was regarded more holistically. Benefactors allowed clients access to their social and economic resources.[26] Christians with moderate surplus resources were encouraged to exercise their beneficence by virtually adopting those to whom they might exercise charity, in imitation of Christ, 'who made us his adopted children, for his own kind purposes' (Eph. 1. 5–6), and in imitation of God, the supreme benefactor, the giver of all good gifts.[27]

Christ, servant and benefactor

Why does Paul single out the two titles *diákonon* and *prostátis*, servant and benefactor, to describe Phoebe as a church leader at Kenchreai? St Paul's Christology is rooted in that of proto-Luke, the parts of Luke's gospel that are likely to form its earliest core. Paul's account of the Lord's Supper, for example (1 Cor. 11. 23–6) is similar to that in Luke, while it is independent of Mark's account. Luke saw Jesus as the great example of a servant benefactor. In the gentile world, a benefactor was at the opposite extreme from a servant, but Jesus united these opposites, and therefore his followers must do so. Luke tells us:

> An argument arose among them concerning which of them was the greatest. He said to them, however, 'The gentile kings lord it over their subjects and are called benefactors. But this must not be so with you. Instead, the greatest among you ought to be like the youngest, and the leader as one who serves [ó diákonon].

For who is greater, the one at table or the one who serves? I, however, am among you as one who serves [ó diákonon]' (Lk. 22. 24–7).

The problem of wealth

Early Christians found it easy to apply this theology to the poor, but difficult to apply it to the moderately well off. In Jewish tradition, riches were understood as a sign of God's blessing, but Jesus had said that it was hard for the rich to enter heaven, and Luke and James echo this (Lk. 6. 24; James 5. 1–6). So what about good Christians who, like Phoebe, were moderately wealthy and possibly well-connected? Clement of Alexandria formulated the question as follows:

What is wrong if a person, by foresight and frugality prior to a life of faith, has enough to live on? What is more, since God is the dispenser of goods to the household of humanity, what if someone was born into a wealthy and powerful family? If such a person is excluded from [heavenly] life and yet has made no choice to be rich, then God, who brought the person into existence, is in the wrong … Why does wealth exist if it is only a vehicle of [spiritual] death?[28]

Luke records Jesus explaining how Christians with resources imitate God when they share their resources not only with their friends, but with everyone. Christians who give generously imitate God, the supreme giver. We must act freely and liberally, as God does:

If you only do good to those who do good to you, how is that to your credit? … Love your enemies and do good; lend with no expectation of return, and your reward will be great; you will be children of the Most High, for he is good even to the ungrateful and evil. Be compassionate as your Father is compassionate (Lk. 6. 33–6).

Clement of Alexandria expanded on this, explaining that charity is an investment for the soul:

What magnificent trading, a godly business! With money you purchase incorruption. In giving up the perishable commodities of the world you receive eternal possessions in heaven. If you are wise, those of you who are wealthy, then set sail for this market. Search the whole earth if necessary. Do not spare any risk or toil, that you might buy a heavenly kingdom.[29]

Phoebe was a woman who had set sail for this market; she understood this magnificent trading, this godly business. In the same way, the author of 1 Timothy requires deacons not to be lovers of money or greedy for gain; instead they should place a higher value on meeting people's needs (1 Tim. 3. 8).

Women servant benefactors

Luke had described a number of women followers of Jesus as servant benefactors. He informs us of a group of women with resources who served with Jesus:

> *Travelling through the cities and villages, Jesus and the twelve with him preached the message of the kingdom of God. Women ..., Mary called Magdalene ..., Joanna, the wife of Herod's steward, Chusa, Susanna, and many others serve them [i.e. provided for them] from their own possessions* (Lk. 8. 1–3).

In the story of Martha and Mary (Lk. 10. 38–42), the two women opened their home to Jesus as benefactors, while Martha was distracted by much service (*diakonían*). In the Acts of the Apostles, Luke portrays other women as servant benefactors including Tabitha, or Dorcas, in Jaffa, whom Peter raised from the dead, 'who never tired of doing good, or giving in charity' (Acts 9. 36). In Philippi, Lydia was 'a devout woman', a benefactor who demonstrated her goodness by inviting Paul to come and stay with her household (Acts 16. 11–15).

Deacons seek the common good

Clement of Rome's Letter to the Corinthians offers us insight into the Christian community in late first-century Corinth, a few decades after Paul worked among them. Clement's chief concern is that a new generation of youngsters have rebelled against their lawfully appointed presbyters, or leaders, and dismissed them from office. He also notes how the community used to live at peace, when their only concern was to do good:

> *You were all humble, not arrogant, submitting yourselves, rather than subjecting others, happier in giving than receiving. You were satisfied with Christ's provision, and you were alert to his words ... Thus a profound and fruitful peace was given to all, and an insatiable desire to do good ... You had no regret in all your good doing, ready for every good work ...*[30] *The more someone seems great, humility is needed and [one must] seek the common good of all, not one's own advantage.*[31]

Deacons such as Phoebe were seen as living examples of Christ's *diákonia*, or service; perhaps the chief task of a deacon was to serve as a role model. Ignatius of Anthioch, writing to the Church in Smyrna in the latter half of the second century,[32] praised the bearer of his letter, a deacon named Burrhus, as a mirror of Christ. He wrote: 'I wish that all imitated him [Burrhus], for he is an embodiment of God's service (*diákonia*)'.[33]

The origin of the early Christian role of deacon may be associated with collecting money for the poor Christians of Jerusalem, a project that greatly concerned Paul: he encouraged all his Asian communities to contribute to this enterprise. Seven of the New Testament passages that refer to the collection use some form of the word *diákonia*.[34] Self-employed, mobile individuals were able to carry both money and correspondence from one Christian community to another, as Phoebe may have carried Paul's letter of commendation (which also includes advice for the community) to the Christians at Ephesus.

Rich and poor

When we read the terms 'rich' and 'poor' in New Testament writings, we tend to think of wealth in modern terms. Steven Friesen has examined the degree of poverty among first-century Christians: in the Roman Empire, which was an agrarian, pre-industrial society, there was no economic middle class. Instead, a very small group of people, the rich nobility, controlled politics and commerce while almost everyone else lived near subsistence level.[35] Friesen uses a seven-point 'poverty scale' to identify various subgroups within this broad outline.

A number of people, including some merchants, traders, freed persons and military veterans, managed to achieve a moderate surplus income, but the majority lived just above or just below subsistence level, either permanently or some of the time. Unattached widows, orphans, disabled persons, unskilled day labourers and some farming families were never able to procure enough food to sustain them. If you were a labourer, artisan or wage earner, a merchant, shopkeeper or tavern owner, you were likely to be able to feed your family and yourself most of the time, but not always.

It is difficult to place Paul within these economic categories;[36] he tells the Corinthians: 'I have been hungry and thirsty and often starving' (2 Cor. 11. 27). In his Letters, when Paul contrasts the rich with the poor, he is likely to be comparing those below poverty level with those slightly above it. When he contrasts those who have enough food with those who have not (1 Cor. 11. 22), he implies that a significant number of Corinthian Christians lived in desperate poverty, and that they were not being cared for by those who lived just above subsistence level.

It is likely that some leaders of Pauline communities had moderate disposable income, and it is even possible that Phoebe may have been wealthy, but since ninety-seven per cent of the urban population did not belong to the wealthy elite, we are unable to assume that Phoebe was rich, without clear evidence. Although she is described as a leader in the Kenchreai assembly, and a patron of Paul and of many in the church (Rom. 16. 1–2), she is likely to have possessed only moderate surplus resources.[37] However, many people had moderate wealth but did not belong to the elite for social reasons, and what Paul meant by 'wealthy' remains unclear. What sociologists term 'status inconsistency' applied to early Christians, as well as to those of today.[38]

Phoebe as a person

What, then, do we know of Phoebe as a person? Phoebe was a common name in the Graeco-Roman world, although she is the only person with this name in the New Testament. Since her name is Greek, Phoebe is likely to have been a gentile Christian, rather than a Jewess.[39] As a woman of moderate means, she became a servant benefactor, in imitation of Christ; she was evidently outstanding in both ministries. As a woman with resources, it is likely that she presided over a house church, and that Paul was her house guest when he came to Kenchreai.[40] The gentle young woman with her elegant coiffure depicted in Figure 4 might have known Phoebe's grandchildren (Fig. 4).[41]

Like many other settlements in the Peloponnese, Kenchreai is in a beautiful setting (Fig. 5), and we can imagine that Phoebe enjoyed walking through the surrounding forests in springtime, when dark red anemones, deep blue grape hyacinths and pale pink cyclamen flower beneath the pine trees. She might have seen the swallowtail butterflies hovering over the shore in the summer and, in September and October, watched the flash of turquoise as kingfishers fly across the bay, often in pairs. Phoebe may have been a widow, since women normally married, and we are not told that she was a virgin, or that she had a husband. We are left to imagine Phoebe's relationship with Paul. What did they eat, for example? The local fish still caught off the north pier of Kenchreai harbour is *tsipoura*, or grey snapper: a stout fish about 30 cm in length (Fig. 6). We can imagine one of Phoebe's servants going down to the quay to buy fresh snapper for dinner.

Paul may have stayed with Phoebe while waiting for a ship to sail from Kenchreai harbour to Ephesus in the spring of AD 53, and from his affectionate

FIGURE 4. Marble head of a woman, probably from Kenchreai, AD 120–40, in the Archaeological Museum, Corinth (5-2585). Photo by Inos Ionnaidou and Lenio Barzotti.

FIGURE 5. Kenchreai harbour in springtime.

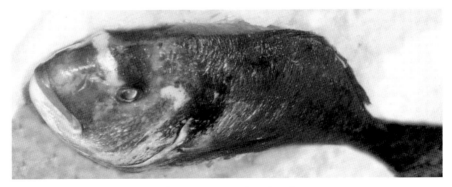

FIGURE 6. Fresh grey snapper in a local restaurant.

description of her, they knew each other well. Paul had worked in Corinth for the previous eighteen months, and since Kenchreai was its eastern port, there was constant travel between the provincial capital and its harbour, 4.5 miles to the south-east. Boats departed from Kenchreai and sailed across the Saronic Gulf and the Aegean Sea to Macedonia, Asia Minor, Syria and Egypt.[42] Perhaps Paul retreated to the peace and comfort of Phoebe's home in the same way that Jesus used to visit Martha and Mary in Bethany, in order to escape the pressure of preaching in Jerusalem in the face of increasing hostility from its religious leaders.

If Phoebe led a house church in Kenchreai, she is likely to have presided over the weekly eucharistic meal. This was a real meal, with much more spontaneity than today's Christian worship. Justin Martyr describes a Sunday gathering in about AD 150 that includes a reading from the Old Testament, a 'gospel', a homily, a Eucharistic Prayer ending with an 'Amen', followed by sharing of food and a collection.[43] However, Thomas O'Loughlin notes that in Justin's account, the prayer of thanksgiving is improvised, its setting is within a real community meal, and there is no mention of who leads the prayer and no hint of ordination, or that the leader has been conferred with any special authority within the group. He adds that the 'memoirs of the apostles' are not treated as a sacred text, and that the collection was not for the upkeep of the clergy or the institution, but for the poor.[44]

St Paul at Kenchreai

St Paul's background was very different from that of Phoebe: while her Greek name suggests that she was a gentile Christian, Paul was thoroughly Jewish. Luke depicts him calling out when on trial in the Sanhedrin, the Jewish priestly court: 'Brothers, I am a pharisee and the son of pharisees!' (Acts 23. 6). As a good pharisee, Paul is likely to have been married; since he does not mention a wife, perhaps he was widowed. We hear about Paul's married sister and his helpful nephew: 'The son of Paul's sister heard of the ambush [the Jews] were laying, and made his way into the fortress and told Paul...' (Acts 23. 16–22). By contrast, the scriptures offer no clues about Phoebe's family.

Paul baptized few Corinthian Christians: he writes to them, 'I am thankful that I never baptized any of you after Crispus and Gaius' and 'the family of Stephanas' (1 Cor. 1. 14–16). Phoebe may have been instructed and baptized before Paul arrived in about AD 50, possibly by Priscilla and Aquila.[45] This married couple were Jewish Christian leather workers who had been expelled from Rome on account of their faith either in about AD 50 or as is now suggested, in the early 40s,[46] which would have been well before Paul came to Corinth.

The development of separate house churches with different approaches to their faith caused tensions among Corinthian Christians – twice Paul refers to their slogans, 'I am for Paul', 'I am for Apollos', 'I am for Cephas' (or Peter) and 'I am for Christ' (1 Cor. 1. 12; 3. 4). The divisions between Christian communities in Corinth will be examined in Chapter 4. Perhaps Phoebe was sufficiently wise and loving that she could reconcile such different approaches to the new Christian faith; Paul certainly valued and respected her ministry.

Paul makes a vow

Paul's Jewishness is evident when, as Luke tells us, 'At Kenchreai he had his hair cut off, because of a vow he had made' (Acts 18. 18). This appears to refer to the traditional conclusion of a Nazirite vow, or one resembling it. Through such a vow, Jews offered themselves to God for a period of time, during which they vowed to abstain from alcohol, to let their hair grow, and avoid defilement by contact with dead bodies. The process is described in detail in the Old Testament Book of Numbers (Num. 6. 2–21).

It is possible that Paul made such a vow prior to travelling to Jerusalem for a festival: his action would also reassure the Jewish community that he respected their laws. In Acts 21, the apostle James, leader of the Christian community in Jerusalem, advised Paul to demonstrate his fidelity to the Law by taking four Jewish Christians to the temple in order to fulfil such a vow, which had to be celebrated with expensive sacrifices:

> We have four men here who are under a vow; take these men along and be purified with them and pay all the expenses connected with the shaving of their heads. This will let everyone know there is no truth in the reports they have heard about you and that you still regularly observe the Law (Acts 21. 24–5).

The reason for Paul shaving his head and making a vow may have been unclear to local Christians in later centuries, who perhaps concluded, based on their own experience, that this was an act similar to becoming a hermit monk. Later tradition recounts that St Paul climbed the mountain range above Kenchreai to pray in a cave, although this is likely to be an anachronistic view of Paul, the holy man, following the model of medieval hermit monks. The mountain-top cave, which can still be reached by the more athletic, may well have been prayed in by medieval monks, and visited by pilgrims. Down below, the ancient road between Corinth and Kenchreai, along which Paul is likely to have walked many times, is named *Odos Apostolou Paulo* or 'Apostle Paul Road'.

Notes

1   Quotations from the Bible are taken from *The Jerusalem Bible: Reader's Edition*, ed. Alexander Jones (London: Darton, Longman and Todd, 1968), with minor alterations.

2   C. Whelan, 'Amica Pauli: the role of Phoebe in the early Church', in *Journal for the Study of the New Testament*, vol. 49, 1993, pp. 71–2.

3   *Ibid*, p. 72.

4   *Ibid*.

5   See P. Lampe, *From Paul to Valentinus* (Minneapolis: Fortress, 2003), ch. 36, which treats Romans 16 as evidence for the fractionisation of the Roman church.

6   J.C. Campbell, *Phoebe, Patron and Emissary* (Collegeville: Liturgical Press, 2009), p. 32.

7   Whelan, 'Amica Pauli', p. 72.

8   E. Goodspeed, 'Phoebe's Letter of Introduction', in *Harvard Theological Review*, vol. 44, Jan. 1951, pp. 55–6.

9   Whelan, 'Amica Pauli', p. 82, n. 38.

10 Chan-Hie Kim, *Form and Structure of the Familiar Greek Letter of Recommendation*, SBLDS4 (Missoula, MONT: Scholars Press, 1972), pp. 110–11.

11 E. Agosto, 'Paul and commendation', in *Paul in the Greco-Roman World*, ed. J.P. Sampley (Harrisburg: Trinity Press/Continuum, 2003), p. 127.

12 Ian Paul, blog 'Psephizo', 1 December 2012, 'Phoebe, carrier of Paul's letter to the Roman Christians'.

13 D. Jankiewicz, 'Phoebe: was she an early church leader?', in *Ministry*, April 2013, pp. 10–14.

14 K. Madigan and C. Osiek, *Ordained Women in the Early Church: A Documentary History* (Baltimore: Johns Hopkins University Press, 2005), p. 203.

15 *Ibid*, p. 18.

16 *Ibid*, p. 14.

17 *Ibid*, p. 13.

18 J.N. Collins in *Diakonia* (Oxford: Oxford University Press, 1990), pp. 224–6, argues against the translation 'servant', however, and argues that Phoebe 'was the community's emissary' (p. 225).

19 Whelan, 'Amica Pauli', pp. 73–5.

20 *Ibid*, pp. 75–7.

21 See S. Friesen, 'Junia Theodora of Corinth: gendered inequalities in the early empire', in *Corinth in Contrast: Studies in Inequality*, ed. S. Friesen, S. James and D. Schowalter (Leiden: Brill, 2014).

22 Quoted in Agosto, 'Paul and commendation', p. 123.

23 Agosto, 'Paul and commendation', pp. 123–4.

24 M. Holmes, *The Apostolic Fathers: Greek Texts and English Translations* (Grand Rapids MI: Baker Academic, 3rd ed., 2007), p. 44 ff.

25 Whelan, 'Amica Pauli', pp. 82–4.

26 *Ibid*.

27 R. Garrison, 'Phoebe, the servant-benefactor and gospel traditions', in *Text and Artifact in the Religions of Mediterranean Antiquity* (Waterloo, ONT: Wilfrid Laurier University Press, 2000), ch. 5, p. 67.

28 Clement of Alexandria, in G.W. Butterworth, transl., *The Exhortation to the Greeks. The Rich Man's Salvation. To the Newly Baptized* (Cambridge, MAS: Loeb Classical Library, 2003), *Divitiae*, 26.

29 *Divitiae*, 27. 32.

30 *Ibid*, 2. 1–2, 7.

31 *Ibid*, 48. 6.

32 It was formerly thought that Ignatius of Antioch wrote his Letters in about AD 100–10, but it is now known that he wrote considerably later, *c.* 150–60 at the earliest. See T.D. Barnes, 'The date of Ignatius', *Expository Times*, vol. 120 (2008), pp. 119–30.

33 Ignatius of Antioch, 'Letter to the Smyrnaeans' 12. 1, in *Early Christian Writings: The Apostolic Fathers*, transl. M. Staniforth (Harmondsworth: Penguin, 1968), p. 123.

34 Garrison, 'Phoebe, the servant-benefactor', p. 69.

35 S.J. Friesen, 'Prospects for a demography of the Pauline mission: Corinth among the churches', in *Urban Religion of Roman Corinth: Interdisciplinary Approaches*, ed. D. Schowalter and S. Friesen, Harvard Theological Studies, vol. 53, 2005, p. 364.

36 *Ibid*, pp. 365, 368.

37 *Ibid*, pp. 367–9.

38 See W. Meeks, *First Urban Christians* (New Haven: Yale University Press, 1984), and R.L. Fox, *Pagans and Christians, The Penguin History of the Church*, vol. 1 (London: Penguin, 2006) for more extensive studies of this subject.

39 J. Miller, 'What can we say about Phoebe?', *Priscilla Papers*, vol. 25 no. 2, Spring 2011, p. 16.

40 C. Osiek and M.Y. MacDonald, *A Woman's Place: House Churches in Earliest Christianity* (Minneapolis, MN: Fortress, 2005), pp. 194–219.

41 Photo ref.: bw_2001_006_33, reproduced courtesy of the American School of Classical Studies at Athens, Corinth Excavations.

42 Miller, 'What can we say about Phoebe?', p. 16.

43 Justin Martyr, *First Apology*, 65–7, in *The First and Second Apologies*, ed. L.W. Barnar, (New York: Paulist Press, 1997).

44 T. O'Loughlin, *The Eucharist: Origins and Contemporary Understandings* (London: T. & T. Clark, 2015), pp. 8–9.

45 E. Adams and D. Horrell, 'The Scholarly Quest for Paul's Church at Corinth: A Critical Survey' in *Christianity at Corinth: The Quest for the Pauline Church*, ed. E. Adams and D. Horrell (Louisville: Westminster John Knox Press, 2004), p. 9.

46 J. Murphy O'Connor, *St. Paul's Corinth: Texts and Archaeology* (Collegeville, MN: Liturgical Press, 2002, 3rd ed.), pp. 52–60.

Chapter 2

KENCHREAI IN EARLY CHRISTIAN TIMES

In chapter one, we explored some of the texts that enable us to catch a glimpse of early Christianity in Kenchreai; in this chapter we shall examine some complementary archaeological evidence. First, however, we shall focus on how Phoebe was remembered in the early Church. We do not know the extent of her cult in Kenchreai, but a sixth-century pillar discovered in Jerusalem recalls her qualities. Next, we shall outline some broad trends demonstrated by early Christian basilicas in the Peloponnese. Finally, drawing on evidence from excavations, we shall take a look at Kenchreai as it would have been in Phoebe's lifetime and in succeeding centuries. Early chambered tombs were used by Christians of Kenchreai from the fourth century onwards, and there are substantial remains of a sixth-century basilica on the seashore,

There is a tantalising gap in our knowledge of early Christianity in southern Greece, from apostolic times until about the late fifth century, when basilicas began to be built. Until recently, it was thought that some of these buildings were constructed at least one hundred years earlier. Indeed, some former archaeologists misinterpreted coin finds, failing to take into account the fact that coins could have circulated for a very long period, first as currency and later as decorative items. Furthermore, accurate dating of pottery from the sites has been refined only in the last two decades.

Respect for Phoebe in the broader Church

It appears that Phoebe was honoured by Christians in this later period, though our strongest evidence for this is found not in Greece but rather in Jerusalem, close to the epicentre of Christianity. A pillar found on the Mount of Olives outside the Old City of Jerusalem bears an inscription that refers to a woman named Sophia (Greek for 'Wisdom'). She is described as a deacon and a 'second Phoebe' (*Sophia, hē diakonos, hē deutera Phoibē*). The pillar was formerly thought to date from the fourth century, but more recently a date of AD 532–62 has been suggested.[1]

The pillar was found below the Tomb of the Prophets in December 1903; it was broken into five pieces. The site, now the property of the Russian Church, is an underground burial complex dating from the first century BC on the upper western slope of the Mount of Olives. This inscription and others in Greek suggest that the burial site was re-used by gentile Christians in the fourth and fifth centuries AD.[2] The pillar is now in the museum of St Anne's Church, in the Old City of Jerusalem.

Like Phoebe, Sophia was a gentile with a Greek name. The text of the first seven lines of the inscription may be translated as '*Here lies the slave and bride of Christ, Sophia, the deacon, the second Phoebe, who fell asleep in peace on 21 March during the eleventh indiction*'.[3] The lower part of the pillar is broken, and subsequent lines of text are incomplete or missing; line 8 appears to name a presbyter (*pres-*), which could have helped to date the pillar.

It is interesting that Sophia is called a deacon, not a deaconess: this suggests that both men and women continued to perform the role of deacon. Sophia was one of a considerable number of deacons serving the Jerusalem churches and those of nearby villages. So far six inscriptions dating from the fifth to the seventh centuries have been found (including three to men and two to women) that commemorate such deacons.[4] When Sophia is described as 'the second Phoebe', however, this is unlikely to refer to her diaconate, since by now there were many women deacons; instead she is more likely to have resembled Phoebe as a patron and benefactor to her local community.[5]

The inscription to Sophia provides fascinating detail concerning women's ministry in the sixth century. She is described by the Christians who erected her funeral monument as a 'slave of Christ': St Paul used the term 'slave' or 'servant' of Christ to describe his own ministry (in Rom. 1. 1; 1 Cor. 4. 1; Phil. 1. 1; Gal. 1. 10, for example). Sophia's second title, 'bride of Christ' tells us that she was dedicated to a life of virginity. The title was originally applied to the Church, and was later given to celibate women, consecrated by their bishop.[6]

The description of Sophia as 'the second Phoebe' means more than it would today. In non-Christian inscriptions, such titles as 'a second Homer' were bestowed by grateful citizens upon individuals who gave outstanding service to their city. Therefore Sophia's title may imply that as well as being a deacon she was a significant benefactor (*prostásis*) in Jerusalem. A number of inscriptions have been found that use the term *prostásis* to describe women who gave financial assistance to their political and religious communities. Both Phoebe and Sophia may have given pastoral assistance to their church while also being businesswomen who gave financial support to their community.[7]

The spread of Christianity in southern Greece

When Christianity became the state religion of the Roman empire in the fourth century, Christians became more visible, but the process of conversion in southern Greece is not well understood. We do not know how strong Christianity already was in the region, neither do we know when and how people were converted, or indeed who converted them. This may have been a gradual, peaceful process, particularly in rural areas;[8] however, archaeological dating of materials from this early period is in the process of revision, and by the time of Justinian, conversion was sometimes carried out by force.[9] By the fourth century, many pagan shrines and temples were falling into disrepair, and Christianity appears to have co-existed with paganism: Plate 20 depicts one of a collection of nine statuettes including gods such as Dionysius, Asclepius and Roma, which were revered in a fourth-century Corinthian home.

Conversion to Christianity appears to have been encouraged rather than enforced. Cyprus, to the south-east, is another example of a region of the Roman empire in which Christianity spread peacefully, in contrast to Syria and Egypt, where pagan sites and people were violently destroyed. The churches of southern Greece are varied in style; this suggests that they were built on the initiative of a local community and their bishop, rather than as a response to an edict from a higher authority,[10] although Lechaion's basilica may have been an imperial project. The construction of so many churches suggests that late Roman communities were relatively wealthy. Local Christians gave generously, in order to gain God's blessing and to create a fitting place in which to celebrate God's goodness. The bishop became a new type of patron, and a wide variety of individuals, both clergy and laity, gave money to churches. Craftsmen might give small amounts of money or offer their labour, free of charge.[11]

Sixth-century inscriptions indicate that, unlike in earlier times when only a small elite possessed wealth, many small donors would help to build and furnish a church. Inscriptions name senators and estate owners, priests and deacons, and a reader in church who carved marble. Texts of inscriptions were intended to be read aloud; three such tablets in Corinthian cemeteries inform us that they were paid for by the driver of a team of oxen, a pickle merchant and a deacon.[12]

Design and location of churches

It is probable that hundreds of churches were constructed in the Peloponnese before the end of the seventh century. Of these, some 130 survive, although only 29 of these are well preserved, or have been excavated, and their plans published; most of them were built in the sixth century.[13] They range in size from very large to quite small, and were generally decorated with marble, sometimes re-cut from earlier buildings; baptisteries have been identified at eleven of them. There is often a monumental door from the *narthex*, or wide corridor at the west end, into the nave, to enable the clergy to process with dignity down the nave and into the sanctuary.[14] External atria, or assembly areas, and baptisteries also exist.

Few wall mosaics or murals survive, but there are fine floor mosaics in a number of churches. Baptisteries were often paved, sometimes with mosaic floors, as at Kenchreai's surviving basilica. Many motifs on mosaics in churches resemble those found in contemporary villas and bath houses. Some were decorated with geometric designs; others, such as one beneath the Apollo Hotel in Kastri near Delphi, depict peacocks, eagles and a deer in a panther's grip.[15] In early Christian iconography, the eyes in a peacock's tail symbolise God's loving gaze, while the majestic eagle conveys God's regal power.[16] Deer often represent the human heart searching for God: Christians chanted the prayer, 'As the deer thirsts for running streams, so my soul thirsts for you, my God' (Ps. 41/42. 1). However, a deer chased by a leopard, a panther or hounds represents the Christian pursued by the forces of evil. Deer are depicted thus on mosaic floors in fourth-century Roman villa house churches at Hinton St Mary and at Frampton (Dorset) in south-west Britain.[17]

Some inland basilicas were built at pre-Christian sanctuaries, such as Epidaurus, Olympia and Nemea. Here, they are not built within earlier sacred spaces, but on the edge of the site, as at Epidaurus, or in a secular building, as at Olympia, where a Christian church was built over the workshop of the famous sculptor, Phidias. Part of its *ambo*, or pulpit, survives. In Athens, Christians built churches inside earlier temples, possibly through lack of space, but in the Peloponnese Christians do not appear to have destroyed pagan holy sites.[18]

The basilicas are concentrated in the north-eastern Peloponnese, particularly on the coast, in towns that were ports. Most churches are found in towns; there were few in the countryside, apart from those at pagan sanctuaries, which might be quite remote. Churches were constructed later in the south, both on the coast and inland; this suggests that the building of churches spread from northern Greece by sea and by inland routes, rather than from the southern ports.[19] The construction of Kenchreai's basilicas, therefore, may have begun relatively early during this process, since it is a north-eastern coastal port.

Roman Kenchreai

In pre-Christian times, the harbour at Kenchreai was much larger than it appears today. It is likely to have extended as far as Loutro Elenis, the small town a mile to the south, before the bay silted up. A large area of ancient Kenchreai probably lies to the south-west of the present village, beneath the army base. North of the village, sections of a Classical Greek city wall are visible, and on the next headland, massive stones that formed the base of an ancient Greek *pharos*, or lighthouse, can be seen in the grounds of the Kalamaki Beach Hotel (Fig. 7). Kenchreai and its sister port of Lechaion were named after Kenchrias and Leches, two sons of the sea god Poseidon and his lover, Peirene, who was the daughter of Achelous, the god of fresh water. The ports were thus aptly named as locations where fresh and salt water meet.

As we shall see in the following chapters, there were really 'two Corinths': the Greek city destroyed by Romans, and the Roman city re-founded in 44 BC. Kenchreai was one of the earliest sites to be refurbished after Corinth's re-foundation. In the first and second centuries AD, Roman Kenchreai grew to become a flourishing port, perhaps twice the size of its northern sister port of Lechaion, and a third of the size of Corinth itself.[20] It became a substantial community in a way that Lechaion did not. In his novel, *Metamorphoses*, referred to by St Augustine as *The Golden Ass*, Apuleius describes Kenchreai in the second century as 'busy with a multitude of people'.[21]

FIGURE 7. Foundations of an ancient Greek *pharos*, or lighthouse, Kenchreai. The sea is visible behind the trees.

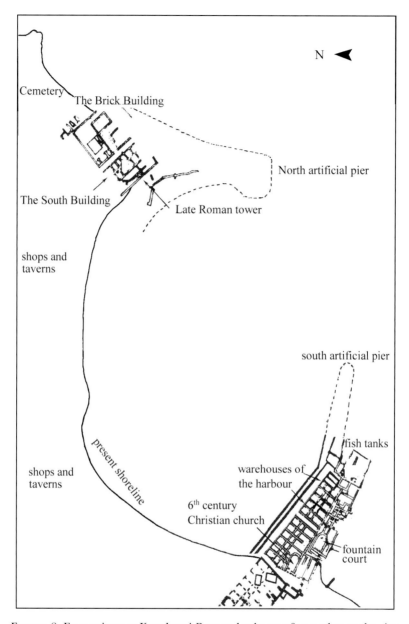

FIGURE 8. Excavations at Kenchreai Roman harbour, after a plan at the site.

Kenchreai was considerably altered and expanded over the following centuries, and no first-century Christian remains have yet been discovered. The same is true of Corinth. House churches leave little evidence, unless archaeologists are fortunate enough to find vessels marked out for Christian use buried within the building, or a later baptistery has been inserted into an earlier mosaic floor, or a villa's living room has been re-ordered for Christian worship.[22]

When the Romans re-colonised Corinth in 44 BC, the harbour that they constructed at Kenchreai (see Plate 2) was smaller than its Greek predecessor. Portions of it were surveyed and excavated by the University of Chicago and by Indiana University, on behalf of the American School of Classical Studies at Athens, in 1963–6 and 1968 (Fig. 8).[23] In 2007–9 Joseph Rife, currently Associate Professor of Classical and Mediterranean Studies, Vanderbilt University, Nashville, Tennessee, conducted further excavations in the port's northern area.

An artificial entrance to the port was created by two great piers, 100 m long, built at right angles to the shore. These provided protection from the prevailing north-westerly winds and created a horseshoe-shaped harbour, which very large ships could enter. At the base of the north pier, a late Roman rectangular building, now ruined, may have been a lighthouse. From the port, cargo ships set sail for the rich cities of Asia Minor, Cyprus, Syria and Egypt.

In the second century AD, the Greek traveller and geographer Pausanias informs us that at Kenchreai there was a temple of Aphrodite, and beyond the temple, a bronze image of Poseidon on the pier that ran into the sea. Pausanias adds that at the other extremity of the harbour there were sanctuaries of Asclepius and Isis.[24] Isis and Aphrodite were deities who protected seafarers, and were especially worshipped at ports. Mindful of Pausanias, the first archaeologists working at Kenchreai were over-hasty in identifying large buildings at each end of the harbour with temples of Aphrodite and Isis. Such conclusions are now considered unlikely because their ground plans do not resemble those of temples.

Northern Kenchreai

On the hillside above the north pier is an impressive Roman brick building, dating from the early second century AD, much of which has been washed away by the sea. A complex of rooms survives, built around a colonnaded court; the walls of the rooms were once covered with marble panels, and some had mosaic floors. It was enlarged at the end of the second century and a new structure erected to the south, named the 'South Building' by its excavators.[25] The two were rebuilt as a single unit after a possible earthquake or tsunami in about AD 370. The excavators thought that this could be the temple of Aphrodite mentioned by Pausanias, since a number of erotically decorated fragments of pottery and clay lamps suggested amorous interests on the part of the building's occupants, but it is more likely that this was the harbour master's offices, or some other public building, or perhaps the residence of a wealthy individual (Fig. 9).[26]

Left: FIGURE 9. Lavish residence at the north end of the harbour, Kenchreai.

Right: FIGURE 10. View from the hilltop tomb across the cemetery site, Kenchreai.

Kenchreai's northern cemetery

Cemeteries surrounded the town on three sides. The limestone ridge above the north pier is honeycombed with underground tombs, one leading into the next through ancient robbers' cuttings; this formed Kenchreai's largest Roman cemetery. Excavations here have yielded well-preserved glass and stone mosaics, monumental architecture, wall paintings, vast quantities of pottery, inscriptions and coins, and even wooden and ivory-sheathed furniture.[27] Part of a sixth-century octagonal baptistery, or possibly a martyr's shrine, was uncovered in 2009 beside the sea cliff: it was dated by a coin of Justinian. They might represent the remains of a Christian basilica. At the top of the hill, a monumental early Roman tomb dominated the skyline; a fragmentary inscription suggests that it was built by a prominent local family in the first century AD.[28] Figure 10 is a view from the site of the imposing Roman tomb across the north cemetery; we must also imagine the coast road below, and boats, plying to and from Asia Minor.

Beyond the remains of domestic buildings, slab-lined (cist) graves surround orderly rows of some thirty chambered tombs constructed in the first three centuries AD. On the high ridge north of the harbour, the tombs would have been visible from the sea and from the coast road below the cemetery. Some tombs

are more elaborate than others, indicating varying degrees of wealth, but their owners seem to have functioned as a social group in creating such memorials. Since Kenchreai was a port rather than a town with its own government, these families are likely to have grown rich and attained status through commerce.[29]

Most of the chambered tombs are arranged in three orderly rows facing the sea; their form is almost unique in this region of Greece and differs from those in such nearby communities as Corinth, where burials are more random and scattered.[30] The chambered tombs fell into ruin in the fourth century, but some were re-used in the fifth, sixth and early seventh centuries. Some of their later occupants were Christian: there are crosses on the interior walls of one tomb, while pious Christian inscriptions are found on another. This is the earliest evidence of Christianity in the port. The tombs may have belonged to the same families as the previous pagan occupants: to be buried with one's forebears was considered important in early times.[31]

At ground level, each tomb consisted of an imposing rectangular building with a large threshold, a door and probably a gabled roof. The building secured the entrance to the tomb and provided space to display an epitaph. Inside, a flight of stairs cut into the bedrock descended into the tomb chamber via a narrow entrance with a second solid door. Inside the tomb chamber there was often a bench carved out of the rock on the front wall and an altar against the back wall; some tombs also had small movable altars. Large numbers of lamps and vessels were found on the floors: these suggest that this is where burial rituals and commemorations took place.[32]

The bodies were placed in long compartments (*loculi*) stretching back into the bedrock, designed to contain several bodies in a slab-lined grave. Sometimes the dead were buried in a wooden coffin or on a bier, with ornaments, small vessels and coins. The tombs remained in use until the end of the third century. Epitaphs indicate that they were built by both men and women for themselves and their families, up to fifty of whom could be buried in each chamber. Above the tombs were niches, some of which contained heavy cylindrical urns with fragments of cremated bones and teeth. Perhaps a family's slaves or freedmen were cremated and placed in the niches above their owners or patrons.[33]

Some tombs were richly decorated with paintings, especially tomb 4, which is decorated in a style found in the Campania region of south-west Italy, where highly-skilled artists' work survives at Pompeii and Herculaneum. Fragments of *amphorae* from Campania were also found in the cemetery at Kenchreai. However, the artist was local: he showed imaginative flair, a sense of design, and an ability to create detailed vignettes. His elongated dolphins are a unique touch.[34]

On the west wall of tomb 4 (see Plate 1), starting from the bottom, there is a row of green branched stems, with imitation column bases painted in purple; the tombs are also outlined in purple. Between the chambers hangs a garland of green leaves and yellow flowers. A bird perches at the centre of the garland; at each end hangs a long, curling tassel, with a knot held in the mouth of an elongated dolphin. Two dolphins are painted above each chamber, tail to tail, with a yellow disc between them. Above are smaller panels, too damaged to be deciphered in the photograph, containing white swans, a hippocamp (or mythical sea horse), and other birds and beasts; at the top are geometric designs. Ochre and maroon add to the rich palette of colours employed by the artist.[35]

Burial rites

The families may have lived in impressive residences such as those to the south of the cemetery (Fig. 9), from which there would have been a procession to the tomb. Since the chambers were not permanently sealed but had accessible entrances, relatives and friends could take part in rituals at the tomb. Cremations may have taken place on the southern slope of the ridge, where pyre debris was found; it seems that animals and small glass bottles (*unguentaria*) designed to hold ointments and aromatic substances were also burnt. Outside the tombs there was no evidence of dining tables, wells or altars; the ridge is quite steep (see Fig. 10) and not conducive to gatherings.[36]

The flight of steps leading down to each tomb would emphasise the transition from the open landscape to the dim underground chamber. There was space for no more than six or seven people to accompany the dead body. Though dimly lit, the tomb chambers that were decorated with painted birds, plants and garlands would convey the atmosphere of a peaceful otherworld. Nails or pins were fixed at regular intervals alongside and above the tombs: this suggests that mourners fixed screens over the tombs or hung garlands round them.[37]

Mourners sometimes placed coins over the face, mouth or chest of the dead person; most of the coins were several hundred years earlier than the burials. There were many incense burners, and clay lamps, and evidence of ritual meals inside the chambers: ceramic stewing pots, basins, casseroles, frying pans and even fragments of a grill with evidence of charring. There were pitchers, jars and amphorae, cups and bowls. Small bone fragments of sheep or goats, pigs and birds indicate what was eaten. Some of the cups and bowls were placed on the altars and in front of the tombs: this suggests that small meals were shared with the dead.[38]

Kenchreai's central shoreline

The ancient road from Corinth, Apostle Paul Road, leads down to the shore at the centre of the harbour. In the first to the third centuries AD, the town was socially and culturally diverse: excavation in the 1960s along the waterfront revealed dense structures and abundant artefacts that indicated the existence of a lively port until the late sixth or seventh century.[39] Further to the west, excavation has been possible only on vacant plots among villagers' homes. Beside the west bank of the coast road, close to Exit A (Odos Apostolou Paulo), an imposing residence with a colonnaded courtyard has been uncovered. On gently rising ground 100 m inland, on the left side of Exit A, what appears to have been a merchant's workshops were excavated in 2011; the small rooms are floored with rough red mosaic pavements and beside the rooms are four circular depressions, surrounded by large white pebbles (Fig. 11). These were designed to contain *pitharia*, or storage bins, in which food might be stored, or possibly olive oil, from which scent might have been made in the adjoining workshops.[40]

FIGURE 11. Merchant's workshops, with three circular depressions for storage jars (centre, left), Kenchreai.

Southern Kenchreai

At the south pier of the harbour, pottery and a few architectural remains indicated a small settlement during the Classical and Hellenistic periods (480–146 BC). In Roman times, a line of warehouses stretched at least 200 m along the south pier. On the shore it housed exports and imports, while at its outer end, six large rectangular fish tanks flowed into each other and through a channel into the sea. They contained fresh fish, which was purchased by those who could afford them.[41]

Land subsidence over the past 1,500 years has resulted in modern sea level being 1.5 m higher than in antiquity, drowning most of the remains. American underwater archaeologists directed by Robert Scranton conducted pioneering shallow-water excavations. They located a sixth-century church (Fig. 12) surrounded by many graves and, further into the sea, what they thought might be the temple of Isis with an apse, a mosaic floor and an octagonal fountain. However its shape is not that of a temple; it is now considered to have been a small pleasure spa, a fountain court or *nymphaeum*.

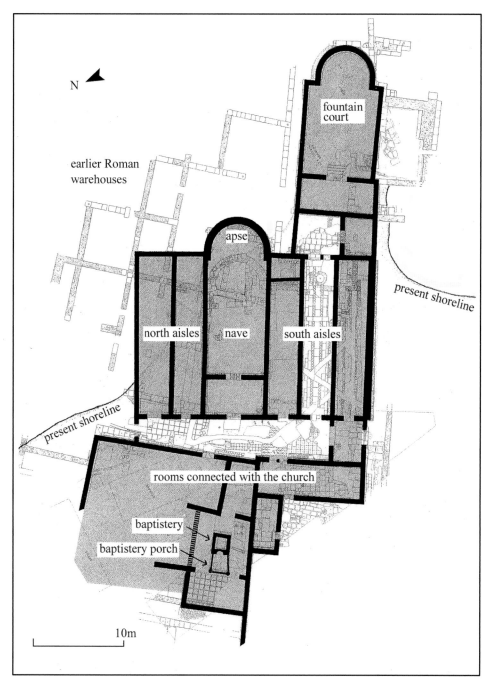

FIGURE 12. Sixth-century basilica, Kenchreai harbour, after a plan by W. Shaw. Courtesy of E.J. Brill.

Originally a *nymphaeum* was a natural grotto to honour water nymphs, but by Roman times such fountain courts might be used both for rituals, including marriages, and for recreation. A third-century date has been suggested for the fountain court; it appears to have been destroyed and partly submerged by earth movements in the 470s.[42] It may have been in the process of redecoration when disaster struck: on the floor of its cellar, large quantities of marble tesserae, marble blocks from which to cut them and polishing material suggest that the fountain court and its surrounding area was in the process of being renovated.[43]

Below the floor of the church, Scranton's most exciting discovery was the original wooden packing cases containing a hundred panels of cut glass (or *opus sectile*), depicting philosophers and scenes with animals, plants and a colonnaded building (Plate 3). They can now be seen in nearby Isthmia Museum. They had been sealed into the building after the earthquake or tsunami in the fourth century. Hector Williams, one of Scranton's team, describes their discovery below the Christian graves:

> There were many associated burials around the ... sixth-century Christian church. Below it were traces of a long corridor that led into the water, to the apse [of the presumed temple of Isis]. A floor almost level with the sea covered the structure, and below the floor was a broad flight of stairs running down into the water. Here, over 100 glass panels ... had been sealed into the building in c. 370 AD.[44]

The glass panels had probably been imported from Alexandria in Egypt, but the crates were never unpacked.

The basilica

The whole complex was later filled in and incorporated into the church.[45] The apsed building with its octagonal fountain may have become the *atrium*, or assembly room of the Christian basilica (Plate 4). A semicircular *agape* table would have been placed in its concave apse, where Christians could enjoy the communal meal that had now become separated from the Eucharist, which took place inside the basilica.[46] The use of *agape* tables will be discussed more fully in Chapter 4.

The ruined sixth-century basilica that can still be explored at the sea's edge was perhaps one of some ten churches in Kenchreai. Since it is located in the harbour, close to the departure point for Ephesus and Asia Minor, it is possible that it was erected in memory of Phoebe, who may have set out from close by, taking with her Paul's letter of introduction. The church was adorned with fine mosaics in the assembly room, the *narthex* (or corridor at the west end), apse and baptistery.

FIGURE 13. Exterior view of Kenchreai basilica from the north: behind a fallen column are two successive semi-circular apse walls, one underwater.

The sanctuary shows evidence of both an earlier and a later apse (Fig. 13). Perhaps the church became ruined and was rebuilt on a smaller scale: the smaller, later apse is constructed inside the earlier one, and built of rougher masonry. In the photograph, flat white slabs (to the right) belong to the larger apse wall; beyond, near the centre of the photo, smaller grey and brown blocks of stone denote the later second apse. A small room to the right of the apse may have been a sacristy, designed to receive the offerings of the faithful.

The nave and aisles

A white marble slab protrudes from the south wall at the junction of the sanctuary and the nave; it formed part of a marble sill, with a groove to support the low, decorated screen that separated the two areas, thus keeping apart the clergy in the sanctuary and the laity in the nave (Fig. 14). The marble sill is roughly dressed, and its carved underside suggests that it may have been recycled from the earlier church. A number of white marble panels, columns and decorated capitals found in the basilica can now be seen in the museum at Isthmia. Some have inscriptions; they are displayed (though not labelled) on the outer wall of the museum, facing the inner courtyard.

Back at Kenchreai, fine striated marble columns of white, grey and green, lie at the edge of the site, together with stacks of white marble floor tiles. Two aisles survive on the north-east side of the church; a third may have been destroyed by the sea. There are three aisles on the south-west side (Plate 5), but the central one is slightly lower than the other two and, unusually, may have been a colonnaded walkway open to the sky. There were mosaic floors, richly decorated with a variety of geometric patterns, in the *narthex* (or corridor at the west end), the apse and the baptistery.

A row of white marble column bases survives; they are in fact Roman representations of Doric capitals, re-used as column bases. It is possible that the three aisles including the colonnaded walkway date from the third century and adjoined the pre-Christian

FIGURE 14. Marble sill separating the sanctuary from the nave, with groove to support a decorated screen, Kenchreai basilica.

fountain court; the glass panels may have been intended to decorate its walls.[47] The fountain court and its surroundings are likely to have remained in ruins from the natural disaster in the fourth century until the Christian basilica was built two centuries later. It appears to have caught fire and collapsed in the early seventh century.[48]

The baptistery

To the north-west of the church, in an area that was formerly warehouses, a small separate building is the baptistery, where candidates were immersed in water by the bishop, during a ceremony that often took place on Easter night or a week after Christmas, on the feast of the Epiphany. The Greek word 'epiphany' means 'revelation', and the feast commemorates the journey of the pagan wise men to Bethlehem, following a star, which revealed to them the newborn King.

Eastern Christians regarded themselves as successors of the pagan magi as they, too, followed the star and found their God. Therefore pagans were baptised on this feast.

The baptistery at Kenchreai had a fine mosaic floor composed of geometric designs, including Solomon's knots, which consist of two interlaced loops: these appear to have been religious symbols, and are often found in both pagan and Christian contexts.[49] The baptistery was later re-ordered, and the foundations of a new font were dug through the room's earlier mosaic floor, damaging it in the process. The new font consisted of a square basin, paved with large terracotta brick tiles (Fig. 15). A porch was added onto its western end, and white columns were erected at the corners of the font and its porch. The walls of the porch were set into roughly trimmed white marble sills, made from small recycled columns. Broad grooves were cut into the sills, in order to support a balustrade, and there was an entrance gate.[50]

FIGURE 15. Kenchreai basilica: the baptistery, with its porch in the foreground. Photo by R. Scranton. Courtesy of E.J. Brill.

Destruction of Kenchreai

In the late sixth century the site was largely abandoned; several hoards of coins, perhaps buried for safety, suggest that by about AD 580 Kenchreai was no longer a flourishing Byzantine town. Small quantities of medieval pottery and coins indicate a modest medieval presence: perhaps Byzantine or Crusader armies still used the dilapidated harbour.[51] By this time, the house church of Phoebe was nothing more than a distant memory, enshrined in the scriptures. Today, the modest village of Kenchries occupies the site.

A mile south of Kenchries, the growing town of Loutro Elenis takes its name from the hot underwater springs of Helen of Troy. In ancient times, this region was sacred to Helen, who was regarded, like Persephone, as a light-bearing, springtime figure. Today the small church in Loutro Elenis stands on a steep hillside above a tiny harbour. It is dedicated to Phoebe, and is administered by an Orthodox nun. Like her predecessor, Helen of Troy, Phoebe's name means 'bright' or 'radiant',[52] in the same way that St Brigit of Ireland's name derives from that of Brígh, the Celtic goddess of fire and light. Many archaic cultures represented springtime as a radiant, happy maiden, who brought flowers and fertility to her people.

Phoebe's cult

Near Sparta, there is a sanctuary dedicated to the goddess Phoebe. Did her Christian counterpart come to replace Helen of Troy as a female figure honoured in the region? There are murals of Phoebe in a number of local churches, including those of Kenchreai and Examilia (Fig. 3), the ancient village between Kenchreai and Corinth, through which St Paul must have passed on his journeys between the two. Beside the sea at Kenchreai, icons of Phoebe can be seen today inside small household shrines, in each of which a family keeps an oil lamp burning, as a symbol of their prayers.

In local churches, Phoebe is depicted on the north wall of the nave, among the female saints to whom the women, sitting on the left side of the church, would naturally pray. Male saints are painted on the south wall, where the men would sit. Phoebe's feast day, often the earliest known fact connected with a saint's cult, is 3 September. A saint's feast day is normally the date of their death, their birthday into heaven. The repopulation of this area by Albanians in the nineteenth century caused a significant loss of oral tradition, although early place names such as Loutro Elenis have survived. Even this small town, however, may have regained its ancient name as a result of later scholars who read its description by Pausanias in the second century AD. Nevertheless, since local saints have been traditionally venerated throughout the centuries, it is just possible that Phoebe's feast day may have been preserved from early times.

Notes

1   Wijngaards Institute for Catholic Research, http://www.womendeacons.org/history-list-women-deacons-palestine-and-egypt/, 'List of women deacons in Palestine and Egypt', accessed 18.04.2020.

2   D. Winter, *Israel Handbook: With the Palestinian Authority Areas* (Bath: Footprint Travel Guides, 1999), p. 169.

3   K. Madigan and C. Osiek, *Ordained Women in the Early Church: A Documentary History* (Baltimore: Johns Hopkins University Press, 2005), Appendix A, Locations of Deacon Transcriptions, entry 139. The indiction was a proclamation made every fifteen years, fixing the valuation of property to be used as a basis for taxation; it was used as a means of dating events and transactions in the Roman empire and in the papal and some royal courts. The system was instituted by the Emperor Constantine in AD 313 and was used in the later Roman empire, and in some places until the sixteenth century.

4   U.E. Eisen, *Women Officeholders in Early Christianity: Epigraphical and Literary Studies*, transl. L. Maloney (Collegeville, MN: The Liturgical Press, 2000), p. 160.

5   Madigan and Osiek, *Ordained Women in the Early Church*, p. 91.

6   *Ibid*, p. 90.

7   Eisen, *Women Officeholders in Early Christianity*, p. 160.

8   R. Sweetman, 'The Christianization of the Peloponnese: the topography and function of late antique churches', in *Journal of Late Antiquity*, vol. 3, no. 2, Fall 2010, pp. 207–9, 243–7.

9   S. Mitchell, in *Anatolia: Land, Men and Gods in Asia Minor* (Oxford: Oxford University Press, 1993), vol. 2, chs. 16 and 17, asks a similar question concerning the spread of Christianity in Asia Minor.

10 Sweetman, 'The Christianization of the Peloponnese', pp. 245, 247.

11 W. Caraher, *Church, Society and the Sacred in Early Christian Greece*, PhD diss., Ohio State University, 2003, pp. 205, 207–9.

12 *Ibid*, pp. 216–7, 222.

13 Plans of over seventy Greek basilicas can be found in Appendix A of Caraher, *Church, Society and the Sacred*.

14 Sweetman, 'The Christianization of the Peloponnese', pp. 219, 235, 239–40.

15 Caraher, *Church, Society and the Sacred*, pp. 169, 192.

16 U. Becker, *The Continuum Encyclopedia of Symbols* (New York, London: Continuum, 1994), p. 91.

17 E. Rees, *Early Christianity in South-west Britain* (Oxford: Windgather Press, 2020), pp. 7–8.

18 Sweetman, 'The Christianization of the Peloponnese', pp. 241–2.

19 *Ibid*, pp. 212–20, 235, 240–1, with map at p. 214.

20 For a full account of Kenchreai and its relationship with Corinth, see D. Pettegrew, *The Isthmus of Corinth* (Ann Arbor, MI: University of Michigan Press, 2016), particularly the two chapters on Kenchreai itself.

21 *Metamorphoses*, 10. 35. See *The Golden Ass*, transl. S. Ruden (New Haven: Yale University Press, 2011).

22 Rees, *Early Christianity in South-west Britain*, pp. 3–17, 21–2.

23 Early photographs and plans of Kenchreai harbour and its basilica can be seen in R. Scranton, W. Shaw and L. Ibrahim, *Kenchreai, Eastern Port of Corinth. Results of Investigations by the University College of Chicago and Indiana University for the American School of Classical Studies at Athens, vol. 1. Topography and Architecture* (Leiden: E.J. Brill, 1978).

24 *Pausanius, Descriptions of Greece, Volume 1: Books I and II, Attica and Corinth*, transl. W.H.S.

Jones, Loeb Classical Library (Cambridge, MA: Harvard University Press, 2005), Book II. 2, 3.

25 H. Williams, 'Kenchreai, eastern port of Corinth', in *The Ancient Eastern Mediterranean: Papers Presented at a Symposium to Celebrate the Centennial Year of the Chicago Society of the Archaeological Institute of America, March 31, 1990*, ed. E. Guralnick (The Chicago Society, The Archaeological Institute of America, 1990), p. 52.

26 J.L. Rife, 'Religion and society at Roman Kenchreai', in *Corinth in Context: Comparative Studies on Religion and Society*, ed. S. Friesen, D. Schowalter and J. Walters (Leiden: Brill, 2010), ch. 13, pp. 381–422.

27 Professor Joseph L. Rife directed field research in the northern cemetery on behalf of the Kenchreai Cemetery Project, 2002–6.

28 Williams, 'Kenchreai, eastern port of Corinth', p. 53.

29 J. Rife and M.M. Morison, 'Space, object and process in the Koutsongila cemetery at Roman Kenchreai, Greece', in *Death as a Process*, ed. J. Pearce and J. Weekes, Studies in Funeral Archaeology, vol. 12 (Oxford: Oxbow Books, 2017), ch. 2, p. 31.

30 *Ibid*, pp. 36–7, 57.

31 I. Mancini, *Archaeological Discoveries Relative to the Judeo-Christians* (Jerusalem: Franciscan Printing Press, 1984), pp. 27–8. Mancini observes that, in a broadly parallel situation, Christians chose to be buried in family tombs owned by Jewish Sanhedrin families.

32 Rife and Morison, 'Space, object and process in the Koutsongila cemetery', pp. 31–2.

33 *Ibid*, pp. 35–6.

34 J. Rife, M. Morison, A. Barbet, R.K. Dunn, D.H. Ubelaker and F. Monier, 'Life and death at a port in Roman Greece: The Kenchreai Cemetery Project 2002–2006', *Hesperia*, vol. 76, no. 1 (2007), pp. 143–81, at p. 165.

35 *Ibid*, pp. 163–6.

36 Rife and Morison, 'Space, object and process in the Koutsongila cemetery', pp. 39–42.

37 *Ibid*, pp. 43–5.

38 *Ibid*, pp. 49, 53–5.

39 *Ibid*, p. 31.

40 Conversation with Professor G.D.R. Sanders, 17.05.2012.

41 Information at the site, 2020.

42 R.M. Rothaus, *Corinth: The First City of Greece. An Urban History of Late Antique Cult and Religion* (Leiden: Brill, 2000), p. 74.

43 *Ibid*, pp. 74–5.

44 H. Williams, 'Kenchreai, eastern port of Corinth', p. 51.

45 *Ibid*.

46 T. O'Loughlin, *The Eucharist: Origins and Contemporary Understandings* (London: T. & T. Clark, 2015), pp. 145–90.

47 Rothaus, *Corinth: The First City of Greece*, pp. 72–3.

48 *Ibid*, pp. 76, 78–9.

49 Caraher, *Church, Society and the Sacred in Early Christian Greece*, ch. 4, p. 162.

50 Scranton, Shaw and Ibrahim, *Kenchreai, Eastern Port of Corinth*, pp. 64, 66.

51 *Ibid*, pp. 50, 52.

52 H.G. Liddell, R. Scott and H.S. Jones, *A Greek-English Lexicon*, 9th ed. (Oxford: Oxford University Press, 1996), entry: *phoibos*.

Chapter 3

ISTHMIA: RUNNING FOR
A VICTOR'S CROWN

Isthmia is two miles north of Kenchreai, along the coast road, and four miles east of ancient Corinth. The sanctuary of Poseidon at Isthmia was the chief shrine of Corinth beyond the city's walls, and there was a long tradition of worship at this early religious centre. In this chapter, after considering its significant location at the south-eastern end of the isthmus, we shall examine some of the ancient rituals that took place at the site, as suggested by the spaces for worship and artefacts found there.

These people also honoured the divine by gratefully celebrating the many talents with which men and women were endowed. This was one of the sites of the pan-Hellenic Games, and we shall focus on how they were celebrated at Isthmia, with crowns accorded to a wide range of people from flute players to female charioteers. The centre of the site was a temple in honour of the sea god, Poseidon, one of the deities most revered by the Greeks. He was believed to drive back and forth in his chariot across the oceans, surrounded by a school of dolphins. Since he embraced the world and influenced it, he was known by such titles as 'World Shaker', 'Ocean-claimer' and 'Emperor of the Sea'.[1]

There is no scriptural evidence that St Paul came to Isthmia, but this is a reasonable deduction. It would seem that he arrived in time to ply his trade and spread the good news of his faith as preparations for the pan-Hellenic Games were underway. It is likely that here he developed his theology of Christians running the race in order to gain the reward of a victor's crown. However, for practising Jews, to focus on the human body could be a divisive issue. For those whose theology was incarnational, based on a risen yet fully human Jesus, the pan-Hellenic Games could be understood and celebrated, but for those whose theology was primarily redemptive, based on the view that humanity is rescued from evil in order to transcend itself, the Games could be problematic. We shall examine such reservations expressed in the Books of Maccabees, for example, later in the chapter.

Isthmia's location at the crossroads between east and west favoured its growth. Travellers and pilgrims who set out from the southern end of the paved road that preceded the Corinth canal, would climb uphill for half an hour and arrive at the sanctuary of Poseidon. The site of Isthmia was first systematically excavated by the American archaeologist Oscar Broneer in 1952, and further excavations were carried out from autumn 1989. There is a small, though significant museum, with a unique collection of artefacts. Isthmia is also a focus for ongoing research and excavation, particularly in the summer, by teams of students from Ohio State University. So far, few indications of early Christianity have become apparent, but there are hints of what still lies buried on the edges of the extensive site.

An attempted canal

Isthmia, meaning 'settlement at the isthmus', stood at the north-eastern end of the Peloponnese, on the land bridge. It was a natural crossroads, and Poseidon's sanctuary became an important roadside shrine. The isthmus was a little less than four miles wide at its narrowest point; although trade flowed easily from north to south, from mainland Greece to the Peloponnese, the isthmus was a barrier to east–west shipping. Since it was dangerous to sail round the southern tip of Greece, the Corinthians had thought of cutting a canal as early as the sixth century BC, but the task proved too difficult. The emperor Nero, who reigned AD 54–68, began work on a canal by digging the first clod of earth with a golden shovel, and emptying it into a golden bucket. Work proceeded, and Nero's image as the god Hercules was inscribed on one wall of the cutting, where it can still be seen, but when he died, the work of digging the canal was far from complete.[2]

A stretch of the canal about 700 m in length was dug out; for this, six thousand Jewish prisoners of war were employed. They had been captured during the war in Galilee. David Romano has suggested that the Jewish slaves may have been sold in local slave markets: if so, this would have greatly expanded their numbers in Corinth.[3] The canal was 40 or 50 m wide: the Jewish slaves began digging from both banks, while a third group drilled deep shafts to test the quality of the rock. The shafts were re-used in 1881 for the same purpose – to detect unstable tectonic plates.[4] Problems with landslides and the discrepancy between tides in the Corinthian and Saronic Gulfs have always dogged attempts to construct the canal. It was completed in 1895, but its narrowness has limited its use in modern times.

A paved road

A simpler and less costly project proved more successful: a paved road (inaccurately termed the *diolkos*), was constructed to join the Corinthian and Saronic gulfs (Plate 6). It was formerly thought that ships were hauled across the isthmus, but scholars now consider that the paved road played a more limited role in moving heavy cargoes, especially construction materials, to the site of Isthmia.[5] It varied in width from 3.4 to 6 m, and contained grooves cut in the pavement 1.5 m apart; these guided the wheels of wooden trolleys, on which goods were hauled across the isthmus. The road was surfaced with gravel, and there were sidings, to allow oncoming traffic to pass. Pack animals used earthen tracks on either side of the paved road. It has been suggested that since the paved road originated when Greece's finest temples were beginning to be erected, it was initially used for transporting marble, monoliths and timber.[6]

Corinth also proved an excellent base for Paul, the missionary. With its close affinities with Rome, Corinth was the launching point for his mission to the

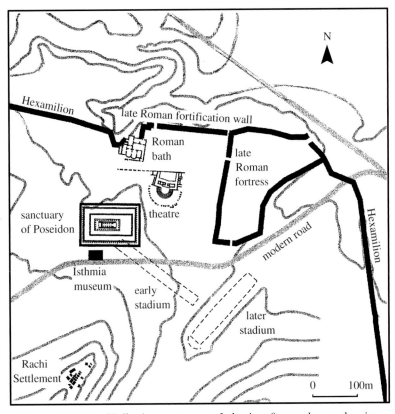

FIGURE 16. Pan-Hellenic sanctuary at Isthmia, after a plan at the site.

41

Romans. From Corinth's harbours he could convey his message as far as Marseilles and Seville in western Europe if he wished, while also staying in contact with his daughter churches in Asia. Having left Athens, Paul's journey to Corinth is likely to have taken him past the temple of Poseidon at Isthmia (Plate 7); the sanctuary lay in ruins, but was now being restored (Fig. 16).

The sanctuary at Isthmia

Isthmia could be considered the most significant sacred site for Corinthians in ancient times. There appears to have been a shrine at Isthmia since the early Iron Age, since cups and bowls were found mixed with ash and the burnt bones of sheep, cattle and goats, dating from the late eleventh or tenth century BC. These were discovered on the site where the altar to Poseidon was later built. At first, sacrifices might be simply made on a flat rock, but in time an imposing sanctuary was built and the pan-Hellenic Games were established to honour the gods.[7] The Isthmian Games were one of the four great pan-Hellenic festivals; as their name implies, these were attended by competitors from throughout Greece. Those held at Olympia were by far the oldest: they are recorded as taking place in 776 BC. The Pythian Games at Delphi were the next to be established: they first took place in 586 BC, and were followed by those of Isthmia (580 BC) and Nemea (573 BC).[8]

At smaller, local festivals, prizes of money were awarded to competitors; the four pan-Hellenic festivals were the only Games at which the victor's sole reward was a wreath. Their standard of performance was also higher than that found in other festivals: an Athenian law of about 430 BC decreed that a man who won at any of the four pan-Hellenic Games would receive free meals at the state's expense for the rest of his life. During the four chief festivals a truce was held throughout Greece, although competitors might be at war for the remainder of the year. The Games took place every four years at Olympia and Delphi and every two at Isthmia and Nemea; those at Isthmia took place in April or May.[9]

The earliest temple of Poseidon at Isthmia was destroyed by fire, but a magnificent marble basin on a stand survives: it contained water for people to purify themselves before entering the sanctuary, and probably dates from the seventh century BC. The shallow circular bowl 1.24 m in diameter rests on a ring supported by columns that depict four women, each standing on the back of a lion, holding its tail in one hand and its leash in the other. The ring between the women's heads is decorated with horned rams' heads; the faces, hair and clothing of the exquisite figures bear traces of paint. The worn surfaces of the handles and rim of the marble bowl suggest that many people reached into it, presumably for water to cleanse themselves before worshipping in the temple.[10]

The basin's magnificence emphasises the prominence that early peoples gave to purifying themselves in order to engage in communion with the divine. The symbolism of washing to cleanse both the outer and the inner self was to deepen over the centuries. It is found in Jewish ritual bathing practices, which were inherited by the early Church. Writing to the Christians at Ephesus, perhaps in the early 80s or 90s, a follower of St Paul reminded his friends:

> *Christ loved the Church and sacrificed himself for her to make her holy. He made her clean by washing her in water with a form of words, so that when he took her to himself she would be glorious, with no speck or wrinkle, or anything like that* (Eph. 5. 25–7).

Isthmia's feasting caves

Two underground caves at Isthmia were used for feasting from the late fifth century BC. Here, worshippers ate a sacred meal in communion with one another and with the gods. One cave is in the north-east corner of the sanctuary of Poseidon; the other, which is better preserved (Plate 8), is on the south-eastern edge of the theatre. Each cave is divided into two chambers, with an unroofed entrance court where meals were prepared; this contained a brazier for cooking and a table. In the court of the theatre cave there is a small, almost circular room where dishes appear to have been washed, since a tiled drain led from a sink into a pit that had been dug out from the hard clay and filled with earth.[11] This elaborate soakaway system has later Christian parallels in Roman baptismal fonts.[12] In many religions, inner purity is symbolised by external cleansing, and the water used is also treated with respect.

In one corner of the entrance court of the feasting cave near Isthmia's theatre, a storage jar contained seventeen pottery vessels of various shapes and sizes, including casseroles blackened by fire.[13] Perhaps they had been washed and left to dry before the cave was abandoned, soon after 350 BC. A doorway led into the cave chamber, which had been given a vaulted ceiling. To the right of the entrance was a niche, perhaps intended for small statues. Along the chamber walls were five couches shaped out of hard clay, each with a head rest at one end; the couches had been later hacked away.[14]

In the north-west corner of the chamber, a doorway leads into a small side chamber, with six couches still intact. These were both dining rooms where worshippers could eat a meal together, in the presence of the divinity. The two chambers in the cave at the edge of the temple of Poseidon were of similar size, again with space for eleven diners.[15] The meals eaten in the caves could be seen as a parallel to the eucharistic meal, in which Christians gratefully share prepared food with one another and with the divine author of such beneficence.

The role of table-sharing, or commensality, throughout human history is now more fully understood. Professor Thomas O'Loughlin has observed:

> *No area of research connected with the Eucharist, the history of liturgy, or early Christianity has seen such an explosion of interest in recent decades as that involving the place of meals and the phenomenon of commensality. This is matched by interest from classicists into the structure and significance of* symposia *and the meals of various associations. To this we might add the results of research by anthropologists and the historians of food, and still the list of contributing disciplines would not be complete.*[16]

He continues to note the ways in which this strand of human life can be traced back through millennia:

> *The effect of this [research] has been to see the gathering for a meal as being a basic element in the formation and maintenance of the early communities of disciples… Indeed, in the small-sized groups [in which] most human beings have lived their lives down through the millennia – the group meal not only gave form to the society, but also enabled the society to express its structure, perform its vision of the universe and maintain the internal bonds that held it together.*[17]

On a grander scale than Isthmia's caves for feasting, there was an enormous banquet hall at Epidaurus, where ritual meals were eaten in honour of Asclepius. A white marble fountain adjoins its eastern wall, where pilgrims could wash before the meal (Fig. 89). The complex will be described in greater detail in Chapter 8.

Washing before a meal was also normal in the Jewish tradition, particularly for solemn meals. In the late first century AD, the followers of St John recorded his memories of the final Passover meal of Jesus, at which he washed the feet of his followers:

> *He got up from table, removed his outer garment and, taking a towel, wrapped it around his waist [as a servant would]; he then poured water into a basin and began to wash the disciples' feet and to wipe them with the towel he was wearing. He came to Simon Peter, who said to him, 'Lord, are you going to wash my feet?' … Jesus replied, 'If I do not wash you, you can have nothing in common with me'. 'Then, Lord,' said Simon Peter, 'not only my feet, but my hands and my head as well!'. Jesus said, 'No one who has taken a bath needs washing, he is clean all over. You too are clean, though not all of you are.' He knew who was going to betray him; that was why he said 'though not all of you are' (Jn. 13. 4–11).*

This final observation tells us that external washing also symbolised inner purity. Excavations of ritual dining rooms in the sanctuaries of Demeter and Kore on the lower slopes of Acrocorinth provide us with further details of banquets eaten in communion with the gods, as they were celebrated in pre-Christian times between the late sixth century and 400 BC. Bathing rooms were often attached to such dining rooms from the fifth century BC onwards; a small number of diners ate in each room.[18] The meals reaffirmed a sense of community, through the equal distribution of food to rich and poor alike. There may have been officials who oversaw its distribution, ensured good conduct and levied fines on those who misbehaved. Meat was served, eaten with the fingers, and crushed grain was boiled into a loose porridge. Other food might include beans, leeks, seeds and nuts, honey and fresh or dried fruit. Wine was a major feature of the meals; olive oil was served as a condiment.[19]

Isthmia's stadium

For travellers by both land and sea, the sanctuary at Isthmia was a testimony to Corinth's wealth and power. It was a natural place for the pan-Hellenic Games and for interstate assemblies. Large quantities of arms and armour brought here as offerings in the Archaic period demonstrate that early on, Isthmia became an important political centre. The first stadium was built in the sixth century BC: the line of wooden starting posts has been reconstructed (Fig. 17). In the following century a theatre was built, probably for musical contests.

FIGURE 17. Isthmia stadium, *c.* 550 BC, with reconstructed wooden starting posts.

At the end of the fourth century BC, a large new stadium was built, lower down the hill – this is the stadium that St Paul would have known (Fig. 18). It can be viewed by walking downhill from the museum and following the first track to the right. The enormous arena is situated in the broad valley to the east of the *rachi* settlement indicated in the lower left-hand corner of Figure 16. This was an early hilltop settlement, *rachi* meaning the 'backbone' of the land.

When Philip of Macedonia was defeated by a combined Roman and Greek army in 196 BC, the victorious Roman general, Titus Quinctius Flamininus, summoned the most famous of the Isthmian assemblies. The Roman historian Livy (59/64 BC–AD 12/17) recounts that when the spectators took to their seats, expecting the opening of the Games, the herald, together with a trumpeter, walked into the middle of the race track and announced that the Greek states would henceforth be free from taxation, and were now free to be governed according to their ancestral laws. The Greek philosopher, Plutarch (AD 46 – after 119), in his biography of the Roman general, adds that afterwards the audience paid no attention to the athletes, but shouted so loudly in approval that ravens flying overhead fell onto the track in shock.[20]

In spite of these political declarations, the Romans sacked Corinth fifty years later, in 146 BC. Control of the Games passed to the nearby town of Sikyon, seven miles north-west of Corinth, while the sanctuary at Isthmia was abandoned, and fell into ruin. We shall examine the town of Sikyon, with its later Christian basilica, in Chapter 6. A new Roman colony was established at Corinth in 44 BC, and a small number of wealthy Corinthians were able to repair the sanctuary at

FIGURE 18. Site of the large stadium familiar to St Paul, Isthmia.

Isthmia, and bring back the Games, perhaps in the early 40s AD.[21] Livy describes the Isthmian Games as both the market and the meeting place of Greece and Asia.[22]

Restoration of the Games

An inscription tells us about the citizen who was chiefly responsible for reinstating the Games. It was the father of one Lucius Castricius Regulus who was the first 'to preside over the [restored] Isthmian Games at the isthmus ... He introduced [poetry contests in honour of] the divine Julia Augusta [patroness of Corinth], and [a contest for] girls ... and gave a banquet for all the inhabitants of the colony.' The inscription adds: 'His son Castricius Regulus erected this monument in accordance with a decree of the city council.' His father would have defrayed the enormous cost of the repairs, and offered free food and drink to all the citizens, from his personal fortune.[23]

An inscription describing the Pythian Games at Delphi confirms the introduction of events for women. It commemorates three female athletes, Tryphosa, Hedea and Dionysia; Hedea was also an outstanding musician:

> *Tryphosa, successively winner of the 200 metres at the Pythian games... and at the Isthmian games ... First of the virgins; Hedea, winner of the race for war-chariots at the Isthmian games, ... and of the 200 metres, both at the Nemean games ... and the games at Sikyon ...; she carried away the prize for young lyre-players at the Sebastea in Athens ... Dionysia, winner of the 200 metres at the Isthmian games, ... and at the Asclepeian games in sacred Epidaurus ...*[24]

These young women appear to have been semi-professional competitors, who earned a considerable income for their families. Amateurs, too, entered the contests, and were often victorious. Hedea won the war-chariot race at Isthmia in AD 43, not long before Paul's arrival in Corinth. She is an example of the liberated women whom he describes in 1 Corinthians 11, when discussing women's behaviour at the Eucharist. He argues that women should cover their heads and, of course, the rest of their bodies. He writes: 'Ask yourselves if it is fitting for a woman to pray to God without a veil...? To anyone who might still want to argue: it is not the custom with us, nor in the churches of God' (1 Cor. 11. 3–16).

Paul's arrival

Paul probably arrived in Corinth nine months after the Games of AD 49.[25] According to the Acts of the Apostles, he was a tent maker or leather worker, as we have seen: Luke describes him arriving in Corinth and meeting a Christian couple who had been expelled from Rome. They were of the same trade, and they evidently invited him to join them in their workshop. We read:

> Paul left Athens and came to Corinth, where he met a Jew called Aquila, whose family came from Pontus. He and his wife Priscilla had recently left Italy because an edict of Claudius had expelled all the Jews from Rome. Paul went to visit them, and when he found they were tent makers, of the same trade as himself, he lodged with them and they worked together (Acts 18. 1–4).

Artisans like Prisca and Aquila worked in small shops scattered throughout Ancient Corinth; these lined busy streets, and were also concentrated in purpose-built commercial developments, a typical example being the North Market complex that was built shortly before Paul's arrival. Excavation has shown that these shops were 4 m high and 2.8 to 4 m wide; they had no running water or toilets. In one of the back corners, steps and a ladder led to a loft that was lit by an unglazed window over the shop entrance. At night it could be closed with wooden shutters, both for privacy and for protection in cold weather. In the shop below, the open doorway was the only source of light: this made it difficult to work in the cold winters.[26]

Professor Jerome Murphy-O'Connor imagines Paul's first months in Corinth:

> Prisca and Aquila had their home in the loft, while Paul slept below amid the tool-strewn work-benches and the rolls of leather and canvas. The workshop was perfect for initial contacts, particularly with women. While Paul worked on a cloak, or sandal, or belt, he had the opportunity for conversation which quickly became instruction, and further encounters were easily justified by the need for new pieces or other repairs.[27]

Paul the tent maker

When Paul arrived at Isthmia, the site was much smaller than its ancient Greek predecessor. By now there were only three significant buildings: the temple of Poseidon (Plate 7), a ruined theatre that would be restored fifteen years later, and the giant stadium (Fig. 18), its white marble gleaming in the sunlight. There would have been other buildings, although we are uncertain about their extent, because excavation at Isthmia has been much less extensive than at Corinth. There were certainly residences and/or villas, and no doubt numerous standing monuments left by former Greeks and Romans. Paul would have realised that there would be plenty of work for him as a tent maker in the fifteen months before the next pan-Hellenic Games at Isthmia, making and repairing tents for visitors and booths for Corinthian shopkeepers who catered for the spectators' needs. Tents were made from both canvas and leather. Paul could also mend the many leather articles used by travellers: wallets, animal harness, shields, and gourds to contain water and wine.[28]

Paul had chosen to support himself as a tent maker for a number of reasons. The skill was in demand throughout the Graeco-Roman world, and it brought him into contact with a wide range of people. The tools were easily portable, simple and light: a knife to cut heavy leather or canvas, an awl to make holes for the waxed thread, and curved needles, all of which fitted into a small wallet. The skill involved was minimal, so it was quickly learnt; the craft was quiet and sedentary, so that Paul could preach as he worked. The phrase that he used when writing to the Christians in Thessalonika, 'working we proclaimed' (2 Thess. 2. 9), suggests that he preached while actually working.[29] His earnings enabled him to preach the gospel free of charge (1 Cor. 9. 17–18) and to earn enough to support his often poor companions.

Athletic imagery

At this time, Paul first developed his theme of Christians resembling athletes competing in the stadium. His focus shifts from runner to boxer to announcer:

> All the runners at the stadium are trying to win, but only one of them gets the prize. You must run in the same way, meaning to win. All the athletes at the Games go into strict training; they do this just to win a withered wreath, but we do it for a wreath that will never wither. That is how I run, intent on winning; that is how I box, not beating the air; I pommel my body and make it obey me, for, having been an announcer myself, I should not want to be disqualified (1 Cor. 9. 24–7).

The withered wreath to which Paul refers was the coveted Isthmian crown awarded to the most outstanding athlete. The crown presented at Olympia was made of wild olive branches; that of the Pythian Games at Delphi was of laurel. At Nemea the crown was woven from broad, wild celery leaves, freshly cut, while at Isthmia, the crowns were of withered celery leaves. In the earliest period, the Isthmian crown was made from tight bunches of pine, attached to a plain headband.[30] The pine tree was, and is, the most common tree in the region around Isthmia, but by at least the 470s BC, wild celery came to replace pine for victory crowns; celery also grows abundantly in the region. We learn of the celery wreath from the four books of Victory Odes (or *epinikia*) of Pindar (*c.* 518–438 BC) composed to celebrate competitors' triumphs: he makes no mention of pine wreaths, but refers to a celery crown four times. He calls the plant 'Corinthian celery', and writes of a successful competitor at both Isthmia and Nemea: 'Two wreaths of wild celery crowned him, when he appeared at the Isthmian festival; and Nemea does not speak differently'.[31]

Pindar describes a charioteer crowned in the same manner: 'I sing the Isthmian victory with horses, not unrecognised, which Poseidon granted to Xenocrates, and sent him a garland of Dorian wild celery for his hair, to have himself crowned, thus honouring the man of the fine chariot...'.[32] Some two hundred years later, pine wreaths are again described at Isthmia: both appear on Roman monuments, and would have been awarded in St Paul's day, perhaps for different events. Pindar describes the celery used in the Isthmian crown as withered, and this appears to be confirmed by depictions of wreaths on later monuments dating from the Roman period.[33]

In the southern *stoa*, or arcade, of Ancient Corinth, a mosaic floor was discovered that may have adorned the office of the director of the Isthmian Games. It depicts a victorious athlete clasping a palm branch in his hand and wearing a crown of withered celery leaves tied at the back. He stands before Eutychia, the goddess of good fortune, as he thanks her for his success.[34] In the last year of his life, aged over seventy, Paul or a close follower returned to athletic imagery: 'In the case of an athlete, no one is crowned without competing according to the rules' (2 Tim. 2. 5). He writes: 'I have finished the race, I have kept the faith. From now on there is reserved for me the crown of righteousness, which the Lord, the righteous judge, will give to me on that day' (2 Tim. 4. 7–8).

Jewish resistance to the Games

It is uncertain whether Paul actually watched the Isthmian Games, since many Palestinian Jews opposed such spectacles. The two Books of Maccabees were compiled by anti-Hellenist Jews some time before 63 BC; they cover the period between 175 and 134 BC, and provide valuable historical information, though with an anti-Greek bias. The second Book of Maccabees is addressed to expatriate Jews in Alexandria, to warn them of the dangers threatening the Temple in Jerusalem. It begins: 'Greetings to their brothers, the Jews in Egypt, from their brothers, the Jews in Jerusalem and in the country of Judaea' (2 Mac. 1. 1).

The author of 2 Maccabees notes with distaste how Joshua became high priest by bribing King Antiochus Epiphanes, and gave himself a Greek name, Jason. The account continues:

> *He went so far as to build a gymnasium at the very foot of the citadel [of Jerusalem], and to fit out the noblest of his youths in the petasos [the hat of the god Hermes, worn by athletes]. Godless wretch that he was, and no true high priest, Jason set no bounds to his impiety; indeed the Hellenising process reached such a pitch that*

the priests ceased to show any interest in the services of the altar; scorning the Temple and neglecting the sacrifices, they would hurry to take part in the unlawful exercises on the training ground as soon as the signal was given for the discus. They disdained all that their ancestors had esteemed, and set the highest value on Hellenic honours (2 Mac. 4. 12–15).

We are also informed that some Jews travelled north to Tyre to watch the Games and – even worse – to make an offering in honour of Hercules, although this was ultimately considered a step too far, so the money was spent on warships instead:

On the occasion of the quinquennial Games at Tyre in the presence of the king, the vile Jason sent some Antiochists from Jerusalem as official spectators; these brought with them three hundred silver drachmae for the sacrifice to Hercules. But even those who brought the money thought it should not be spent on the sacrifice – this would not be right – and decided to reserve it for some other item of expenditure; and so what the sender had intended for the sacrifice was in fact applied, at the suggestion of those who brought it, to the construction of triremes (2. Mac. 4. 18–20).

In the time of Christ, Jewish towns adopted different degrees of adherence to the detailed laws contained within the Torah. Nazareth, where Jesus was brought up, observed these laws more strictly than Sepphoris, three miles to the north, where Graeco-Roman culture was stronger. Recent excavation directed by Dr Ken Dark of Reading University, funded by the Palestine Exploration Fund, indicates that Nazareth was larger than previously thought, with up to 1,000 inhabitants. Nevertheless, only rough stoneware pottery is found in first-century Nazareth, while in Sepphoris a range of ceramic and wooden vessels were also used.[35]

These were avoided by strict Jews, because wooden vessels and unglazed pottery cannot be purified as thoroughly as stoneware, which can be vigorously cleansed, soaked in water or passed through fire. Nazareth's stoneware was almost all made in the Jewish village of Kefar Hananya, twenty-three miles north of Nazareth. No human manure is found around Nazareth, whereas human faeces was used liberally by the inhabitants of Sepphoris to fertilise their soil. Ultra-religious Jews, such as the Essenes, regarded human excrement as ritually impure.[36]

This provides a possible context for the words with which Jesus challenged the worshippers in the synagogue at Nazareth. Perhaps his proclamation of freedom for the poor, the blind and the downtrodden (Lk. 4. 18–19), who were often considered to be ritually unclean, was more than his fellow townsmen could accept. The dialogue grew more hostile until, according to Luke, '...everyone in the synagogue was enraged. They sprang to their feet, hustled him out of the town; and they took him up to the brow of the hill their town was built on, intending to throw him down the cliff' (Lk. 4. 28–9).

Freer attitudes to the Games

Among the Jews dispersed beyond Palestine, it is likely that attitudes were freer. In the theatre at Miletus in western Asia Minor, Jews had specially reserved seats,[37] presumably in order to stay separate from gentile spectators, and so avoid defilement. The Jewish philosopher, Philo, who was born in about 20 BC and died around AD 50, came from a Jewish priestly family (*de genere sacerdotum*),[38] and was one of over a million Jews living in Alexandria, where he was also trained in Greek and Roman thought.[39] Philo frequently attended horse and chariot races; he also enjoyed watching boxing and wrestling matches, and the Olympic Games. He attended the theatre to watch plays by Euripides and other dramatists, and went to concerts, especially of choral music, since he loved harmony.[40]

Paul may have been too busy making and repairing items to attend the Games at Isthmia but if, like Philo, he watched wrestlers, their bodies glistening with oil, did it remind him of Jesus naked on the cross, wrestling with evil, and of the many baptismal candidates whom Paul had anointed, in order to join Christ in his mighty struggle against the 'principalities and powers' (Col. 2. 15)? Greek athletes were anointed to stimulate the body before exercise, and to reduce the loss of body fluids, and thereby increase their stamina. The oil also protected them from the sun's rays, and was considered to enhance their physical beauty.[41]

Christian lamps

A few early Christian lamps were discovered at Isthmia. Examples of a Christian type of boat-shaped lamp were found: prototypes of this kind of lamp had reached Greece from north Africa. They have a solid knob handle, a broad flat rim, and two or three holes in the upper surface; many date from the sixth century AD.[42] The lamps are carved in a variety of designs, often with biblical motifs taken from both the Old and New Testaments. The most common design features a pair of palm branches round the rim, and a cross on the disc. The palm branch symbolised the tree of life, and the branches spread before Christ by his followers on Palm Sunday, as he rode triumphantly into Jerusalem. Martyrs in heaven were also depicted carrying palm branches, an image taken from scripture (Rev. 7. 9). However, the use of such themes is likely to denote a ready market for Christian designs, rather than Christian owners, or use in worship.

One fragmentary lamp from the south-western part of the temple of Poseidon is made of red clay, with bright red glaze, and is decorated with one studded arm of a cross.[43] On another fragment, the lower part of the *chi-rho* monogram for Christ can be seen, above a palm leaf.[44] A third lamp fragment has a design in the form of a chalice on its rim, and part of a fish, another symbol for Christ, on the body of the lamp.[45] They appear to have been stored, together with other late Roman lamps, in a cave above the theatre.[46] Christian graves scattered across the extensive site suggest a sizeable Christian presence at Isthmia, and there are likely to be several basilicas as yet undiscovered, including one at the end of the Hexamilion Wall, where there is evidence of a possible Christian community.[47]

The fortress and the Hexamilion Wall

At the eastern end of the site, a late Roman fortress dates to the fifth century AD. Its north-east gate incorporates a monumental arch that would have served as a majestic entrance to the fortress, the sanctuary and perhaps to the entire Peloponnese. Excavation in the northern area of the fortress revealed many graves, some of which contained several bodies, not only of soldiers but also of women and children. This suggests that families lived within the fortress both in times of war and of peace. It was refurbished and used during the later Byzantine, Turkish and Venetian periods, at least until the seventeenth century.[48]

In AD 395 the Goths, under the leadership of Alaric, devastated southern Greece. Twelve years later, the Emperor Theodosius II (407–50) began to reign at the age of seven, on the death of his father. His elder sister Pulcheria acted as co-regent for the next eight years, and continued to influence her younger brother. Theodosius decided to protect the Peloponnese from invasion from the north by constructing a wall across the entire isthmus, from the Corinthian to the Saronic Gulfs. The Hexamilion (or 'six mile') Wall protected Isthmia's northern and eastern boundary and required an enormous quantity of stone.

The ruined temple of Poseidon was torn down to its foundations and its stone plundered, together with that of the surrounding buildings – the bath, theatre and athletic structures that by now were no longer in use. The trans-Isthmian wall was faced on both sides with large ashlar (squared) masonry blocks and filled with mortar and rubble, and was designed to repel Visigoth invaders; much of it still survives. Archaeologists are continuing to examine the *spolia*, or recycled materials found in both the wall and the fortress, in order to locate, identify and record blocks that originate from pre-existing buildings at Isthmia.[49]

Justinian's dedicatory inscription

A final Christian artefact on display in Isthmia museum dates from this time: carved within the outline of a cross is a dedicatory inscription of the Hexamilion Wall, found nearby. It was one of a pair of two blocks of stone that were probably placed above gateways in the wall; they commemorate Justinian and an official or engineer named Victorinus. The first gives thanks to God using words from the Nicene Creed (Fig. 19) and reads in translation,

FIGURE 19. Dedicatory inscription from the Hexamilion Wall (AD 548–60), in Isthmia Museum (I-1390). Courtesy of Timothy Gregory.

> *Light from light, true God from true God, guard the Emperor Justinian and his faithful servant Victorinus along with those who dwell in Greece according to God.*[50]

The inscription on the second block calls upon Mary, Mother of God, to protect Corinth's Christians:

> *Holy Mary, God-bearer, guard the empire of Christ-loving Justinian and Victorinus who serves him wisely, along with those who dwell in Corinth living according to God.*[51]

The inscriptions indicate that Justinian's agents were involved in the construction of the Hexamilion Wall, although it is likely that the provincial governor and a host of local officials were primarily responsible for urban change. There is no unequivocal evidence that Justinian attempted to force the conversion of the population of Achaia, although there is evidence for this elsewhere.

Reviewing Isthmia's archaeology, it is apparent that while a remarkable number of artefacts and buildings survive from Isthmia's pagan past, little evidence of Christian Isthmia has so far been discovered. It is to be hoped that future excavations in the area surrounding the sanctuary will yield finds that shed further light on the development of early Christianity in Isthmia.

Notes

1   N. Karela, *Greek Mythology* (Athens: Michalis Toubis, 1998), p. 33.

2   D. Pettegrew, 'The Diolkos and the Emporion: how a land bridge framed the commercial economy of Roman Corinth', in *Corinth in Contrast: Studies in Inequality*, ed. S.J. Friesen, S. James and D. N. Schowalter (Leiden: Brill Academic Press, 2013) pp. 126–42.

3   D.G. Romano, 'Urban and rural planning in Roman Corinth', in *Urban Religion in Roman Corinth: Interdisciplinary Approaches*, ed. D.N. Schowalter and S. J. Freisen, Harvard Theological Studies no. 53 (Cambridge, MAS: Harvard University Press, 2005), ch. 2, pp. 27–9.

4   B. Gerster, 'L'Isthme de Corinthe: tentatives de percement dans l'antiquité', *Bulletin de correspondance hellénique*, vol. 8, no. 1 (1884), pp. 225–32.

5   D. Pettegrew, *The Isthmus of Corinth* (Ann Arbor, MI: University of Michigan Press, 2016).

6   Raepsaet and Tolley, 'Le Diolkos de l'Isthme à Corinthe', p. 256.

7   E. Gebhard, 'The evolution of a pan-Hellenic Sanctuary: from archaeology towards history at Isthmia', in *Greek Sanctuaries: New Approaches*, ed. N. Marinatos and R. Häg (London, New York: Routledge, 1993), pp. 157, 164, 168.

8   S.G. Miller, 'The date of the first Pythiad', *California Studies in Classical Antiquity* (CSCA), vol. 11 (1978), pp. 127–58.

9   S.G. Miller, *Nemea: A Guide to the Site and Museum* (Athens: Ministry of Culture Archaeological Receipts Fund, 2004), pp. 12–13.

10 *Ibid*, p. 168.

11 O. Broneer, 'Paul and the pagan cults at Isthmia', in *Harvard Theological Review*, vol. 64 (1971), pp. 169–87, at p. 178.

12 For a later Christian parallel in a villa at Bradford on Avon (Wiltshire) in south-west Britain, see E. Rees, *Early Christianity in South-West Britain* (Oxford: Windgather Press, 2020), pp. 14–15.

13 A complete example of a two-handled casserole with a lid, dating from the sixth to the fourth century BC, can be seen in the Ancient Agora Museum, Athens, housed in the Stoa of Attalus. It can be viewed online at https://en.wikipedia.org/wiki/Cookware_and_bakeware (accessed 30.05.2020). The casserole rests on a solid cylindrical brazier, perforated with holes for the smoke to escape.

14 Broneer, 'Paul and the pagan cults at Isthmia', pp. 178–9.

15 *Ibid.*

16 T. O'Loughlin, *The Eucharist: Origins and Contemporary Understandings* (London: T. & T. Clark, 2015), p. 85.

17 *Ibid*, p. 86.

18 N. Bookidis, 'Ritual dining at Corinth', in Marinatos and Hägg, *Greek Sanctuaries: New Approaches*, pp. 45, 51–2.

19 *Ibid*, pp. 54–6.

20 Plutarch, *Vita Flaminini* 10. 3–11, in Gebhard, 'The evolution of a pan-Hellenic Sanctuary', p. 168.

21 M. Kajava, 'When did the Isthmian games return to the Isthmus? (Rereading "Corinth" 8. 3. 153)', in *Classical Philology*, vol. 97, no. 2 (April 1, 2002), pp. 168–78.

22 Livy, *Ab Urbe Condita Libri*, 32. 33, in *The Rise of Rome*, transl. T.J. Luce, bks. 1–5 (Oxford: Oxford University Press, 1998).

23 J. Murphy-O'Connor, *St Paul's Corinth: Texts and Archaeology* (Collegeville, MN: Michael Glazier, Liturgical Press, 1983), pp. 14–15.

24 *Ibid.*

25 J. Murphy-O'Connor, *Paul: His Story* (Oxford: Oxford University Press, 2004), p. 81.

26 *Ibid*, p. 84.

27 *Ibid*.

28 Murphy-O'Connor, *St Paul's Corinth*, p. 176.

29 *Ibid*, p. 177.

30 O. Broneer, 'The Isthmian victory crown', in *American Journal of Archaeology*, vol. 66 (1962), pp. 261–3.

31 Pindar, Olympian Victory Ode no. 13, in F.J. Nisetich, *Pindar's Victory Songs* (Baltimore: Johns Hopkins University Press, 1980).

32 Pindar, Isthmian Victory Ode no. 2, Nisetich, *Pindar's Victory Songs*.

33 Broneer, 'Paul and the Pagan Cults at Isthmia', p. 186.

34 O. Meinardus, *St Paul in Greece* (Athens: Lycabettus Press, 2006), p. 88.

35 K. Dark, 'A liminal landscape? Living between Nazareth and Sepphoris in the Roman and Byzantine periods', in *Roman-Period and Byzantine Nazareth and its Hinterland*, K. Dark (London, New York: Routledge, 2020), ch. 3.

36 *Ibid*.

37 Murphy-O'Connor, *St Paul's Corinth*, p. 17.

38 Jerome, *De Viris Illustribus*, ed. and transl. T. P. Halton, *Fathers of the Church*, vol. 100 (Washington, DC: Catholic University of America University Press, 1999), ch. 11.

39 Philo, *Against Flaccus*, chs. 6–9, in *Philo with an English Translation*, transl. F. H. Colson, Loeb Classical Library, vol. 363 (Cambridge, MAS: Harvard University Press, 1929–62).

40 M.L. Samuel, *Rediscovering Philo of Alexander: A First Century Torah Commentator. Volume 1: Genesis* (Sarasota, FL: First Edition Design Publishing, 2016), p. 18.

41 Miller, *Nemea: A Guide to the Site and Museum*, pp. 209–10.

42 O. Broneer, 'Terracotta lamps', in *Isthmia: Excavations by the University of Chicago under the auspices of the American School of Classical Studies at Athens*, vol. 3 (Princetown, NJ: American School of Classical Studies at Athens, 1977). This comprises a 124-page catalogue of all the lamps discovered at Isthmia prior to 1977.

43 *Ibid*, no. 3145.

44 *Ibid*, no. 3147.

45 *Ibid*, no. 3152.

46 *Ibid*, p. 89.

47 T.E. Gregory, 'Religion and Society in the Roman Eastern Corinthia', in *Corinth in Context: Comparative Studies on Religion and Society*, ed. S.J. Friesen, D.N. Schowalter and J.C. Walters (Leiden: Brill, 2010), pp. 433–76.

48 J.M. Frey and T.E. Gregory, 'Old excavations, new interpretations: the 2008–2013 seasons of the Ohio State University excavations at Isthmia', in *Hesperia*, The Journal of the American School of Classical Studies at Athens, vol. 85, no. 3 (2016), pp. 437–90.

49 *Ibid*.

50 The inscription was discovered by M. Paul Monceaux (1859–1941) and taken to New Corinth, where it was given the ref. no I-1390. After an earthquake it was recovered from the rubble and taken to Ancient Corinth. It was returned to Isthmia in 2005; inscription ref. nos. IG IV 204; SEG 46 344. See T. Gregory, *The Hexamilion and the Byzantine Fortress: Isthmia V* (Princeton, NJ: American School of Classical Studies at Athens, 1992), pp. 12–13, plate 1a.

51 A.R. Brown, *Corinth in Late Antiquity: a Greek, Roman and Christian City* (London: Tauris/Bloomsbury, 2018), pp. 153–4.

Chapter 4

CORINTH: A DIVERSE COMMUNITY

In this chapter we shall focus on Corinth, the ancient capital of the province of Achaia, the north-western portion of the Peloponnese. St Paul's Letters to the Corinthians and the Acts of the Apostles provide evidence of the early Church in Corinth, but both these sources also raise further questions: they will be examined in this chapter. There is a gap of some centuries before the appearance of either Jewish or Christian artefacts in Corinth. A number of Corinthian basilicas have been excavated, dating from the sixth century onwards, and inscriptions commemorating the dead provide information about the social strata from which worshippers came. Late Byzantine accounts tell us the legends of early martyrs and inform us about the lives of subsequent monks and bishops.

The Greek city of Corinth was established in the eighth century BC; it flourished until 146 BC when it was sacked and burned by the Roman general, Lucius Mummius. It was re-founded in 44 BC on the orders of Julius Caesar. Most of the early colonists were freedmen: many were probably Greek, but others came from across the Roman empire. Newcomers migrated to the city, attracted by its economic growth. It was a thriving colony when Paul arrived, where Greek and Roman gods were venerated, as well as local Corinthian hero-gods such as Bellerophon, and Egyptian gods including Isis and Serapis. Poseidon and Aphrodite, both associated with the sea, were popular in Corinth. The elite preferred Roman cults, including worship of the emperor. Latin was the official language, though Greek was normally spoken.[1]

St Paul arrived in Corinth in AD 50, having walked or sailed from Athens. The great university city of Athens might have seemed the ideal place for Paul to begin his ministry in central Greece. In Paul's time, however, the university was becoming conservative; the great philosophers of the past had not been replaced by creative successors; those who listened to Paul's new ideas do not appear to have welcomed them. Writing in about AD 80 or even later, Luke, the author of the Acts of the Apostles, recalls: 'At the mention of rising from the dead, some of them burst out laughing; others said, "We would like to hear you talk about this again"' (Acts 17. 32). Luke names two Athenian converts, Damaris and Dionysius the Areopagite, but it is unclear whether Paul was able to establish a Christian community in the city.

He therefore set out for its more prosperous neighbour, Corinth. Its citizens were efficient businessmen; it had no university, but its inhabitants were open-minded.[2] It lay close to trade routes, with sailors and merchants travelling in every direction, which made Corinth an ideal location for Paul to receive news from and send letters to his other churches. It was also the final stopping point on sea routes westwards to Italy and Rome. Corinth was an ideal centre for Paul to preach to his fellow Jews: Philo tells us that they were to be found 'in most of the best parts of the Peloponnese',[3] and the largest Jewish community was in Corinth.

Jews in Corinth

There is evidence of a Jewish presence in the city in later centuries. Carved on the back of a block of stone that was first used in the second century AD is a Greek inscription that reads [SYNA]GOGE EBR[AION], or 'the synagogue of the Hebrews', in debased lettering (Fig. 20).[4] It is likely to date from the fifth or sixth century, and could have been a practice model for an inscription on the lintel of a synagogue doorway. The block was found by the gateway steps leading into the *agora*, or town square, from the road to Lechaion. A marble impost (or upper course of a pillar, supporting an arch) survives, dating from the sixth or seventh century, on which is carved a design including three seven-branched candlesticks, or *menorah*, with palm leaves (Fig. 21);[5] it was found in the theatre.[6]

FIGURE 20. Greek inscription: [SYNA]GOGE EBR[AION], in the Archaeological Museum, Corinth (MF-13302). Photo by I. Ionnaidou and L. Barzotti.

FIGURE 21. Marble impost depicting the *menorah*, in the Archaeological Museum, Corinth (MF-13303). Photo by I. Ionnaidou and L. Barzotti.

Often, the gentile population was more receptive to Paul's message than were the Jews, but in Corinth, according to the author of the Acts of the Apostles, Crispus, the ruler of the synagogue, became Christian, together with his family (Acts 18. 8). This may have contributed to the growing opposition of the Corinthian Jews to Paul who, we are told, left the synagogue and moved next door to the house of a convert named Titius Justus (Acts 18. 7). The Jews attacked Paul and brought him before Gallio, the proconsul of Achaia, who, however, refused to listen to them (Acts 18. 12–17).

St Luke and Acts

Some scripture scholars have urged caution when attempting to reconstruct Paul's time in Corinth from Acts 18, since this account differs considerably from Paul's own correspondence with the Corinthians: Paul gives little hint that there was hostility to Christians in Corinth, either from Jews or Romans. Thirty years ago, Professor Lawrence Willis suggested that Luke's account, written some decades after St Paul's own letters, might fall within the genre of a historical romance, drawing on traditions that are later than Paul's own time. This view has now been considerably modified, but some aspects of his argument are, nevertheless, interesting. Willis points out that the agents in the narrative behave in a stereotyped way: as in some other chapters of Acts, the Jews form a mob and attack Paul, while Roman officials find no fault with Paul's ministry. Throughout the Acts of the Apostles, the Jews are presented as a threat to Roman order, while the Christians are presented as good citizens of the empire; this is a message that Luke is keen to convey.[7]

Willis observes that Luke consistently presents the young Church in the context of the Roman empire. At the beginning of his gospel, he situates the birth of Jesus within the chronology of the Caesars (Lk. 2. 1); Jesus heals a centurion's favourite servant (Lk. 7. 1–10). Roman officials comment favourably on Christianity; a spirit of orderly citizenship pervades Christian activities (Acts 9. 31), and Roman officials hand down decisions in their favour (Acts 18. 15–17). Paul declares his loyalty to Roman law. He appeals to Caesar: 'If I am guilty of committing any capital crime, I do not ask to be spared the death penalty ... I appeal to Caesar' (Acts 25. 11).[8]

Following from this, Willis notes that, as a loyal Roman citizen himself, Luke wrote the Acts of the Apostles during the seventy years in which the Jews were involved in three bloody rebellions. Luke presents a gentile Church whose members have by now split away from Judaism: from Luke's perspective, 'the Jews' are people who make life miserable for the young Church. He constructs sections of the Acts of the Apostles as a repeating cycle of three dramatic moments – firstly positive missionary activity, which then causes opposition and persecution, often by 'the Jews', but which results in Paul's release and the expansion of the new Christian movement. Luke's description of Paul's activities in Corinth (Acts 18. 1–17) follows this threefold pattern: Paul preaches successfully; he is persecuted by 'the Jews' (18. 12), whose charges are dismissed by the consul as falling outside Roman law (18. 15); Paul remains in Corinth 'for some time', and then proceeds on his travels (18. 18).[9]

Luke's actual account of Paul's troubles in Corinth is as follows:

> *But while Gallio was proconsul of Achaia, the Jews made a concerted attack on Paul and brought him before the tribunal. 'We accuse this man', they said, of persuading people to worship God in a way that breaks the Law'. Before Paul could open his mouth, Gallio said to the Jews, 'Listen, you Jews. If this were a misdemeanour or a crime, I would not hesitate to attend to you; but if it is only quibbles about words and names, and about your own Law, then you must deal with it yourselves – I have no intention of making legal decisions about things like that'. Then he sent them out of the court, and at once they all turned on Sosthenes, the synagogue president, and beat him in front of the courthouse. Gallio refused to take any notice at all (Acts 18. 12–17).*

In this account, it is unclear whether Sosthenes was, in fact a Christian, so the situation is more complex than it might appear.

A more recent interpretation of Acts

It is now considered that Luke presents a nuanced and observant view of Paul's persistent difficulties with the Roman authorities. This can be seen in the four civic conflicts that Paul experienced on his 'second missionary journey', at Philippi (Acts 16), Thessalonika (Acts 17), Corinth (Acts 18) and Ephesus (Acts 19).[10] At Corinth, instead of being tried by a local magistrate, Paul was brought before Gallio, a confident and experienced proconsul. Professor Loveday Alexander observes that it took time for a proconsul to tour his province and important trials could only be judged by the provincial governor, therefore 'the arrival of a new proconsul tended to trigger a flurry of prosecutions'.[11]

Luke describes Paul as a tent-maker lodging with other migrant artisans who had been expelled from the Jewish population of Rome (Acts 18. 1–3); the artisans' quarter where they lived may also have been an ethnic Jewish quarter of Corinth. The charge against Paul was brought by the Jewish community against a sectarian splinter group. Paul's successful mission just next door to their synagogue is likely to have irritated the members of what was probably a house-synagogue in a centre of Jewish community life.[12] The charge originated from traders and artisans, rival immigrants within the Jewish community, which Paul had destabilised. Gallio dismissed the case, not because Paul was a Christian but because he was a sectarian Jew.[13]

Where did these events take place?

It is uncertain where these events took place. The location of the *bema*, or rostrum used by officials for public appearances was identified, perhaps inaccurately, by the early archaeologist Oscar Broneer at a point facing the *agora*, or central square (see Fig. 22). A three-apsed church was built on this site; it was dated by its sculpture and coins to the ninth or tenth century, and may have been built on the ruins of an earlier, smaller church. Many Christian graves were dug into the hard rubble that surrounds it.[14] The foundations of the church and its carved gravestones can still be seen. However, archaeologists now consider it equally possible that the events took place closer to the Julian basilica (Fig. 23), a building reserved for the imperial court, further to the north; here judicial trials took place away from the public eye. However, Luke explains that no trial took place – Gallio refused to hold one. To the west of the Julian basilica lies the magnificent ruined Greek temple of Apollo, dating from the mid-sixth century BC, which still dominated the city in Paul's day (Fig. 24).

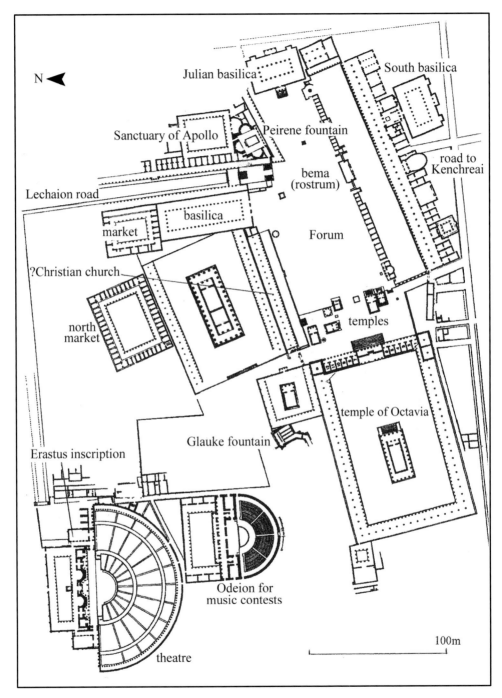

FIGURE 22. Corinth city centre, around AD 150. Courtesy of the American School of Classical Studies, Athens (with added text).

FIGURE 23. The Julian basilica, Corinth, where trials took place in the time of St Paul.

FIGURE 24. The Ancient Greek temple of Apollo, Corinth.

Paul's first converts

The First and Second Letters to the Corinthians enable us to reconstruct in part the early history of the Christian cells established by Paul around the Mediterranean Sea in the late 40s and 50s AD.[15] However the two letters raise numerous questions: there are four references to other letters (1 Cor. 5. 9; 2 Cor. 3–9; 7. 8–12; 10. 10), eight allusions to visits promised, delayed or accomplished, and numerous shifts in tone, content, and in the relationship between Paul and the Corinthian Christians. Paul's Second Letter may be compiled from as many as five letters or portions of letters.[16] They cannot therefore be read as a chronological account of Paul's ministry in Corinth.

It appears that Paul's first Corinthian converts were not the very poor: Paul needed benefactors with moderate resources, who could open their homes as house churches, and slaves had neither the leisure nor the means to do so. At first, as we have seen, he lodged with his fellow tent makers, Aquila and Priscilla, but their small shop could not accommodate a group of worshipping believers. Paul tells us the names of his first Corinthian converts: 'I am thankful that I baptised none of you except Crispus and Gaius ... I did baptise also the household of Stephanas. Beyond that, I do not know if I baptised anyone else' (1 Cor. 1. 14–16).

All three men must have had surplus resources. Crispus, Luke tells us in the Acts of the Apostles, was an *archisynagogos* (Acts 18. 8): this was an honorary title awarded to a benefactor by a Jewish community in gratitude for a sizeable donation to their synagogue. Paul describes Gaius as 'host to me and to the whole church' (Rom. 16. 23). Not only could he host a house church: his home seems to have been large enough for the members of all the Corinthian house churches to meet together. Stephanas was perhaps self-employed: he had the leisure and the financial freedom both to assume leadership in the Corinthian church and to take part in the delegation to Paul at Ephesus (1 Cor. 16. 17).[17]

Erastus, the city steward

It is possible that another successful Corinthian Christian was 'Erastus, the city steward' (or *oikonomos*) whom Paul greets in his Letter to the Romans (16. 23). However, this was not a municipal office, nor does it imply that Erastus was a member of Corinth's elite. An inscription from Thessalonika uses the same Greek title for a poor city slave.[18] A Corinthian inscription commemorating a person named Erastus was found on a block of stone used in an ancient repair to a pavement in the small square at the northern end of the street leading past the theatre (Fig. 25). The letters are deeply hollowed out; they were once filled

FIGURE 25. Pavement with inscription to Erastus, Corinth.

with bronze and held in place with lead. They read: ERASTUS PRO AEDILITATE S[UA] P[ECUNIA] STRAVIT, or 'Erastus laid this pavement in return for being treasurer, at his own expense'.

The Latin word *aedilis* means 'treasurer' or, more accurately, 'commissioner of public works'. The inscription does not include his father's name, which implies that Erastus had once been a slave, before achieving Roman citizenship and acquiring the surplus money necessary to hold public office. However, some scholars consider that the Greek term *oikonomos* employed by Paul refers to a less high-ranking official than the *aedilis* of Corinth; the debate remains open, however.[19]

Paul names sixteen individuals at Corinth, of varied status and origins. Six are Jewish, while at least three are gentile. Most of the Corinthian Christians must have been gentile converts from paganism, for Paul writes to the entire community, 'You remember that, when you were pagans, whenever you felt irresistibly drawn, it was toward dumb idols' (1 Cor. 12. 2). The households of Stephanas and Crispus probably included slaves, but domestic slaves, unlike those who worked in the fields or down the mines, often enjoyed a reasonable standard of living and education.[20]

House churches

Until recently it was thought that early Christians met almost exclusively in each other's houses, but this has been challenged by Professor Edward Adams. He has re-examined both literary and archaeological data and demonstrates that evidence for assembling in house churches is less extensive than was previously thought, while at the same time there is considerably more evidence for Christians meeting in settings other than their homes. Adams suggests that in the first two centuries, early Christians gathered in a range of venues, rather than almost entirely in private houses.[21]

In Acts 16, Luke describes women gathered for prayer on the riverbank outside Philippi:

> *After a few days in this city we went along the river outside the gates as it was the sabbath and this was a customary place for prayer. We sat down and preached to the women who had come to the meeting. One of these women was called Lydia, a devout woman ... The Lord opened her heart to accept what Paul was saying. After she and her household had been baptized she sent us an invitation: 'If you really think me a true believer in the Lord,' she said, 'come and stay with us', and she would take no refusal* (Acts 16. 13–15).

Nevertheless, a number of the first Christians' meetings to celebrate the eucharist would have taken place in family homes. Because of their layout, these homes had limited space for eucharistic meals. A typical Corinthian villa has been excavated at Anaploga; it dates from the second century AD, but is similar in plan to those of Paul's time. Its dining room (or *triclinium*) has a magnificent mosaic floor; it was customary for the family and their close friends to eat together here. The room measures 5.5 by 7.5 m, and with couches around the walls, there would have been space for about nine people to recline during a meal.[22]

The dining room was approached through an internal courtyard (or *atrium*) that was almost as large, but contained a square pool (or *impluvium*) to collect the rain that poured through a hole in the roof of similar size, which also let in the light. Thirty or forty people could stand in the courtyard, including children, servants, slaves and others. Thus in a typical Corinthian house church, some fifty people could meet together for worship. The whole community might meet as a single group from time to time at the house of Gaius, but normally each house church formed a sub-group consisting of a family, their servants and a few nearby friends. This fostered intimacy, but also tended to encourage divisions, as each group developed its own theology, which had time to take root before it was challenged by others' views.[23] Factions arose easily, to Paul's dismay: 'I do appeal to you... to make up the differences between you, and instead of disagreeing among yourselves, to be united again in your belief and practice' (1 Cor. 1. 10).

Problems sharing food

Since the dining room was so small, the believers were separated into two groups: firstly the favoured friends, who reclined to eat, and secondly everyone else, who sat or stood in the courtyard. In John's gospel we read that Jesus reclined to eat the Passover meal with his disciples (Jn. 13. 23), but there is no mention of second-class followers in the courtyard outside. However, Corinth was a Roman colony, and according to Roman custom, different types of food were served to different categories of guests. Roman satirists of the first century AD noted the inequality of this system. In his *Epigrams*, Martial writes sharply to his former friend Ponticus:

> *Since I am asked to dinner..., why is not the same dinner served to me as to you? You take oysters fattened in the Lucrine lake,*[24] *I suck a mussel through a hole in the shell. You get mushrooms, I take hog funguses. You tackle turbot, but I, brill. Golden with fat, a turtledove gorges you with its bloated rump, but there is set before me a magpie that has died in its cage. Why do I dine without you, Ponticus, though I dine with you?*[25]

It would make financial sense for the host of a Corinthian house church to serve cheaper food to the less important members of the community. His friends would belong to the leisured class, and so could arrive early and feast on larger helpings of better food, while awaiting the arrival of lower-class believers, who could only arrive after work. Paul is displeased with the situation: the *agape* or love feast that constitutes the eucharist has become a parody:

> *When you hold these meetings, it is not the Lord's Supper that you are eating, since when the time comes to eat, everyone is in such a hurry to start their own supper that one person goes hungry while another is getting drunk. Surely you have homes for eating and drinking in? Surely you have enough respect for the community of God not to make poor people embarrassed? ... When you meet for the Meal, wait for one another. Anyone who is hungry should eat at home* (1 Cor. 11. 20–22, 33–4).

Meat offered to idols

Another problem that concerned Paul was the scandal that Corinthians of stronger faith gave to those of weaker faith when the former ate meat offered to idols. Meat was generally sold in the markets after pagan festivals, during which it had been offered in sacrifice to the gods. This caused no moral problems to those whose faith was strong, but scandalised the less confident. Christians might also be invited to participate in temple banquets to celebrate the marriage of a relative, or a birth or a coming of age, in a pagan complex such as the Asclepieion on the edge of Corinth. The Asclepieion had three dining rooms and facilities for swimming; in Paul's time, it was perhaps the equivalent of a country club.[26]

Commenting on meat offered to idols, Theissen suggests that since the wealthy often ate meat, they may not have associated it with cultic feasting in the same way as the poor who rarely ate meat, and only at pagan festivals. As new Christians, the poor may have considered that eating meat must therefore be wrong.[27] Although Theissen's views have been challenged,[28] Paul was evidently concerned that pressure was being put on those of weaker faith by those whose faith was stronger:

> *If anyone sees you, a man of knowledge, reclining at table in an idol's temple, might not the conscience of the weak person be encouraged to eat food offered to idols?... And so by your knowledge this weak person is destroyed, the brother for whom Christ died... That is why, since food can be the occasion of my brother's downfall, I shall never eat meat again, in case I am the cause of a brother's downfall* (1 Cor. 8. 10–13).

As Paul walked through the artisans' quarters of Corinth, various images must have come to mind. Perhaps he was strolling through the Potters' Quarter, to the west of the theatre, when he thought to himself: 'We are only the earthenware jars that hold this treasure', the treasure that is Christ (2 Cor. 4. 7).

Corinthian women

Paul worked alongside both male and female missionaries. As we saw in Chapter 1, in his letter of introduction for Phoebe, Paul describes a woman named Junia as outstanding among the apostles; she was a missionary who laboured before he did, and, like Paul, she had been imprisoned for her fearless witness (Rom. 16. 7). Although most post-Reformation scholars claimed that she was male, Eldon Jay Epp has convincingly demonstrated that all major patristic sources regarded Junia as a woman.[29]

In Corinth, Paul found a vibrant Christian community that was apparently led by women prophets. In a seminal work entitled *The Corinthian Women Prophets*, Antoinette Clark Wire examined Paul's First Letter to the Corinthians as a carefully constructed rhetorical address. Paul was trained in the art of rhetoric, and skilfully used the language of those whose minds he wished to influence. By examining the words and phrases that Paul quotes in order to challenge them, Wire reconstructs the beliefs and practices of the Corinthian Church. Two of Paul's chief concerns are what he regards as chaotic community gatherings, in which everyone prays and utters prophecies, and women who speak with unbound hair in the assembly. Greek prophetesses declaimed oracles with their hair unbound, and Wire proposes that women uttered prophecies in a similar manner in the Corinthian Church.[30]

Women prophets

Wire suggests that, according to Greek religious custom, these prophetic women remained chaste; this enabled them to retain their independence, and to regard the Christian community as their new family. They possibly prepared the food for eucharistic meals. Paul approves of the celibate state of these unmarried women and virgins (1 Cor. 7. 34), but would prefer them to eat at home (1 Cor. 11. 22) and to remain silent in the gatherings, keeping quietly in the background (1 Cor. 14. 34–5). In the assembly, they rise to speak in the Spirit, not necessarily waiting for others to finish, for all are endowed with ecstatic speech in praise of God (1 Cor. 14. 1–40).

Paul accepts that God's Spirit has been given to them, and inspires them to move beyond speech into 'tongues of angels' (13. 1). Anyone may receive the Spirit, and prophecy becomes a communal experience, so that voices blend and combine as people inspire each other to chant their praise of God. Paul observes how they teach one another and declaim insightful, wise words (or oracles, in Greek understanding); they express what they had not known before, and so come to discover more fully that God is present among them.[31] However, Paul would prefer a tidier, more formal style of worship, as he spells out firmly and at length (13. 1–14. 40). In his demand that prophecy should be regulated, he orders women to be silent; he invokes Jewish Law, tradition, and his own authority to enforce his opinion (14. 34–8). All this suggests the key role of the women prophets in Christian Corinth. Paul was evidently uncomfortable about their Spirit-inspired style of leadership.[32]

Corinthian theology

Their theology, too, differs from Paul's: while Paul focuses on the crucified Christ, and his own personal struggle to follow Christ in a world that is not yet fully redeemed, these charismatic women claim access to risen life in Christ, through God's Spirit. They take part in the Lord's joyful meal, and God's word goes forth through them into the Christian community and beyond. There is now neither male nor female, for they are all one in Christ (Gal. 3. 28). God's Spirit has been poured out on them, giving them wisdom and insight (1 Cor. 1. 26; 4. 10). Paul is unhappy with this theology, as he makes clear: 'Is it that ... you are rich already, in possession of your kingdom, with us left outside? ... Here we are, fools for the sake of Christ, while you are the learned ...' (4. 8, 10).[33] Paul's First Letter to the Corinthians thus offers a fascinating glimpse of a Christian community whose belief and practice differed considerably from his own.

While Wire's conclusions are cogent, it is now considered that we know too little of Corinthian religious thought to be able to arrive at satisfactory theories concerning Paul's difficulties with Corinthian Christians.[34] Some scripture scholars have concluded that the paragraph in 1 Corinthians 14 (vv. 34–5) that orders women to be silent in the community are a non-Pauline addition, since it interrupts the flow of thought in chapter 14, and since some early manuscripts place verses 34–5 later, after verse 40. Epp summarises the debate, and comments that, either way, the ambiguity in the variant readings makes clear that ecstatic female leadership was evidently a concern of the early Church.[35]

Christians and outsiders

Despite Luke's portrayal of Paul's struggle with the Corinthian Jews, it appears that there was little conflict between Christians and outsiders at Corinth. This stands in marked contrast to the situation in other towns where Paul established Christian communities. His First Letter to the Thessalonians, for example, emphasises the persecution and social harassment that he and they suffered (1 Thess. 3. 2–5). In the same letter, he recalls his suffering and mistreatment at Philippi (1 Thess. 2. 1–2). In 1 Corinthians there is no sign of such opposition or alienation; Christians do not suffer at the hands of outsiders. On the contrary, they receive invitations to dine with pagans, both at home and in communal settings (1 Cor. 10. 27–11. 1). Some Christians believe it appropriate to attend cultic meals in pagan temples (8. 7–13). Outsiders are welcomed at Christian gatherings for worship: Paul advises Christians not to speak 'in tongues' (in an unknown language, inspired by the Spirit) unless someone can interpret their speech, in case unbelievers enter the house and 'think you are mad' (14. 23).[36]

Such lack of external conflict may have been a contributory factor to the emergence of conflict within the Christian community: it was unusually open-minded, and its members had social ties with pagans across the city. Corinth was a more tolerant town than Thessalonika, for it had been re-founded only recently, with a mixed population of Greeks and Romans. The Christian community was diverse, which facilitated the attraction of new converts. It was easier for people from different social strata to interact, and their outlooks and beliefs varied.[37]

It is interesting that although Paul was deeply engaged with a lively church in Corinth, there is little evidence of its survival. As we saw in Chapter 1, Clement of Rome's *Letter to the Corinthians* describes how, in the late first century, younger Christians dismissed their own older leaders from office. Perhaps the conflict and tensions among its members caused the Corinthian church to dwindle, unlike the more peaceful communities that Paul established elsewhere. It may have been too divided to survive amid the worship of Greek divinities whose temples surrounded the *agora* in Corinth. This was Paul's most troublesome community and so, paradoxically, it called forth his finest rhetoric, his most personal outpourings and his most developed theology. His Letters to the Corinthians reveal Paul more fully than any of his other writings.

Later Christian Corinth

Christianity continued to develop in Corinth: fragmentary letters survive written by a second-century bishop of Corinth, Dionysios, who worked to build a network of churches along trade routes in the eastern Mediterranean. The letters throw light on various Christian communities who followed somewhat differing lifestyles. This was a period of significant debates concerning issues of celibacy, marriage, the re-admission of sinners, Roman persecution, and the economic and political interdependence of churches. The letters provide insight into a fluid, emergent Christianity at a pivotal moment of its evolution.[38]

By the late fourth century Christianity had become the norm, although there is little evidence of church buildings in Corinth before the third quarter of the fifth century. In about AD 400, John Chrysostom (c. 347–407), the archbishop of Constantinople, wrote to bishop Alexander of Corinth. In his homily on Paul's first letter to the Corinthians, Chrysostom refers to Corinth of his own era as the 'first city of Greece';[39] later in the homily he describes St Paul as similar, though superior, to Diogenes the Cynic (412/404– 323 BC), who lived in Corinth for much of his life.

In 553 a Corinthian bishop named Photius sent two deacons, Dionysius and Callinicus to the Fifth Church Council in Constantinople. Photius is the first Corinthian bishop to be named in an inscription: his name appears in an invocation inscribed on a column on the hill of Acrocorinth, where a small church was built.[40]

There is no evidence of buildings dedicated to Christian worship before at least AD 475. Oscar Broneer suggested that the central shop in a row of fifteen,

FIGURE 26. A second-century shop in the Corinthian *agora*, with Christian graffiti on its walls.

71

built in the second century AD on the north-west side of the *agora*, was later turned into a small church, since Christian graffiti are carved on its walls (Fig. 26): traces of a mural, with its red and blue paint, are still visible on its walls. However, more recent interpretation of the evidence has cast doubt upon Broneer's conclusion.

At the same time, the Corinthians experienced a series of natural disasters that their own gods, Poseidon, Demeter and Asclepius were powerless to avert. An earthquake in AD 525 killed half the population of Corinth. This was followed by a severe global climatic event lasting for about five years from around 536 onwards. This catastrophe is thought to have caused famine and perhaps to have precipitated the plague of the early 540s which, according to Procopius, killed almost half of the earthquake's survivors throughout the Roman empire. To the demoralised Corinthians, a Christian God, who was both creator of the universe and committed to healing humanity, must have acquired a new appeal.[41]

Corinthian bishops acted as emissaries between the patriarch in Constantinople and the pope in Rome until the 680s. Bishop Stephanos of Corinth represented the pope at the sixth ecumenical council in 680, and another Corinthian bishop took part in an embassy from the patriarch to the pope in 689. Although Slavic and Arab raids began in the seventh century, Corinth's clergy remained active; several small churches were built around the *agora* at the centre of ancient Corinth in the seventh and eighth centuries.[42]

The first basilicas

A third-century urban house in the Panayia Field, south-east of the forum, was replaced in the fifth century by a new house with a dining room, its apse designed to accommodate an *agape* table with radiating couches. Its bath suite, dating from the mid-sixth century, is modelled on the sixth-century baptistery at Lechaion which will be described in the following chapter. A long structure south of the bath complex appears to be related to it. With his trowel, a plasterer has incised fish, a symbol for Christ, on the inside walls of one of the basement rooms in the long building.[43] The structure could have been used for worship; this site may be an example of the evolution of a fifth-century house church into a later basilica.

Five Corinthian churches have been excavated, most of them dating from the sixth century; the outlines of four are depicted in Figure 27. All five have aisles and a semi-circular apse, and a number of them were constructed in several phases. It is not known why so many churches were built in a relatively small area: perhaps there was a large population, or there was now more money to erect basilicas, or wealthy households commissioned family churches. It is possible that bishops commissioned churches, together with wealthy donors eager to make their mark, or to ensure their entry into heaven through virtuous deeds.[44]

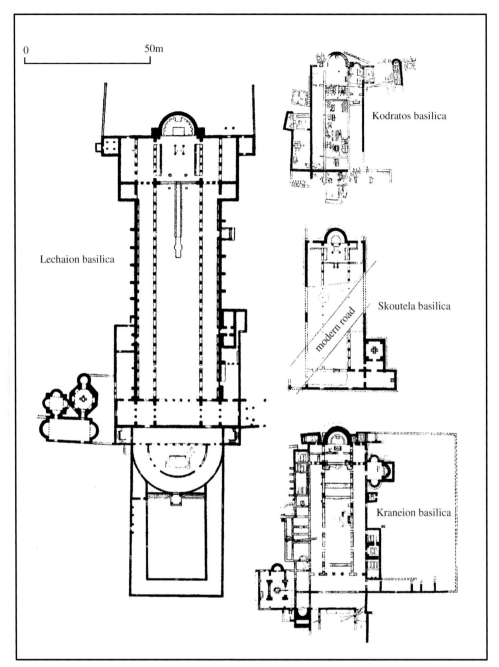

FIGURE 27. Four Corinthian basilicas, showing their relative sizes. Courtesy of the American School of Classical Studies, Athens.

Inside the basilicas, the men were separated from the women, while catechumens, or candidates for baptism, observed the first half of the eucharist from galleries above ground level. In Corinthian basilicas there was as much space in the galleries as there was in the church below: this might suggest that there were as many candidates for baptism as there were Christians at this time. In the basilica at Lechaion, a very large baptismal pool could have enabled forty or fifty people to be baptised at the same time. Later, as the number of new Christians diminished, a new type of font was created for individual baptism. The candidate climbed into it on a step ladder, to be immersed in the water by the bishop. However, it is necessary to remember that size does not equate neatly with function in Christian architecture in the eastern empire. Since Lechaion's basilica is likely to have been an imperial church constructed under the aegis of Corinth's archbishop, it may have had symbolic purposes beyond the simple function of managing converts.[45]

The Kraneion basilica

Three Corinthian basilicas have been excavated. The largest is the Kraneion basilica outside the late Roman city wall, where the land rises towards the hill of Acrocorinth, near the gate on the road leading to Kenchreai. Kraneion, or 'Place of the Skull', was the eastern quarter of Corinth: it was famous in literature for its expensive villas, market, gymnasium and its connection with the life and death of Diogenes the Cynic. Here there were ancient Greek grave monuments and sanctuaries alongside new houses, burials and, later, churches.[46] Burials continued around the Kraneion basilica into the Venetian era (1687–1715), when the Venetian Republic captured the Peloponnese for almost thirty years.[47]

Pottery, lamps, coins and architectural sculpture date the basilica's construction to the first half of the sixth century. The threshold of the north doorway of the *narthex*, or corridor at the entrance to the church, consists of a recycled statue. Its arms, head and drapery were trimmed down and its back was cut flat, except for a narrow raised door sill with a socket hole at each end to secure the door. The statue is one of seven such figures found in Corinth: all were carved in the early fifth century, though none of the others was reused in such a way, or remains in its sixth-century context.[48]

These life-sized marble figures would have been impressive in their original position; in their turn they were often re-carved from earlier marble statues. They are the last examples of an ancient tradition of public sculpture; they are carved in the round, in a shallow, schematic style. Each depicts a man draped in a distinctive long cloak or *chlamys*, pinned with a brooch on the right shoulder. This was the professional robe of a late antique imperial official, perhaps a governor

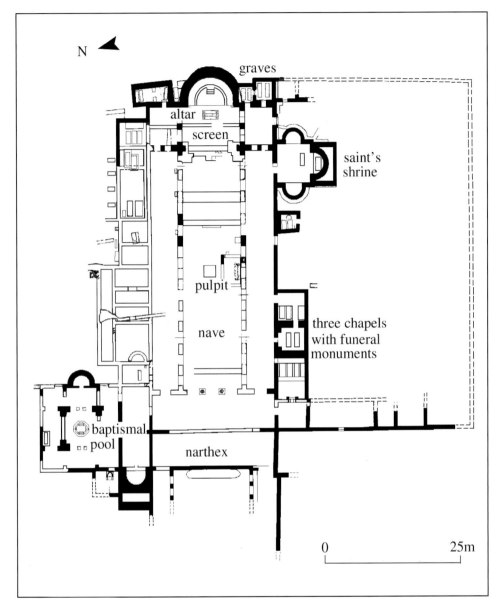

N

graves

altar

screen

saint's shrine

pulpit

nave

three chapels with funeral monuments

baptismal pool

narthex

0   25m

FIGURE 28. The Kraneion basilica, Corinth. Courtesy of the American School of Classical Studies, Athens (with added text).

of Achaia based at Corinth, or a local civic benefactor who held imperial office beyond Achaia, and returned to endow the city. These marble statues provide some of the clearest evidence of activity in Corinth's city centre, where they were carved, displayed and eventually reused.[49]

FIGURE 29. The Kraneion basilica, with steps down into the octagonal baptistery pool in the foreground.

FIGURE 30. Deep brick-lined graves beside the apse of the Kraneion basilica (foreground), with the hill of Acrocorinth in the background.

The Kraneion basilica has a baptistery on its north-west side (Figs 28 and 29) containing an octagonal pool, into which candidates for baptism descended down a shallow flight of steps. There were many burials around the church to the south and west, in vaulted and cist (or slab-lined) graves, both types being built of brick (Fig. 30); burials continued well into the seventh century. Inside the church, chapels adjoining the aisles contain burial monuments: in the central chapel of three on the south side, a fine marble pavement survives, with pale pink and blue slabs arranged in geometric patterns (Fig. 31). Burials within churches emphasised the bond between the living and the dead in a sacred space: this was a unique feature of Christianity, arising from their belief that we all belong to Christ.[50]

FIGURE 31. Marble pavement surrounding funeral monuments in a chapel adjoining the south aisle, the Kraneion basilica.

There is a saint's shrine in what was a semi-domed, tri-conch apse on the south-east side of the basilica, near the sanctuary, with a tomb in the central conch (Fig. 32); alternatively, it might be a family mausoleum.[51] It could only be approached from inside the church: this ensured privacy and respect for the person(s) buried there.[52] A complete *agape* table (these will be described more fully below) was found in the cemetery to the south. Some later grave slabs are recycled portions of the sixth-century church: a white marble slab with a carving of the cross as the tree of life, which was cut in the eleventh or twelfth century, may once have formed part of the marble screen, or *templon*, that separated the chancel from the nave (Fig. 33).[53]

FIGURE 32. Saint's shrine on the south side of the Kraneion basilica, near the sanctuary.

FIGURE 33. The cross as the tree of life, on a grave slab from the Kraneion basilica, now in the Archaeological Museum, Corinth (AM-10). Photo by I. Ionnaidou and L. Barzotti.

The Kodratos basilica

Just beyond the city, to the north, a sixth-century basilica honours a martyr named Kodratos (or Quadratus in Latin), north-east of the ruined Asclepieion; it was associated with a healing spring that was known in late antiquity; together with the basilica, it attracted Orthodox pilgrims to Corinth between the ninth and the eleventh centuries. Joseph the Hymnographer (816–86) refers to the basilica and its cult. The spring above the basilica flows from a cave; its current size and shape appear to date from the medieval period. It could supply water for farmers, travellers and funeral rites.[54]

The Kodratos basilica is the smallest of the three Corinthian churches that have been excavated; it had three aisles, but no baptistery or *atrium*, where converts might gather for instruction. There is a possible platform to support a ceremonial seat for the priest who presided over the liturgy, and numerous basins with hydraulic systems for conveying water to them.[55] It has been associated with St Kodratus because E.G. Stikas identified an early inscription on a marble lintel honouring the saint; the lintel had later been re-used in a grave within the basilica. The latest coins from the excavation date from the reign of Manuel I Commenous (1143–80). Beside the west side of the church is a medieval belfry or watchtower.[56]

Like the Kraneion, the Kodratos basilica was a cemetery church; there are fifty-five burials around its exterior walls. Attached to the aisles are funeral monuments, and there are graves within the aisles and the nave, including what appears to be the tomb of a bishop named Eustathios. However, the inscription appears to date from a century later than the church, so it may commemorate the bishop, rather than marking his burial site.[57] There are also graves in chambers to the north and south of the church, and in the *narthex*.[58] Burials within a city were uncommon at this time, for the living had no wish to be haunted by the spirits of the dead. However, as we saw in Chapter 3, the emperor Justinian had moved the city eastwards, and so the Classical forum and the Christian basilicas lay outside the new city.

Kodratos is probably Corinth's most famous saint; he was commemorated in churches as far away as Carthage in north Africa and Lyon in France. The story of Kodratos is told in various collections of saints' lives, including the ninth-century *Parvum Romanum* and the *Menologion*, dating from 800–900; it is also recounted by the fourteenth-century Byzantine scholar, Nicephorus Gregoras. However, since these sources are late, their historical accuracy is questionable.[59] There were at least four individuals named Kodratus, whose lives became conflated: one was an early theologian, a second was a bishop of Athens, a third was a prophet in Asia, and a fourth was a Corinthian martyr. According to the *Menologion*, under the persecutions of Decius (reigned 249–51) and Valerian (253–60), Corinthian Christians fled to the mountains, including a young woman who gave birth to Kodratos in her mountain hideaway. As he grew up, many came out from the city to be instructed by him; their fame spread from the mountains into the town, where Kodratos and five or more of his followers were denounced, arrested and martyred.[60]

Other Corinthian basilicas

Further out of the city, to the north-west, the Skoutelas basilica was a little larger than that of St Kodratos; it had a large and elaborate baptistery at its south-western end (see Fig. 27), but no cemetery. The church is bisected by a modern road. Inside the basilica, against the wall of the apse is a large semi-circular *synthronon* where officiating clergy could sit. Stone benches flank a central rostrum (or *bema*) that projects into the nave; this contains a short paved pathway (or *solea*) that might have led to a pulpit. There was an *enkainion* that contained a saint's relics under the altar; a *baldachino*, or decorative canopy, emphasised the altar's importance.[61]

Near the amphitheatre, north-east of the city, a Christian structure appears to have been a baptistery or perhaps a *martyrium* (saint's shrine). It dates from the sixth century and was a circular or octagonal building 12 m in diameter, related to a larger rectangular building, perhaps a church. Many cist graves were built close to the site, north of the city wall.[62] A fragment of a column found nearby bears a worn inscription of three lines: PAULOU / LAMPROTATOS / CLARISSIMUS. It can be translated as '[the memorial of] Paul, a most eminent man'. The second (Greek) word is followed by its Latin equivalent; the inscription might commemorate a Corinthian official or a bishop.[63]

A basilica was built in the sixth century in a dramatic location at the highest point on Acrocorinth, where it would have been visible from a distance. It was constructed on the site of a temple of Aphrodite, dating from the fifth or fourth century BC. The church was later replaced by an Islamic sanctuary. As we saw earlier, the name of Photius, a sixth-century Corinthian bishop, is inscribed on a nearby column. At the foot of Acrocorinth, the Fountain of Haji Mustafa, or Joseph the Tailor, yields such pure water that today's residents of Old Corinth and the surrounding villages still collect it. An inscription informs us that it was built in the seventeenth century; a traveller writing in 1670 described the excellence of its water. Material used in its construction includes two large white marble column capitals inscribed with the *chi-ro* monogram, and pieces of enormous double columns designed to support window jambs from a large Christian basilica that has not yet been discovered (Fig. 34).[64]

FIGURE 34. Column capital inscribed with *chi-ro* monogram, built into the Fountain of Haji Mustafa, Corinth.

Agape tables

A number of D-shaped *agape* tables ('love tables' or '*sigma* tables') dating from the sixth and seventh centuries have been found in Corinth. Several of these can be seen in the Archaeological Museum: a beautiful deep red marble table from a possible Christian context beside the Lechaion Road (Plate 9), a white marble table from the Kraneion basilica, and another white marble example found

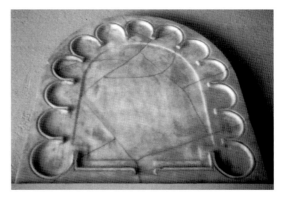

FIGURE 35. White marble *agape* table, found near the *Asclepieion*, in the Archaeological Museum, Corinth (MF-13303).

in a healing context near the *Asclepieion* (Fig. 35). In secular society, a party of a dozen people could recline around an *agape* table for a meal, while watching dancing girls, or some other entertainment. At the Peirene Fountain, three spaces for such tables enabled families to picnic while a fountain played in the central court (Plate 10; Fig. 36).[65]

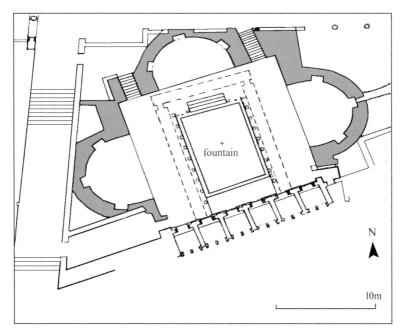

FIGURE 36. The Peirene fountain, Corinth, in the fourth century AD. Courtesy of the American School of Classical Studies, Athens.

The Peirene fountain was itself a pre-Christian holy place: it was one of the locations at which an abducted maiden who represented springtime vegetation was snatched into Hades. It was also believed to be the site where the Corinthian hero Bellerophon tamed Pegasus, the winged horse, aided by the goddess Athena. A wall painting in the *triclinium*, or dining room, of a villa at Pompeii dating from the late first century BC depicts the scene.[66] Bellerophon became a model of pious, enterprising Corinthians. Peirene, too, came to represent both Corinth and the Isthmian Games. In one version of her story, she was a woman who became Poseidon's lover: because of her continuous weeping over their dead son she was transformed into a spring.[67]

At the Peirene fountain, water flowed from four ancient rock-cut reservoirs into three long underground basins created in the sixth or fifth century BC, from which residents drew water. In Roman times, the fountain's six antechambers were converted into smaller basins; people leaned through the arches in order to collect water. At the beginning of the second century AD the fountain's court and façade were redecorated with marble; throughout the Roman period it was periodically renovated.[68] By the fourth century, access was gained to the fountain via a staircase to the pool, from which people could draw water, filling their amphorae from lions' head spouts.

Pagan families might enjoy a meal beside the Peirene fountain for both religious and social reasons. Christians would recline around an *agape* table for the communal meal that constituted the eucharist. Similar tables have been found in the Roman catacombs, where they are likely to have been used for funeral meals. In the Lerna Court to the west of the Corinthian *Asclepieion*, a large number of sixth- and

seventh-century Christian graves have been excavated. There were spaces among the graves, perhaps for celebrating burial liturgies, with attendant mourners. One of the *agape* tables (Plate 9) was found in the largest of the open spaces at the centre of the court.

A sixth-century mosaic in the basilica of S. Apollinare Nuovo, Ravenna (Fig. 37) depicts Jesus and his apostles reclining around an *agape* table for their

FIGURE 37. The Last Supper, with Jesus and his apostles reclining around an *agape* table, from a sixth-century mosaic in S. Apollinare Nuovo basilica, Ravenna. Courtesy of Ravenna archdiocese.

Left: FIGURE 38. Jesus and his apostles seated around an *agape* table at the Last Supper, from an icon in Agia Ekaterina church in the Plaka, Athens.

Below: FIGURE 39. Wedding guests at Cana sit around an *agape* table, from a Greek icon designed as a wedding gift.

final solemn Passover meal, the Last Supper, which took place on the night before Christ died. In later Greek icons of the Last Supper, the apostles are often portrayed around an *agape* table, although they are now depicted sitting upright (Fig. 38), since people no longer reclined at meals. In western art, by contrast, the apostles sit at a long trestle table, as in Leonardo da Vinci's famous painting.

An icon that is a popular Greek Orthodox wedding gift depicts the wedding feast at Cana in Galilee, described in John's gospel (Jn. 2. 1–10). The host runs out of wine and, at his mother's request, Jesus tells the servants to draw water, which then becomes wine. In the

icon, the young married couple preside at the feast, which often takes place around an *agape* table (Fig. 39); the participants sit upright. Mary appeals to her son to address the problem (left); a servant pours water into stone jars (foreground).

Funerals and burials

Many sixth-century Christian burials were found around the Corinthian temples of Demeter (a goddess of resurrection) and Asclepius (a healing god), both of whom were traditionally compassionate; perhaps the new Christians still honoured their pagan roots. Sixty or seventy years later, in the seventh century, grave goods began to appear in Christian graves: pitchers for water or wine, and lamps, as are used in the Orthodox burial rite today. This syncretic element is typically Greek, having been employed from 2,000 BC to AD 2,000. In modern Orthodox practice, the priest anoints the body of the dead person with oil, water and wine at the graveside. The containers are now plastic bottles, which are then thrown away, but until recently, ceramic pitchers were used. They were then broken at the graveside, or placed in the grave.[69]

There was a communal meal at the funeral, and perhaps at later intervals. Large quantities of lamps, possibly lit for these occasions, were found in the *Asclepieion* cemetery, dating from the second half of the fifth century onwards. Many of these have Christian symbols: usually a cross, or sometimes a shell: this was originally symbolic of the birth of Aphrodite, but later came to represent the resurrection, or rebirth, of the Christian. Vigil lamps were also lit during the graveside liturgy, and were presumably periodically renewed.[70]

The Christian rock-cut tombs around the edges of the *Asclepieion* date from the mid-sixth century; the tombs are oriented east–west, and the bodies are laid out with their heads facing west. Some 65 epitaphs found nearby record details of their sellers and owners, who were not wealthy: they were gardeners, goatherds, merchants and bath attendants. One burial inscription describes the owner of a tomb named Eusebius, a merchant who had travelled from what is now Turkey before settling in Corinth: '+ A sepulchre belonging to Eusebius the Anatolian, a shoe and clothing merchant, purchased from Leonidus the fuller [one who cleaned and thickened cloth]. Here lies Noumenis of blessed memory, who died the fifth day of the month of June, in the sixth year of the indiction.+' Four skeletons were found in the grave.[71]

Corinthian martyrs

In the sixth century, the Corinthian Church flourished: as we have seen, the first basilicas, those of Kodratus, Skoutela and Lechaion, were built in the plain to the north of the city, and at Kraneion to the east. Sadly, at a time when the new religion was about to grow and blossom, Corinth was struck by bubonic plague, which caused high mortality in the region. Archaeological evidence demonstrates that this was followed by a deep economic depression, lasting five hundred years. Later Christian Corinth bore little resemblance to its sixth-century forerunner.[72]

However, Corinthians treasured the memory of their saints: an early account of an anonymous virgin martyr is recorded by Palladius in his *Lausiac History*, which he wrote in AD 419–20. It tells the story of a beautiful virgin from a prominent Corinthian family, who was denounced to the pagan magistrate. Inflamed with passion for her, he had her sent to a brothel, where she kept would-be clients away by saying that she had an offensive sore. She prayed fervently, until a Christian youth tried to help her by exchanging his clothes with her, so that she could escape. She did so, wearing his cloak, while he was caught, thrown to wild animals and devoured.[73]

Dionysius and Victorinus

Late texts relate that one of the Corinthian Christians who went out into the mountains to visit St Kodratos 'for Christian instruction in the truth' was a man named Dionysius. At the end of his account of Kodratos, the ninth-century author of the *Menologion* (or calendar of saints) recounts the deeds of St Dionysius, who was denounced to the *archon*, or magistrate, of Corinth as 'one of those who were familiar with holy Kodratos, for not having obeyed the mandate of the emperor, and for looking down on the great gods'.[74] In the short account of his life, we are told how his persecutors summarised the teaching of Dionysius:

> He proclaims some other god who was crucified, saying that he was the maker of heaven and earth and sea, and all creatures in them, the very one who would, in the future, come out of heaven and judge the living and the dead, and give back to each according to his works.

The primary purpose of this credal statement was to strengthen the faith of the ninth-century worshippers who heard the story proclaimed during the liturgy; it is unlikely to have come from the mouth of the torturer. The account then relates that after being offered a final opportunity to renounce Christ, Dionysius was killed by the sword.[75]

The *Menologion* also commemorates St Victorinus and his six companions, who were martyred in Corinth on 31 January, again during the persecution of Decius. The seven men were handed over to the proconsul, Tertius, who tortured them with unusual ferocity. There were also female saints: St Helokonis of Thessaloniki was arrested and eventually martyred in Corinth during the reigns of the emperors Gordian III (AD 238–44) and Julius Philippus (244–49), known as Philip the Arab. The Life of Helokonis relates that orders to have Christians arrested were sent throughout the prefectures, including Achaia and Macedonia. Helokonis was sent to Corinth to appear before the duke, Perinius. She refused to offer sacrifice to idols, and courageously proclaimed Christ as the true God. She was hideously tortured, and eventually decapitated.[76]

Monks and bishops

Eventually, the persecutions ended, and martyrs were no longer the only models for attaining sanctity; monks, nuns and hermits were now considered as worthy models for holy living. A long and somewhat tedious *Life of Kyriakos* survives that describes a fifth-century hermit. Kyriakos was born in Corinth at the end of the reign of the emperor Theodosius II (d. 450); his parents were John, a priest, and his wife, Eudoxia. Her brother, Peter, was the metropolitan bishop of Corinth – the chief bishop of the region; letters survive that were written by Bishop Peter to Pope Leo VII (d. 939). Kyriakos grew up in Corinth and travelled to Palestine in search of monastic life; pilgrims from Corinth visited the holy man in his monastery. The *Life of Kyriakos* hints at a growing ecclesiastical upper class, to which his family belonged, yet the clergy of this fifth-century capital of Achaia are not known for their contribution to doctrinal theology or for producing outstanding monks or bishops.[77]

The Christian community that Kyriakos left behind in Corinth was evidently alive and well-established, but the city remained a provincial capital. In the fifth and sixth centuries, Corinth was overshadowed by larger cities and their more charismatic bishops. Justinian's legislation from 535 to 556 consolidated the strength of central imperial government. This created a vacuum in leadership at regional levels; as a result, local bishops came to exercise the power that had formerly been wielded by city magistrates. At the same time, the influence of the Corinthian Church was curtailed by the fact that, as a Roman settlement in Greece, Corinth also became a political pawn between papal power in the west and imperial authority in the east.[78]

Growth of the church

Nevertheless, the Corinthian Church quietly flourished, and by the twelfth century there were perhaps 160 churches in Corinth, compared with some 60 in Athens. The Peirene Fountain became a monastic compound, with a bell tower and a small burial chapel dedicated to the Virgin Mary to the right of the fountain, and a monastery to the left; bones dating from this period were found in the tunnel behind the fountain. The present church above the Peirene fountain dates from 1924, and is built on tenth-century foundations. Looking at ancient Corinth today, it is difficult to imagine the streets alive with monks, priests and nuns, and bells tolling, each calling its community to prayer.

High above the city, a cave with wall paintings on Acrocorinth is dedicated to one of three saints named Paul, though it is uncertain which one: it might honour Paul the apostle, or a third-century follower of St Kodratus, who along with many others including Crescens, Cyprian and Dionysius was martyred in AD 251. A third possible saint honoured at the cave is a Corinthian holy man who lived in the ninth and tenth centuries known as St Paul the Dribbler, who chose to play the fool.[79] From at least the sixth century, Eastern Orthodox holy men might express their faith by pretending to be fools (or *saloi* in Greek). Instead of retreating into a hermitage or monastery, a *salos* lived among ordinary people. In his first Letter to the Corinthians, St Paul wrote: 'it was to shame the wise that God chose what is foolish by human reckoning' (1 Cor. 1. 27). Holy fools avoided being praised for their holiness, and by feigning madness they could offer profound advice, much as court jesters could speak truths that others dared not voice.

It has been difficult for archaeologists to glean evidence of Corinth in the Byzantine period, for much of it lies beneath the homes of today's inhabitants of Old Corinth. For some years, however, members of the American School of Classical Studies have been excavating areas around the edge of the ancient Forum, with interesting results. In 2008 a monastic complex was uncovered, to the south-west of the Corinthian *agora*, or town square; it belonged to the Knights Hospitallers, and dates from the mid-thirteenth to the early fourteenth century. A row of shops includes a metal workers', a fast-food butcher's shop, a pharmacy, and an office that maintained banking standards through discarding counterfeit coinage issued by banking families. Occupying the main portion of the site was a hospital, which may have been that of St Samson.[80]

Around the hospital were many burials, including males aged forty to fifty, placed in *arcosolia*, or arched recesses containing tombs. There were graves of 230 younger males buried hastily, perhaps during an epidemic, and many babies, including a pair of twins who died at birth. Among the males was a Mongolian mounted bowman.[81] The landlocked nation of Mongolia, situated between China and Russia, greatly expanded its borders westwards in the twelfth century, as far as Poland and Turkey: this would account for a bowman who died so far from home.

To summarise: after St Paul's dynamic ministry, Christianity in Corinth began to develop. It flourished in the fifth and sixth centuries, when Corinthians lovingly remembered their martyrs who had perished during former persecutions; new churches were dedicated to their memory. In medieval times, however, the Corinthian church became less important than that of Athens. Ironically, Athens was the city that Paul had left behind in order to focus his energy on Corinth.

Notes

1   E. Adams and D. Horrell, 'The scholarly quest for Paul's church at Corinth: a critical survey', in *Christianity at Corinth: The Quest for the Pauline Church*, ed. E. Adams and D. Horrell (Louisville: Westminster John Knox Press, 2004), pp. 2–7.
2   J. Murphy-O'Connor, *Paul: His Story* (Oxford: Oxford University Press, 2004), pp. 77–8.
3   Philo, 'Legatio ad Caium imperatorem' ('Embassy to Gaius') in *Philo with an English Translation*, transl. F. H. Colson, Loeb Classical Library (Cambridge, MAS: Harvard University Press, 1929–62), vol. 10.
4   Photo ref.: bw_1990_054_23, reproduced courtesy of the American School of Classical Studies at Athens, Corinth Excavations.
5   Photo ref.: bw_1990_054_21, reproduced courtesy of the American School of Classical Studies at Athens, Corinth Excavations.
6   O. Meinardus, *St Paul in Greece* (Athens: Lycabettus Press, 2006), pp. 76–7, with revised dating.
7   L .Willis, 'The depiction of the Jews in Acts', *Journal of Biblical Literature*, no. 110, vol. 4 (1991), pp. 637, 640, 648–53.
8   *Ibid*, p. 651.
9   *Ibid*, pp. 639, 653.
10   L. Alexander, 'Silent witness: Paul's troubles with Roman authorities in the Book of Acts', in *The Last Years of Paul*, Essays from the Tarragona Conference, June 1013, ed. A. Puig i Tàrrech, J.M.G. Barclay and J. Frey (Tübingen: Mohr Siebeck, 2015), pp. 153–174, at p. 159.
11   *Ibid*, pp. 156, 164.
12   *Ibid*, p. 165.
13   *Ibid*, pp. 166, 170.
14   Meinardus, *St Paul in Greece*, pp. 80–81.
15   M.M. Mitchell, 'Paul's Letters to Corinth: the interpretive intertwining of literary and historical reconstruction', in *Urban Religion in Roman Corinth: Interdisciplinary Approaches*, ed. D. Schowalter and S. Friesen, Harvard Theological Studies, vol. 53 (Cambridge, MAS: Harvard University Press, 2005), ch. 11, p. 307.
16   2 Cor. 2. 14–7. 4 (minus 6. 14–7. 1); 2 Cor. 10. 1–13. 10; 2 Cor. 1. 1–2. 13, plus 7. 5–16, plus 13. 11–13; 2 Cor. 8; and 2 Cor. 9. See Mitchell, 'Paul's Letters to Corinth', pp. 317–8.
17   Murphy-O'Connor, *Paul: His Story*, p. 85.
18   S.J. Friesen, 'Prospects for a demography of the Pauline Mission: Corinth among the churches', in *Urban Religion in Roman Corinth*, ch. 13, p. 369.
19   J.K. Goodrich, 'Erastus of Corinth (Romans 16. 23): responding to recent proposals on his rank, status, and faith', in *New Testament Studies*, vol. 57, no. 4 (2011), pp. 583–93; S.J. Friesen, 'The wrong Erastus: ideology, archaeology, and exegesis', in *Corinth in Context: Comparative Studies on Religion and Society*, ed. S.J. Friesen, D.N. Schowalter and J.C. Walters (Leiden: Brill, 2010), pp. 231–56; J. Walters, 'Civic identity in Roman Corinth and its impact on early Christians', in *Urban Religion in Roman Corinth*, ch. 15, pp. 415–6; J. Murphy-O'Connor, *St Paul's Corinth: Texts and Archaeology* (Collegeville, MN: Michael Glazier, Liturgical Press, 1983), pp. 173–6.
20   Murphy-O'Connor, *Paul: His Story*, pp. 87–8.

21 E. Adams, *The Earliest Christian Meeting Places* (London: T & T Clark, 2015).

22 Murphy-O'Connor, *St Paul's Corinth: Texts and Archaeology*, pp. 161–3.

23 *Ibid*, pp. 163–6.

24 A lake close to the sea in Campania in southern Italy: its oyster-beds were renowned, as they still are.

25 Martial, *Epigrams*, 3. 60; see J.F. Donahue, *Food and Drink in Antiquity: Readings from the Graeco-Roman World* (London: Bloomsbury, 2014), p. 177.

26 Murphy-O'Connor, *St Paul's Corinth*, pp. 169–73.

27 G. Theissen, *The Social Setting of Pauline Christianity: Essays on Corinth*, transl. J. H. Schultz (Philadelphia: Fortress Press, 1982), pp. 121–43; repr. in *Social-Scientific Approaches to New Testament Interpretation* (Edinburgh: T. & T. Clark, 1999), pp. 249–74.

28 A.T. Cheung, *Idol Food in Corinth: Jewish Background and Pauline Legacy, Journal for the Study of the New Testament: Supplement Series no. 176* (Sheffield: Sheffield Academic Press, 1999), Appendix, pp. 311–13.

29 E.J. Epp, *Junia: The First Woman Apostle* (Minneapolis: Fortress Press, 2005).

30 A.C. Wire, *The Corinthian Women Prophets: A Reconstruction through Paul's Rhetoric* (Minneapolis: Fortress Press, 2nd ed. 2003).

31 *Ibid*, p. 187.

32 *Ibid*, pp. 181–4.

33 *Ibid*, pp. 184–7.

34 Mitchell, 'Paul's Letters to Corinth', p. 314.

35 Epp, *Junia: the First Woman Apostle*, pp. 12, 16–17.

36 J. Walters, 'Civic identity in Roman Corinth', p. 399.

37 *Ibid*, pp. 411–5.

38 C.W. Concannon, *Assembling Early Christianity. Trade, Networks and the Letters of Dionysios of Corinth* (Cambridge: Cambridge University Press, 2017).

39 John Chrysostom, *Homiliae in 1 Cor.*, Argument 1–2, in J.-P. Migne, ed., *Patrologiae cursus completus, series graeca* (Paris: Imprimerie Catholique, 1857–66), vol. 61. 9.

40 A.R. Brown, 'Medieval pilgrimage to Corinth and Southern Greece', in *Journal on Hellenistic and Roman Material Culture* (HEROM), vol. 1 (2012), p. 210.

41 G.D.R. Sanders, 'Archaeological evidence for early Christianity in Corinth', in *Urban Religion in Roman Corinth*, ch. 16, pp. 419–42.

42 Brown, 'Medieval pilgrimage to Corinth', p. 210.

43 Sanders, 'Archaeological evidence for early Christianity in Corinth', pp. 419–42. See A.R. Brown, *Corinth in Late Antiquity: A Greek, Roman and Christian City* (London, New York: Bloomsbury, 2018) for a more recent survey of early Christianity in Corinth.

44 R. Sweetman, 'The Christianization of the Peloponnese: The Topography and Function of Late Antique Churches', in *Journal of Late Antiquity*, vol. 3, no. 2 (Fall 2010), pp. 222–3.

45 W. Caraher, 'The ambivalent landscape of Christian Corinth: the archaeology of place, theology, and politics in a late antique city', in *Corinth in Contrast: Studies in Inequality*, ed. S.J. Friesen, S. James and D. Schowalter (Leiden: Brill, 2013), pp. 143–65.

46 Brown, *Corinth in Late Antiquity*, p. 137.

47 Brown, 'Medieval pilgrimage to Corinth', p. 209.

48 A.R. Brown, 'Last men standing: Chlamydatus portraits and public life in late antique Corinth', in *Hesperia*, vol. 81 (2012), pp. 141–76, at pp. 144–5, 159–60.

49 *Ibid*, pp. 141, 169–71.

50 A.M. Yasin, 'Commemorative Communities: The Dead in Early Christian Churches', in *Saints and Church Spaces in the Late Antique Mediterranean: Architecture, Cult and Community*, A.M. Yasin (Cambridge: Cambridge University Press, 2009, repr. 2012).

51 R.M. Rothaus, *Corinth: The First City of Greece. An Urban History of Late Antique Cult and Religion* (Leiden: Brill, 2000), p. 98.

52 Sweetman, 'The Christianization of the Peloponnese', p. 232.

53 Photo ref.: bw_2000_001_26, reproduced courtesy of the American School of Classical Studies at Athens, Corinth Excavations.

54 M.E. Landon, *Contributions to the Study of the Water Supply of Ancient Corinth*, PhD diss. University of California, Berkeley, 1994, 'Spring of Ayios Kodratus', pp. 207–18, no.12

55 W. Caraher, *Church, Society and the Sacred in Early Christian Greece*, PhD diss., Ohio State University, 2003, p. 461.

56 Brown, 'Medieval pilgrimage to Corinth', pp. 216–7.

57 Caraher, *Church, Society and the Sacred*, p. 312.

58 Rothaus, *Corinth: The First City of Greece*, p. 97.

59 St Quadratus is named in the *Carthaginian Martyrology*, and in the recension by Florus of Lyons of the *Roman Martyrology*. See V. Limberis, 'Ecclesiastical Ambiguities: Corinth in the Fourth and Fifth Centuries', in *Urban Religion in Roman Corinth*, pp. 452–3.

60 *Ibid.*

61 Caraher, *Church, Society and the Sacred*, p. 462.

62 G.D.R. Sanders, 'Problems in interpreting rural and urban settlement in southern Greece, AD 365–700', in *Landscapes of Change: Rural Evolutions in Late Antiquity and the Early Middle Ages*, ed. N. Christie (Aldershot: Ashgate, 2004), ch. 5, pp. 163–93.

63 Brown, 'Medieval pilgrimage to Corinth', p. 210.

64 Lecture by Professor G.D.R. Sanders to the Phoebe Institute, Corinth, 26.09.2007.

65 Conversation with Professor G.D.R. Sanders, 17.05.2012.

66 Pompeii, Casa di Virnius Modestus, IX 7, 16.

67 B.A. Robinson, 'Fountains and the formation of cultural identity at Roman Corinth', in *Urban Religion in Roman Corinth*, ch. 4, pp. 118–21.

68 *Ibid*, pp. 118, 121, 123.

69 G.D.R. Sanders, 'Archaeological evidence for early Christianity in Corinth', pp. 419–42.

70 *Ibid.*

71 *Ibid.*

72 G.D.R. Sanders, 'Urban Corinth: an introduction', in *Urban Religion in Roman Corinth*, ch. 1, p. 24.

73 Palladius, *Lausiac History*, transl. W. Lowther Clarke (London: Society for the Promotion of Christian Knowledge, 1918), ch. 65, pp. 171–3.

74 *Menologion*, in Migne, *Patrologiae graeca*, vol. 117, cols. 345–8.

75 Limberis, 'Ecclesiastical Ambiguities', p. 45.

76 *Acta Sanctorum*, ed. The Bollandists, *Propylaeum Novembris Synaxarum Ecclesiae Constantinopolitanae* (Brussels, Antwerp: Société des Bollandistes, 1902), pp. 713–4; Limberis, 'Ecclesiastical Ambiguities', pp. 454–5.

77 Recounted in Migne, *Patrologiae graeca*, vol. 115, cols. 919–44; Limberis, 'Ecclesiastical Ambiguities', p. 455.

78 Caraher, 'The Ambivalent Landscape of Christian Corinth', pp. 143–65.

79 Information from Professor G.D.R. Sanders, October 2015.

80 Lecture by Professor G.D.R. Sanders to the Phoebe Institute, Corinth, 11.04.2008.

81 *Ibid.*

Chapter 5

LECHAION AND ST LEONIDAS

The port of Lechaion was a trading centre of major significance in the ancient world: its quays and warehouses were active from the sixth century BC to the fifth century AD, and probably beyond. In the last decade, extensive excavation has revealed that the harbour town was more important than was previously thought.[1] From Lechaion's jetties and warehouses, ships set out laden with cargo, sailors and colonists bound for Corfu, Sicily and ports throughout the Mediterranean and its northern arm, the Adriatic, reaching into the Balkans. Corinth's unique access to the West helped to shape the Hellenisation of the region; this led to the evolution of Europe as we know it.[2]

It was far safer to set out from Lechaion's wharfs than to sail round Cape Malea at the south-eastern end of the Peloponnese. In the first century BC Strabo quoted a proverb 'If you have rounded Cape Malea, forget your home'.[3] There was a thriving ship-building industry at Lechaion: the Athenian historian Thucydides (460–395 BC) claimed that the trireme was introduced to Greece by Corinthian ship-builders in the late eighth century BC.[4] This was a fast and agile galley with three rows of oars: it became the dominant warship in the Mediterranean between the seventh and the fourth centuries BC.

As we have seen, the Romans destroyed Corinth in 146 BC during their conquest of Greece, but Julius Caesar rebuilt the city and its harbours in 44 BC; this resulted in several centuries of prosperity. Corinth's northern port of Lechaion was much larger than her southern harbour of Kenchreai. There was extensive settlement around the busy northern port, which rivalled the great harbour of Piraeus at Athens. Lechaion included a series of at least four landlocked harbour basins, accessible from the sea through a large entrance canal and several inland canals. Offshore structures included three long wharves outside the harbour, two of which created a square basin for shipping; a third protected the entrance to an inner harbour (Fig. 40).[5]

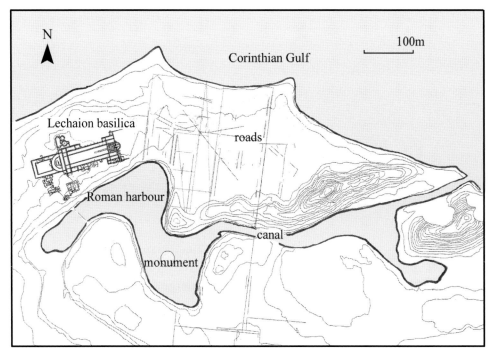

FIGURE 40. Lechaion Roman harbour and basilica. Courtesy of the American School of Classical Studies, Athens (with added text).

The silted wetland basins that formed the inner harbour were once lagoons within an ancient river delta. It is unclear how shipping moved between the busy offshore quays and the more protected inner basins.[6] On Figure 40, the roads marked to the east of the basilica indicate the work of surveyors during the last third of the first century AD. Shallow trenches divided the land into strips of one *actus* (or 120 Roman feet) in width, separated by roads 30 feet wide. This appears to indicate the outline of a harbour installation that was not completed.[7] Monumental architecture is preserved underwater as far as 80 m offshore; it has been systematically charted by the Lechaion Harbour Project. In 2019 its archaeologists uncovered the remains of a large lighthouse that featured on ancient coins depicting the harbour.[8]

The Lechaion Harbour Project

This extensive programme includes divers and archaeologists from the Greek Ministry of Sports and Culture and from the University of Copenhagen. This unique interdisciplinary collaboration ensured a combination of skilful diving and archaeological expertise. Excavation began in 2013 under the joint direction of Dr Bjørn Lovén and Dr Dimitris Kourkoumelis.[9] Divers were essential to the project, since much of the excavation has been conducted underwater, with the attendant difficulty of accurately recording data. Additional problems have been caused by the fact that although the water is shallow, excavation trenches quickly fill with sediment from wave action: overnight several tons of sand can be deposited across the site.[10]

Beyond the shoreline, the Lechaion Harbour Project team have discovered artefacts preserved for 1,400 years by the salt water, including fishing lines and hooks; even food has survived, including nuts and seeds. Ceramic containers were found: they would have transported goods from Italy, Tunisia and Turkey.[11] Perhaps most significant are well-preserved wooden artefacts including part of a wooden pulley, foundation posts and carved pieces of wood. Such organic material is rarely found on land in the central Mediterranean region, but woodworm does not survive in salt water, and divers have recorded evidence of the harbour's wooden constructions over many centuries.[12] By the first century AD, Lechaion had a large outer harbour of 40,000 square metres. The large piers and quays of the outer harbour and the inner basins were built of finely-dressed ashlar stone blocks, each weighing five tons.[13]

The entrance canal

The stone-lined entrance canal protected ships entering and leaving the town's inner harbours; in 2015 the team uncovered some 55 m of its sides.[14] Large stone blocks from the harbour front area were held in place with metal clamps. A great wooden bulwark formed part of the piers flanking the western side of the entrance canal. Forty vertical wooden posts that shored up rubble foundations have been carefully conserved underwater, since this is the first bulwark of its kind to be found in Greece. Divers working at a depth of 1–3 m of water also examined the eastern side of the entrance canal to a distance of 46 m offshore. Adjoining it they discovered strong stone foundations, perhaps for a tower to protect the harbour entrance. Nearby were two column drums; they may have been intended to support a portico that would have created an impressive entrance to the harbour.[15]

The complex harbour evolved over time. The entrance canal was up to 30 m wide in the fourth and third centuries BC, but became narrower in later centuries, as sediment accumulated. A sand spit separated the inner basins of the harbour from the sea, and a monument was erected on a small island in the long, sheltered inner harbour (see Fig. 40). This could have been a religious sanctuary, a large statue or a customs office. The monument was destroyed by an earthquake some time between 50 and 125 AD. Professor Guy Sanders has suggested that this may be our first surviving evidence of an earthquake that occurred around AD 70 in the time of the emperor Vespasian.[16]

The harbour in late Roman times

By the late Roman period, while still linked with Corinth, Lechaion had developed its own identity as a town and a religious centre. By the sixth century AD, sediment had filled areas of the earlier harbour basins, and an earthquake had raised the area around Lechaion by over a metre; an extensive new basin was therefore carved out.[17] Towering above the ships in the harbour, an imposing basilica was built on the sand spit in the mid-sixth century, the size of two football pitches; it was one of the largest of its kind, 180 m long, and was comparable in size with the original basilica of St Peter's in Rome. It would have been a prominent landmark for travellers approaching by land or sea. The basilica was dedicated to the Corinthian martyr Leonidas; it was excavated in the 1960s by Demetrios Pallas and the Greek Archaeological Society.[18]

In 2015 the Lechaion Harbour Project's divers excavated six well-preserved wooden *caissons*: these were single-use barges filled with rock and concrete that were sunk in order to create quays and a harbour frontage. The barges and their cargo formed a solid foundation stretching 57 m; they held back the sea along this exposed coastline. They were the first of their kind to be discovered in Greece with their wooden elements still preserved. Until recently, it had been thought that such facilities dated from earlier times, and were merely maintained and repaired in the late Roman period, but initial carbon dating suggests that this was a unique early Byzantine construction, created at the same time as the Leonidas basilica that was begun in the mid-sixth century. It was to be a short-lived project, however – Lechaion and its basilica were destroyed by an earthquake in the seventh century.[19]

Lechaion's magnificent basilica

At first, archaeologists assigned dates for the basilica's construction and destruction that are now considered too early. A coin of Marcian (450–57) was found in its foundations, while a coin of Anastasius I (491–518) was found under a section of its interior pavement. The outer *atrium* at the basilica's west end does not bond with the rest of the building; a later coin of Justin I (518–27) was discovered in its foundations. Pallas suggested that the basilica was destroyed by the earthquake of 551/2, but scientists now doubt that these distant quakes affected Corinth, so the dating by Pallas is probably incorrect.[20]

The church is built on an unstable sandbar; if it had been completed by AD

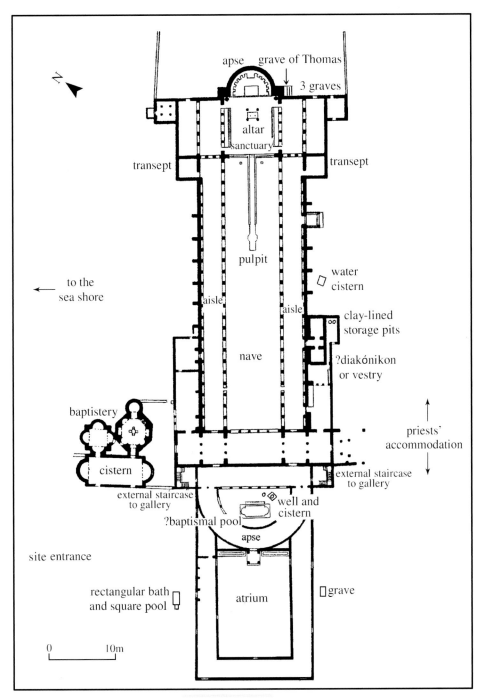

FIGURE 41. Lechaion basilica, Courtesy of the American School of Classical Studies, Athens (with added text).

525, one would expect it to have suffered major damage during the earthquake of 525 that destroyed Corinth, according to Procopius. It is therefore more likely that the basilica was constructed after this date. Vessels used in burial liturgies were found in two of three brick-built graves immediately south of the basilica's apse, one belonging to Thomas the Presbyter; they will be described later. The ceramic vessels date from about AD 600, and the graves predate the destruction of the basilica; thus it could not have been destroyed in the mid-sixth century.[21]

The enormous basilica would have come alive during the liturgy each Sunday. It is probable that the clergy entered the *narthex*, or entrance corridor at the western end of the church, where they performed opening prayers (see Fig. 41). Meanwhile, the people could have gathered in the *atrium*, a large courtyard with colonnades on three sides, further to the west, and then filed into the aisles. Since Corinth had been re-founded as a Roman colony in 44 BC, it had a considerable Roman population, and its government was modelled on the Roman pattern. Until the eighth century AD, Corinthian churches, including the Leonidas basilica, followed the Roman custom whereby a bishop and his clergy processed in last, unlike the normal eastern practice, in which they processed in first.[22] Professor Guy Sanders paints a vivid picture of a Sunday liturgy:

> *The congregation entered first and filed into the aisles, perhaps women on one side and the men on the other. From here they were afforded a ringside view of the advent of the [book of the] gospels, the bishop and the attendant clergy [processing] down the nave and into the sanctuary. During the liturgy ... the empty nave enabled efficient distribution of the communion over the nave barrier.*[23]

At the basilica's eastern end is a spacious sanctuary with an altar, behind which, set against the semi-circular wall of the apse, is the *synthronon*, a semi-circular podium with seats for officiating clergy. There is a small transept at the junction of the sanctuary and the nave: this is the only church in the Peloponnese in which the transepts, or arms of the holy space, extend beyond the width of the aisles.[24] There were ample galleries for catechumens above the aisles. These candidates for baptism would listen to the Liturgy of the Word, including the scripture readings and the sermon, before descending down two external staircases at the west end of the basilica, for further instruction on their own. This is likely to have taken place in a large *atrium* that was added to the west end of the basilica in the sixth century.

A central paved pathway, or *solea*, extends westwards through the enormous nave, a full third of its length, to the *ambo*, or pulpit, from which the bishop preached. The cool, resonant marble walls would have amplified his voice (Plate 11). The *solea* was perhaps marked out by low screens; the *solea* is found

FIGURE 42. Pediment and giant column in the north aisle of Lechaion basilica, near the sanctuary.

in Constantinople, but less frequently in Greece, since the laity were already separated from the clergy behind low screens in the aisles.[25] There were elaborate *opus sectile* floors, made of pieces of marble and slate, cut into geometric patterns. The columns, capitals and screens are of elegant white Proconnesian marble, delicately streaked with pink, blue and green (Fig. 42). Their fine quality suggests that the church may have been a donation by the emperor Justinian, as part of his restoration of Corinth after the earthquake of 551/2.[26]

The Proconnesian marble came from imperial quarries on islands in the Sea of Marmara: it was used extensively to adorn the basilica of Hagia Sophia in Constantinople, built in AD 537. On a number of Lechaion's column capitals, a cross surrounded by fine-toothed acanthus foliage is carved; both the cross and acanthus foliage represent the tree of life (Fig. 43). The capitals may have been carved in the imperial workshops that supplied churches in Constantinople (such as the Studios basilica), Thessaloniki (the Acheiropoeitos basilica) and Philippi (basilica 'B'). This style was widely imitated by local craftsmen in the early sixth century.[27]

FIGURE 43. Column capital in the north transept of Lechaion basilica, decorated with a cross surrounded by acanthus foliage, to represent the tree of life.

A combination of imperial and local elements

The elaborate building and the fine quality of the materials used in the basilica's construction reflect Justinian's policy of founding churches in significant locations throughout the empire, in a style that reflected imperial liturgical practice. The long pathway down the nave and its centrally placed pulpit imitate imperial worship in Constantinople, although other aspects of the basilica's design are Greek. This combination of liturgical features from the imperial capital with features from the provinces is found elsewhere in the West: in the sanctuary of the church of San Vitale in Ravenna, completed in 547, two mosaics that depict Justinian and his wife Theodora surrounded by court officials appear to present them within the context of a liturgy celebrated in Constantinople.[28] This conveys an image of political authority, in a church setting.

Worship in Lechaion's basilica may also have reflected the political scene: in the fifth and sixth centuries, Greece was ecclesiastically part of the Western province of *Illyricum Orientalis* (which included both Macedonia and areas around the River Danube); this province lay within the jurisdiction of the pope, the bishop of Rome. Sometimes, the emperor Justinian exerted his authority by interfering in papal politics. The design of Lechaion's basilica suggests that Justinian also sought to influence liturgical practice. In the fifth and sixth centuries, worship could be used to political effect: imperial or church policies were opposed by excluding the name of the emperor or offending bishops from those commemorated in the liturgy. However, the Greek features in the design of Lechaion's basilica suggest that the local hierarchy also asserted control over the space and style of worship celebrated there. The church is a fascinating example of a hybrid space in which imperial and local liturgical style co-existed and overlapped.[29]

FIGURE 44. Giant masonry block from the vault over the apse, east of the sanctuary, Lechaion basilica.

Collapsed portions of the apse are strewn close to the tomb of Thomas the Presbyter (Fig. 44). As we have seen, grave goods in the tomb date from around AD 600; thus the basilica was still in use in the early seventh century. It is possible that, during its short lifetime, the enormous basilica became the seat of the archbishop of Corinth, who, as the Metropolitan, exercised oversight of southern Greece.[30] South of the inner *atrium* there are rooms with apsidal dining areas that might have been the Corinthian bishop's quarters in the sixth, seventh and perhaps eighth centuries. In medieval times, Corinth's cathedral is likely to have been closer to the centre of ancient Corinth.[31]

St Leonidas

The great church appears to have been a shrine dedicated to Corinth's most famous saint, the martyr Leonidas, who was hung at Corinth and thrown into the sea at Lechaion. It also commemorated the seven virgins, perhaps women deacons, who mourned his death and were drowned at Troezen, south-east of Corinth, on Easter Monday in AD 240 or 250. These events took place during the persecution initiated by the emperor Decius, under the consul Venustus. Leonidas and the women were buried in a shrine on the beach, probably at Lechaion.[32] According to tradition, the women's names were Chariessa, Galina, Nike, Kallida, Nunexia, Vasilissa and Theodora.

The cult of Leonidas and his female companions is attested relatively early, in the Syriac Martyrology composed around AD 411 and in the later so-called Martyrology of St Jerome, an Italian source dating from the second half of the fifth century and surviving in a late sixth-century manuscript, probably from Auxerre in Gaul. These sources give the date of the martyrdom of Leonidas as 16 April; by the thirteenth century, when Athens had become more powerful than Corinth, Leonidas was conflated with an Athenian bishop, whose death was celebrated on 15 April, the date on which the Orthodox Church honours the martyr to this day.[33]

The story of the martyrdom of Leonidas and his companions is related in MS Patmos 254.[34] This manuscript in the monastery of St John on the island of Patmos is the April volume of a late tenth-century *menologion*,[35] or Greek Orthodox calendar of saints, containing their biographies. The story recounted in Patmos 254 goes as follows: Leonidas and the seven women were known in Corinth for their prayer, fasting and bold preaching. They were arrested, and the women were separated from Leonidas. When they were brought before the consul, the magistrate demanded that the young man should sacrifice to the gods; otherwise he would be tortured.[36]

Leonidas replied in rather philosophical language that although the body is perishable, and can be destroyed by objects of a similar nature, the invulnerable soul will perceive rational objects more clearly when it is set free from what is material. When he refused to offer sacrifice, Leonidas was removed and the women were brought in. The leader told them, 'Leonidas, who at first was in error, now promises to sacrifice'. Recognising his deception, the women replied that they would indeed sacrifice, but to God and his Son, Jesus Christ, for it was to these that Leonidas had promised to sacrifice, and not to idols. The leader urged them to sacrifice to the twelve gods who protect the world, but the virgins replied that these so-called gods were merely matter shaped in human form, unable to see or move. At this the Corinthian leader grew angry, and sent the women to prison.[37]

The consul ordered Leonidas to be brought back, again failed to persuade him to sacrifice to the gods, and sent him to the torturers, who flogged him and eventually burnt him to death. The women were summoned again, and asked: 'Of what rank and family are you? And what kind of relationship (*koinonia*) do you have with Leonidas?' They replied that they were 'Christians, just as our companion Leonidas is'. They explained that although they came from separate physical families, they were one in their way of life and were united by their faith. On hearing this, the consul promised them the same punishment as Leonidas. They were flogged, chained, weighted down with rocks, and thrown into the sea. After a day or two, their bodies were washed up on the shore. Devout Christians gathered up their remains, buried them, and built a shrine over their bodies, where the saints were honoured by the faithful and performed cures.[38]

Martyrdom in Maccabees

The story of the torture and death of Leonidas and the seven women follows a traditional formula intended for the edification of a worshipping community, in a style that had been established in pre-Christian times. It was employed from at least the first century BC, when the Second Book of Maccabees was written, a book that describes the Jewish resistance against compulsory Hellenisation by the Seleucid kings. As we saw in Chapter 3, the First and Second Book of Maccabees were addressed to the expatriate Jews of Alexandria, to arouse their concern for the dangers threatening the Temple in Jerusalem. After a period of doubt, the two books were accepted by various Christian Churches into the canon of scriptures to be read during worship.[39]

Book 2 chapter 7 describes the arrest and torture of a mother and her seven sons. Here, the king plays off the mother against her children, and asks her to persuade them to defy their religious beliefs by eating pork. Both the sons and their mother refuse, explaining their motives in theological language. The mother encourages her sons in a discourse similar to that of Leonidas, saying:

I do not know how you appeared in my womb; it was not I who endowed you with breath and life, I had not the shaping of your every part. It is the creator of the world, ordaining the process of man's birth and presiding over the origin of all things, who in his mercy will most surely give you back both breath and life, seeing that you now despise your own existence for the sake of his laws (2 Mac. 7. 22–3).

After this reflection, which was actually intended as instruction for those who heard the account read aloud, we are told that the whole family was tortured to death.

As in this pre-Christian narrative, the author of the account of Leonidas and the seven holy women brings the story forward into his own time. Like the scribes who compiled the books of Maccabees, he speaks directly to his listeners by putting theological reflections into the mouths of the martyrs. These Acts of the Martyrs were designed to be read on their feast day during worship at the place where their relics were enshrined and, if the saints were well-known, in churches elsewhere. Ann Marie Yasin considers that in worship, the increasing use of the Lives of martyrs and stories of their miracles enabled the listeners to become more united with their forebears, as they gained inspiration from them and sought their prayers, particularly when a local saint was celebrated on their individual feast day or 'birthday into heaven'.[40]

The baptistery at Lechaion

The bodies of Leonidas and his companions may have been washed ashore at the site of Lechaion's basilica, and it is possible that the large baptistery complex to the north, the seaward side of the church, was originally a shrine to the martyrs. Perhaps their relics were later moved to another part of the great church, where they could be more fittingly venerated. When the basilica lay in ruins, a later chapel was built in the sanctuary, where medieval pilgrims may have continued to honour the martyrs.[41]

In its later form, the baptistery complex includes two elaborately-designed square buildings (Fig. 45;

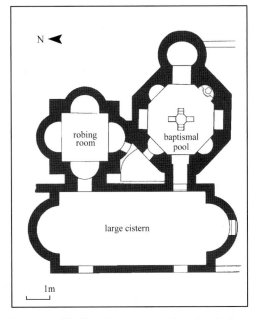

FIGURE 45. Baptistery complex, Lechaion basilica. Courtesy of the American School of Classical Studies, Athens (with added text).

Plate 12): that to the north is likely to have been the room where candidates assembled and robed, before entering the adjacent baptismal pool. The design of the cruciform baptismal font suggests baptism by immersion. It was later replaced by a new font placed in one corner, access to which was more restricted.[42] To the west is a large rectangular cistern, designed to contain water for baptisms; there are foundations of what may have been a similar large cistern, or perhaps a baptismal pool, in the *atrium* which was added on to the west end of the basilica, and there is a smaller tank with a blue tiled floor to the north of the *atrium*. The unusual number of baptismal facilities suggests that many Corinthians were still unbaptised in the sixth century.

Four graves

It was common for Christians to seek burial at martyrs' shrines, but there are only four graves at Lechaion. To the south of the *atrium* is a single tomb (Fig. 46). A red cross and the letters *alpha* and *omega* are painted on its white plastered walls, a testimony to Christ, the beginning and the end of all life. At the opposite end of the basilica, three more graves are situated near the altar, outside the sanctuary, adjoining the apse: the northernmost grave, closest to the church wall, contained the body of a presbyter (or 'elder') named Thomas; as we have seen, it dates from about AD 600.

Pallas reported the discovery of these three brick-built graves in 1961. That of Thomas was covered with limestone slabs and fragments of what had formerly been the marble screen that separated the chancel from the nave. As in the single tomb south of the *atrium*, red crosses are painted on its walls, with *alpha* and *omega* pendants. Three *lekythoi*, or narrow vessels with a single handle attached to the neck, were found in the grave: they would have contained oil for use in graveside burial liturgies. The tomb also contained a red slipware pitcher with +TOMA[S] PR[ESBYTER] incised on its shoulder.[43]

The basilica's walls are constructed of rubble and cement. Around the building, even in places that were intended to be covered, plasterers incised

FIGURE 46. Tomb painted with a cross and *alpha* and *omega*, Lechaion basilica.

FIGURE 47. Two incised fish swim from left to right above the tomb of Thomas the presbyter, Lechaion basilica.

at least fifteen fish, a symbol for Christ; two such fish can be seen in the cement above Thomas's tomb (Fig. 47). Perhaps it was these plasterers who also carved fish on the inside wall of the building in the Panayia Field to the south of central Corinth, described in Chapter 4. Similar incised fish are found in the Hexamilion Wall, in the walls of Corinth's south *stoa*, or colonnade alongside the forum, in a small bath near Sparta and a basilica at Chersonisos on the island of Crete.[44]

Adjoining the south wall of the nave of Lechaion's basilica, a range of rooms may have formed the *diakónikon*, or vestry, one of whose functions was to house the offerings of the faithful. The room at the east end contains two storage pits lined with clay (Fig. 48), in which grain or other commodities could be preserved.

FIGURE 48. Two clay-lined storage pits, Lechaion basilica.

Further to the south are extensive ruins, perhaps of accommodation for clergy, including a circular building at the south-west corner that may have been a kiln. Pottery dating from the mid-sixth century was discovered in the houses built up against the basilica.[45] Small booths attached to the basilica's south wall might have been shops.

A marble slab from the baptistery

In 1984 remains of an off-white marble slab that may have been associated with the shrine of St Leonidas was found at Lechaion in the early baptistery structure: it could have adorned a sacred fountain (or *hagiasma*) dedicated to Leonidas and his companions. It is approximately half a metre in both height and width, and can be seen in the Byzantine and Christian Museum, Athens (Fig. 49).[46] On one side is carved the head of Medusa, the terrible Gorgon whose glance, according to Greek mythology, turned onlookers to stone, and on the other side a large cross is depicted. The grim Gorgon is portrayed in a typical Graeco-Roman style, with wings on its head.[47]

The Gorgon mask is surrounded by a double-banded interlace with swastikas arranged in the shape of a cross: interlinked swastikas are a common Graeco-Roman design, and in early Christian iconography the swastika was a version of the cross, a symbol of Christ's victory over death. In the space between the swastikas, a dog wearing a collar is depicted running, perhaps chasing an animal on the missing portion of the slab. In similar contexts, a hound chasing a deer represents evil forces hounding the human soul.[48] On the reverse side of the slab is a large Latin cross with flared arms and a fragment of a palmette motif of symmetrical leaf fronds. The slab is finely carved and belongs to a type found in Greece, Italy, Syria, Palestine, Egypt and Constantinople. The imagery is intended to convey that the demonic power of the Gorgon is neutralised by the power of the Christian cross, depicted on each side of the slab.[49]

FIGURE 49. Gorgon's head: detail on a marble slab from Lechaion, in the Byzantine and Christian Museum, Athens (BXM 317).

Lechaion's other churches

The remains of what appears to be the west end of a smaller basilica have been found near Lechaion harbour. Its *narthex*, or entrance corridor at the western end, and its *atrium*, or gathering space, have been identified. Fragments of columns, capitals and ceramics were discovered, together with clay lamps; coins dating from the eleventh century suggest that the building was also in use at a later period.[50] To the west of Lechaion, architectural fragments and tesserae from mosaics indicate another possible early Christian basilica on the hill of Agios Gerasimos.[51]

It is difficult to glimpse the early Church at Lechaion: the town is not mentioned in the New Testament, although it is likely that Priscilla and Aquila sailed from one of Rome's two ports, Ostia or Puteoli, and arrived at Lechaion harbour before settling in Corinth and inviting St Paul to lodge with them (Acts 18. 1–3). Later, Paul wrote of his intention to travel through Rome to Spain on his next visit to Corinth (Rom. 15. 28). This would have entailed his departure from the port of Lechaion.

St Leonidas and his seven women deacons were honoured at Lechaion, but they lived in the third century, while their cult developed considerably later, by which time little was actually known about them. Since Lechaion's great basilica did not become a cemetery church, there are no early monuments with inscriptions that might provide insight into the lives of the men and women who inhabited the port, but at least we know of Thomas the priest and the anonymous plasterers who carved fish on the walls of the basilica, as a testimony to their faith.

Notes

1   'Underwater Archaeology: Lechaion Harbour Project', The Carlsberg Foundation, 20.12.2016. ww/carlsbergfondet.dk>ENG>Lechaion_Loven, accessed 30.05.2020.

2   B. Lorén, 'At the crossroad of the ancient world: Lechaion – the main harbour of ancient Corinth', lecture at the University of Louisville, KY, 9.02.2017.

3   Strabo, *Geographica*, ed. and transl. H.L. Jones, in 8 vols., Loeb Classical Library (Cambridge, MAS: Harvard University Press, 1917), bk. 8. 6.

4   Thucydides, *History of the Peloponnesian Wars*, bk. 1. 13. 2–5, transl. M. Hammond (Oxford: Oxford University Press, 2009).

5   Scuba Hellas underwaterworld: Lechaion Harbour Project, 5.01.2016, www.scubahellas. com>Lechaion-harbour-project-2, accessed 30.05.2020.

6   'Underwater Archaeology: Lechaion Harbour Project'.

7   They were photographed from a low-level balloon by Dr and Mrs J. Wilson Meyers in 1986. See D.G. Romano, 'Urban and rural planning in Roman Corinth', in *Urban Religion in Roman Corinth: Interdisciplinary Approaches*, ed. D. Schowalter and S. Friesen, Harvard Theological Studies, vol. 53 (Cambridge, MAS: Harvard University Press, 2005), ch. 2, p. 51.

8   'Underwater Archaeology: Lechaion Harbour Project'.
9   *Ibid.*
10 P.B. Campbell, 'New underwater discoveries in Greece reveal ancient Roman engineering', *The Guardian*, 14.12.2017.
11 *Ibid.*
12 'Underwater Archaeology: Lechaion Harbour Project'.
13 Campbell, 'New underwater discoveries in Greece'.
14 Scuba Hellas underwaterworld.
15 'Underwater Archaeology: Lechaion Harbour Project'.
16 Campbell, 'New underwater discoveries in Greece'.
17 *Ibid.*
18 Pallas reported his findings almost annually in the Greek journal *Praktika*, between 1953 and 1965.
19 Scuba Hellas underwaterworld.
20 K.W. Slane and G.D.R. Sanders, 'Corinth: late Roman Horizons', *Hesperia*, vol. 74, no. 2 (Spring 2005), pub. The American School of Classical Studies at Athens (ASCSA), p. 291.
21 *Ibid.*
22 W. Caraher, 'The ambivalent landscape of Christian Corinth: the archaeology of place, theology, and politics in a late antique city', in *Corinth in Contrast: Studies in Inequality*, ed. S.J. Friesen, S. James and D. Schowalter (Leiden: Brill, 2013), pp. 143–65.
23 G.D.R. Sanders, 'Archaeological evidence for early Christianity and the end of Hellenic religion in Corinth' in *Urban Religion in Roman Corinth: Interdisciplinary Approaches*, pp. 419–42.
24 R. Sweetman, 'The Christianization of the Peloponnese: the topography and function of late antique churches', in *Journal of Late Antiquity*, vol. 3, no. 2 (Fall 2010), p. 238.
25 W. Caraher, *Church, Society and the Sacred in Early Christian Greece*, PhD diss., Ohio State University, 2003, ch. 3, p. 107, n. 174.
26 G.D.R. Sanders, 'Problems in interpreting rural and urban settlement in southern Greece, AD 365–700', in *Landscapes of Change: Rural Evolutions in Late Antiquity and the Early Middle Ages*, ed. N. Christie (Aldershot: Ashgate, 2004), ch. 5.
27 K.M. Hattersley-Smith, *Byzantine Public Architecture between the Fourth and Early Eleventh Centuries AD with Special Reference to the Towns of Byzantine Macedonia* (Thessaloniki: Society for Macedonian Studies, 1996), pp. 60–2, 146–7, 160.
28 Caraher, 'The ambivalent landscape of Christian Corinth', pp. 143–65.
29 *Ibid.*
30 A.R. Brown, 'Medieval pilgrimage to Corinth and Southern Greece', in *Journal on Hellenistic and Roman Material Culture* (HEROM), vol. 1 (2012), p. 214.
31 *Ibid*, pp. 213, 217.
32 *Ibid*, p. 212.
33 V. Limberis, 'Ecclesiastical ambiguities: Corinth in the fourth and fifth centuries', in *Urban Religion in Roman Corinth: Interdisciplinary Approaches*, ch. 13, p. 450.
34 MS Patmos 254, in 'Sainte Léonide et ses sept compagnes martyrs à Corinthe', ed. F. Halkin, in *Recherches et documents d'hagiographie byzantine*, Subsidia Hagiographica Graeca, vol. 5 (Brussels: Société des Bollandistes, 1971), pp. 60–6.
35 F. Halkin, 'Un Ménologue de Patmos (MS. 254) et ses Légendes Inédites', *Analecta Bollandiana*, vol. 72 (1954), p. 15.
36 Halkin, 'Sainte Léonide et ses sept compagnes', pp. 63–4; Limberis, 'Ecclesiastical ambiguities', p. 451.

37 Halkin, 'Sainte Léonide et ses sept compagnes', pp. 64–5; Limberis, 'Ecclesiastical ambiguities', p. 451.

38 Halkin, 'Sainte Léonide et ses sept compagnes', p. 65; Limberis, 'Ecclesiastical ambiguities', pp. 451–2.

39 A. Jones, 'Introduction to the Books of Maccabees', in *The Jerusalem Bible, Reader's Edition*, ed. A. Jones (New York: Doubleday, 1968), p. 569.

40 A.M. Yasin, 'What Saints Do in Church, Part II: Community Connections', in *Saints and Church Spaces in the Late Antique Mediterranean: Architecture, Cult and Community*, A.M. Yasin (Cambridge: Cambridge University Press, 2009, repr. 2012), ch. 6.

41 Brown, 'Medieval pilgrimage to Corinth', p. 213.

42 Sanders, 'Archaeological evidence for early Christianity', pp. 419–42.

43 Slane and Sanders, 'Corinth: late Roman Horizons', p. 291, n. 93.

44 Sanders, 'Archaeological evidence for early Christianity', pp. 419–42.

45 Sanders, 'Problems in interpreting rural and urban settlement', ch. 5.

46 Athens, Byzantine and Christian Museum, exhibit no. BXM 317.

47 Y. Theocharis, in *Transition to Christianity: Art of Late Antiquity, 3rd–7th Century AD*, ed. A. Lazaridou (Onassis Cultural Centre, NY: Alexander S. Onassis Public Benefit Foundation, 2011), Exhibition Catalogue no. 116, p. 149.

48 J. Toynbee 'Pagan motifs and practices in Christian art and ritual' in *Christianity in Britain, 300-700* (Leicester: Leicester University Press, 1968), ed. M.W. Barley and R.P. Hanson, pp. 181, 186; E. Rees, *Early Christianity in South-west Britain* (Oxford: Windgather Press, 2020), pp. 7–9.

49 Y. Theocharis, *Transition to Christianity*, p. 149.

50 A. Avramea and M. Kyrkou, 'Inventaire topographique de Corinthe et sa région à l'époque Chrétienne et byzantine', in *Géographie historique du monde méditerranéen*, Byzantina Sorbonensia, no. 7, ed. H. Ahrweiler (Paris: Publications de la Sorbonne, 1988), pp. 44–5; Caraher, *Church, Society and the Sacred*, p. 464.

51 Caraher, *Church, Society and the Sacred*, p. 465.

Chapter 6

CHRISTIAN COMMUNITIES
AT NEMEA AND SIKYON

Ten miles south-west of Corinth, the scenery changes: now the soil is yellow and dry, but until the fifth century AD, the Nemea valley was mainly an uninhabitable swamp. This is the region that surrounds the ancient Greek sanctuary of Nemea, which was tended by the citizens of Kleonai, in the hills two miles east of Nemea. In this chapter, we shall first focus on Kleonai and its association with the hero Hercules (or Herakles in Greek). Most of the chapter will be concerned with Nemea, which has been the subject of detailed excavation, largely under the direction of Stephen G. Miller, Emeritus Professor of Archaeology at the University of California, Berkeley. The site offers a fascinating glimpse of the evolution of a Classical pagan sanctuary into a Christian one. Finally we shall examine the nearby acropolis of Sikyon, and consider some neighbouring sites.

Kleonai and Hercules

The fortress city of Kleonai lay on an ancient route leading from Corinth to Argos. During the Classical period Kleonai became a political ally of Argos against its northern neighbours, even though Kleonai was nearer to Corinth than to Argos.[1] Kleonai possessed only a small territory; it largely owed its importance to the Nemean Games celebrated on its land. Indeed, Pindar (c. 518–438 BC) described them as 'the Kleonian games'.[2] Close to the town, the remains of many sarcophagi have been found along the route that passed below Kleonai's walls; they indicate roadside burials in the Classical era.[3] Little is known about later burial practices, but Anna Avramea records the site of an early Christian basilica at Kleonai; it was built over the remains of a temple dedicated to Athena.[4]

Writing in the second century AD, Pausanias recounts that, according to mythology, Hercules waylaid and killed the two sons of Actor near Kleonai, as they were on their way to the Nemean Games.[5] Two centuries earlier, Diodorus of Sicily wrote an extensive three-part *Bibliotheca historica,* or 'Historical library' between 60 and 30 BC. He stated that a temple of Hercules was built in the neighbourhood of Kleonai in memory of the slaughter.[6] A more well-known account of the hero's exploits associates the area with his defeat of the Nemean lion. Kleonai's temple of Hercules (Plate 13) can be seen below the hilltop settlement.

In one version of the myth, in a bout of madness caused by the jealousy of Hera, the wife of Zeus, Hercules had murdered his wife and children. He consulted the Delphic oracle, and was told to expiate his crime by serving his cousin, the king of Argos, for twelve years. He was given twelve dangerous tasks, the first being to slay a fierce lion, which Hera had sent to terrorise Nemea. The lion's lair was a cave with two entrances; Hercules walled up one entrance, and drove the lion inside with his club. He wrestled with the lion in the darkness, strangled it, skinned it, and thereafter wore its hide.[7] After being killed, the Nemean lion was transformed into the constellation Leo, for one function of the twelve Labours of Hercules was to explain the great constellations: each of his tasks is related to a sign of the zodiac.

Hercules prefigures Christ

In early Christian times, pagan heroes were seen to prefigure Christ, in a manner similar to the ancient Jewish prophets such as second Isaiah, who was described as 'the Suffering Servant'. Hercules was believed to be partly human and partly divine, as Jesus was both God and man. In early Christian iconography, Jesus is often depicted as a youthful hero like Hercules, Orpheus or Dionysus. In mythology, these three each descended into the underworld, as Jesus was believed to have suffered death and risen from the tomb. Hercules entered Hades in order to guide Alcestis back to her husband. In the Via Latina catacomb in Rome, where Christians worshipped and buried their dead in the mid-fourth century, Hercules is depicted performing his labours.[8]

Hercules engaged in single combat with a lion, just as the youthful King David had done in the Old Testament (1 Sam. 17. 34–5). In the same way, Jesus mounted the cross, locked in combat with Satan, with whom each Christian also struggles: 'Your enemy the devil is prowling around like a roaring lion, looking for someone to devour. Stand up to him, strong in faith' (1 Pet. 5. 8, 9). Hercules survived in the lion's cave, like the prophet Daniel in the lion's den (Dan. 6. 17–25); this is another theme often depicted in early Christian art, including on the panels of high crosses in Celtic monasteries of Ireland and Scotland. A ninth-century cross slab from a Pictish monastery at Meigle near Brechin in Perthshire, Scotland, depicts Daniel in the lions' den. He wears a pleated kilt and stands vulnerable and open, with outstretched arms like Christ on the cross, while the lions lick him and paw at his body.[9]

In Jewish-Christian theology, God's faithful will perform labours like Hercules:

> *On the lion and the viper you will tread,*
> *and trample the young lion and the dragon* (Ps. 90. 13).[10]

On an almost daily basis each monastic community entered into the imagery of fighting the lion of evil as they chanted the psalms, in such words as:

> *My soul lies down among lions*
> *who would devour the sons of men* (Ps. 56. 5).

> *Lord God, I take refuge in you.*
> *From my pursuer save me and rescue me,*
> *lest he tear me in pieces like a lion*
> *and drag me off with no one to rescue me* (Ps. 7. 2–3).[11]

Nemea's origins

There was no permanent settlement in ancient Nemea: the geology of the valley inhibits drainage and it reverted to marshland for several months each winter. The annual flooding of the valley made agriculture impossible, but it could offer pasture to sheep and goats. The region of Nemea appears to derive its name from *némo*, meaning 'I pasture'. In the summer, the area was sufficiently dry for the pan-Hellenic Games to take place.[12] According to mythology, the Nemean Games began as a funeral festival after the death of Opheltes, the infant son of Lycurgus, King of Sparta. Opheltes was killed by a snake while left unattended by his nurse: she had placed him in a bed of wild celery at Nemea. For this reason, successful competitors at the Nemean Games were crowned with wreaths of wild celery leaves, freshly cut.[13]

The first recorded pan-Hellenic Games at Nemea were held in 573 BC; a temple was built to honour Zeus, but it was destroyed in the late fifth century BC during the Peloponnesian Wars. The site was abandoned and the Games were relocated to Argos, fifteen miles to the south. The Games returned to Nemea in about 330 BC. Most of the pre-Christian remains visible at Nemea today were built between then and 271 BC, when Argos returned the Games to its city and Nemea fell into ruin once more. When Pausanias visited the site in the mid-second century AD, it had been a ruin for some four hundred years. He observed that the temple roof had collapsed and the statue of Zeus was missing.[14]

Excavations at Nemea

The site was first excavated by a French team in 1884. Forty years later, the American School of Classical Studies at Athens examined the area for two years in 1924–6; they conducted further excavations in the 1960s. From 1971 onwards, Professor Stephen Miller led an ongoing programme: he began by fundraising and working on a grid reference system to map the site. He started his first season of excavation in 1974, with four teams working in Nemea's sanctuary and one in the stadium. A sacred way led to the stadium, which was dug out of the hillside 500 m away. In 1974, the stadium's starting line was discovered, 6.85 m below the modern surface. In 1978 Miller's team found the vaulted entrance tunnel that led to the stadium, built in 320 BC.[15]

The following year the shrine of the hero Opheltes was identified: since the Nemean Games centred upon the worship of Opheltes, this was a significant discovery. A great deal of evidence about the cult was uncovered, which was all the more important because no comparable Greek hero's cult site had been examined.[16] In 1983–4, work began on the reconstruction of the enormous temple of Zeus, but this was suspended for economic reasons. In 1999 work on restoring the temple began once more. Many of the drums from the temple's exterior Doric colonnade still litter the ground around the temple; some have now been restored to their original position.

Meanwhile, Professor Miller had organised the first re-enactment of the Nemean Games in 1996; this is repeated every four years. Miller saw it as an opportunity to re-connect both Greeks and competitors worldwide with the best of their heritage, to celebrate human endeavour in a climate of peaceful competition.[17] Every two years in ancient Nemea, thousands of athletes, trainers, spectators and merchants arrived in Nemea for about a month to celebrate the Games. During this time there was a national truce – Athenians and Spartans competed side by side, though they might be at war for the remainder of the year. As Director of the Nemead, Miller aimed to revive the Olympic spirit in Nemea's stadium. Today's contestants do not run naked, but all dress in plain ancient-style tunics. They run barefoot, change clothes in the original locker room and place their toes in the starting blocks that were used by competitors over two thousand years ago.[18]

Christian Nemea

After the temple of Zeus at Nemea fell into ruin, a small agricultural community lived in its shadow; it flourished in the fifth and sixth centuries. In the late fourth century AD an artificial river had been created to drain the valley and enable arable farming. The people lived in scattered dwellings and grew vegetables by digging rows of narrow, oblong irrigation trenches between the plants. The trenches were then filled with water that soaked into the ground alongside the vegetables; this is a technique still employed in Greece today. Unfortunately, the use of this method of farming destroyed much of the archaeological evidence at Nemea.[19] Meanwhile, Christianity had spread to the region: as we have seen, there is evidence of a basilica at nearby Kleonai, and there is another at the summit of Evangelistria Hill, high above the sanctuary at Nemea.

It appears that Nemea acquired a bishop: this would have been unusual for a recently formed agricultural community outside a town. Possible evidence for this is found in the *Synekdemos* attributed to Hierokles, written during the reign of the emperor Justinian, before AD 535. The *Synekdemos* is a unique source of information about Byzantine political geography during the lifetime of Hierokles. It contains a table of administrative divisions of the Byzantine empire, and assigns 912 listed cities to their respective eparchy, or archdiocese, of which there were 64. Where previous editors had rendered the text as *Νέα Σικύων* ('New Sikyon'), its most recent editor, Honigmann, emended the text to *Ν[εμ]έα Σικύων* ('Nemea, Sikyon'). This suggests that there was a bishop at each location, and that Nemea was a recognised entity.[20]

The agricultural community began around AD 400. A significant increase of population, and perhaps trade, in the valley may be indicated by the number of coins excavated: only 152 coins were found dating from the period 200 BC to 300 AD, with the number rising dramatically to 813 for the following 200 years. The valley had evidently become habitable throughout the year, perhaps for the first time. This was made possible because of the artificial river mentioned above. Excavation revealed a channel 15 m wide; it had been created by digging a series of steps down into the virgin soil, to a depth of 2 m. Thick layers of gravel in the corners of the steps suggested that a large volume of water flowed through the channel. Part of the river was re-excavated in the twelfth century.[21]

Professor Miller suggests that such a large and unusual undertaking might have been initiated by the central government in Constantinople. This was a time when barbarians were attacking the empire: the Goths and their allies defeated the Eastern Roman army and the emperor Valens lost his life at Adrianople in AD 378. The Visigoths, led by King Alaric, sacked Rome in 410. The establishment of a community at Nemea might indicate the resettlement of former citizens of the empire.[22] It is possible that civilians, perhaps accompanied by a bishop and some monks, were relocated to Nemea, which was then a peaceful region far from barbarian invasions.

It would have made sense for the patriarch at Constantinople to send a bishop and a group of monks to enable Christian formation and worship in a newly-developed region. Pope Gregory the Great (*c.* 540–604) sent St Augustine, together with a band of monks, to work among the Saxons in Britain; Gregory appointed Augustine a bishop in order to give him the necessary authority for the task. At Nemea, clerics of some type might have lived with their bishop in the domestic buildings south-west of the basilica (see Fig. 56 below). The large number of coins found at the site suggests the presence of lay people also, who grew and perhaps traded foodstuffs; these could have been sold to the inhabitants of nearby Kleonai.

Where did Nemea's Christians worship?

At first, Nemea's inhabitants buried their dead in cemeteries at the south-east and north-west corners of the temple of Zeus. This suggests that at least part of the pagan temple had been re-roofed and converted into a Christian church. In the first quarter of the fifth century a new basilica was built: trenches were dug and filled with broken stone from the temple, bound together with cement. A large fragment of a Corinthian interior column from the temple is still visible in the foundations of the basilica's south wall. Above the foundations, at floor level, the basilica's walls were built using over a thousand blocks from the temple wall. A baptistery was added soon afterwards, in the second quarter of the fifth century, on the north side of the basilica. Coins found in the construction fill of its drain suggest that it was built early in the reign of the emperor Theodosius II; other coins found during its excavation suggest a similar date.[23]

The inhabitants may have built a basilica for two reasons: a purpose-built church would better suit their needs, and the central government in Constantinople also required temples to be destroyed. In AD 407 a decree directed that pagan temples be used henceforth for public, secular activities. One of the last decrees of the Theodosian Code in AD 435 ordered magistrates to destroy all remaining pagan shrines and replace them with the 'sign of the venerable Christian religion ... if any shrines still remain intact'.[24] This may have been already largely accomplished by missionary bishops, zealous monks and pious lay people. Coins found beneath the church floor suggest that Nemea's basilica had been completed by this date.[25]

The community's artefacts

Grain provided a basic part of the diet of Nemea's Christian inhabitants: fragments of two disc-shaped grinding stones were found, and also a eucharistic bread stamp made of terracotta (Fig. 50), or fired clay, not produced on a wheel. The bread stamp indicates that some of the bread baked at the site was regularly set aside for use in worship: it is circular, and engraved with a superimposed cross and a *chi* symbol for Christ. Today, nuns make altar breads by stamping them in a similar way. The bread stamp was broken long ago, which has caused grey mineral encrustations to form on the broken surfaces and elsewhere.

Pieces of an earthenware jug were found: it was decorated with a large, elegant cross and a *chi*; small circles are carved between the arms of the cross and the *chi*, and palm branches adorned vessel's neck. It may have contained wine or blessed oil intended for use in the liturgy (Fig. 51). The surface design was incised in the clay before the pot was fired. These Christian artefacts can be seen in the museum at Nemea, together with numerous everyday implements, such as sickles, bronze pruning hooks and spindle hooks.

FIGURE 50. Eucharistic bread stamp, Nemea Museum (TC 100). Photo by Stephen Miller.

Left: FIGURE 51. Jug used for the liturgy, Nemea Museum (P 160). Photo by Stephen Miller.

Above: FIGURE 52. Oil lamp with palm branches round the rim and a central cross, Nemea Museum (L 216). Photo by Stephen Miller.

Oil lamps were found, a number of them decorated with Christian symbols such as a cross, palm branches (Fig. 52), or a scallop shell to symbolise rebirth. The shell was associated with the Greek goddess Aphrodite (Venus was her Roman equivalent) who, in mythology, was born from the sea and floated ashore in a shell; it came to symbolise the Christian reborn in the waters of baptism. In ancient Greece the palm branch symbolised victory: on vases and mosaics it is frequently depicted being presented to victorious competitors in the pan-Hellenic Games. The palm tree was portrayed in the Scriptures as growing beside the river of life (Ezk. 47. 12; Rev. 22. 1–2), an image derived from the date palms growing alongside the Nile, ancient Egypt's most significant river.

The date palm was revered as life-giving, and still is in some cultures, on account of its many uses, including its nourishing dates, its oil used for anointing the body and tending wounds, and its branches, which had many uses including roofing, clothing (some icons depict the Desert Fathers wearing a loincloth of palm leaves) and shrouds. Palms also symbolise the victory of good over evil: Christ's followers waved branches as he triumphantly entered Jerusalem before his passion and death (Mt. 21. 8), while in the Book of Revelation the just are portrayed holding palm branches as they worship God (Rev. 7. 9).[26]

Over two hundred Christian graves were excavated, north-west and south-west of the basilica. A number of the dead wore crosses round their necks. Those illustrated include a silver cross with diamond-shaped pendants (Fig. 53), a bronze cross with a suspension hole, a pivot for closing, and an inscription (Fig. 54). The inscription, ΣΜΥ ΘΙΣ, is difficult to decipher but might mean 'My God'.[27] A third cross of bronze has a suspension hook and a pivot for closing (Fig. 55).

FIGURE 53. Silver cross with diamond-shaped pendants (GJ 80). Photo by Stephen Miller.

FIGURE 54. Bronze cross with suspension hole, pivot for closing, and inscription (GJ 85). Photo by Stephen Miller.

FIGURE 55. Bronze cross with suspension hook and pivot for closing (GJ 86). Photo by Stephen Miller.

Was this a monastic community?

It is possible that Nemea's Christian community was a monastic village consisting of both clerics and married lay people: one might find such a grouping of people in the countryside rather than in a town, since agricultural labour was conducive to prayer. The large number of burials around a sanctuary in a rural setting is typical of a religious community in which, as well as clerics honouring their own deceased, lay people from the surrounding area desired to bury their dead. The remarkable number of Christian artefacts also suggest an active worshipping community – a eucharistic bread stamp, a jug with a cross and a *chi* to symbolise Christ, and oil lamps with Christian themes (although these are widely found in non-Christian settings). As we have seen, some of the dead wore Christian crosses round their necks. At this early date, a religious community was more like a village than the highly organised medieval monasteries of Benedictines with which we might be more familiar, or the less structured Greek Orthodox monasteries of today.

At this period, monks enjoyed the favour of emperors and patriarchs, and might be highly educated. In Constantinople, the monastery of St John the Baptist known as the *Stoudium* was founded in 462 by a Roman patrician and former consul, Flavius Studius, in the south-western part of the city, near the sea.

In their previous secular life, some monks were university professors, scientists and engineers. In his seminal book, *The Desert a City*,[28] Derwas Chitty observed that the desert monks of Egypt lived in isolated places, but generally also near to cities. One of them taught local farmers living beside the Nile how to mix silt with desert sand, in order to grow better crops. Monks were content to live in marshy areas that offered a liminal space beyond towns, and they might possess the technology to cultivate such land.

Nemea's basilica

The Christian community erected their basilica (Plates 14 and 15) beside the ruined bath house, where athletes might wash after competing in the Games; its water flowed into the River Nemea that runs alongside it. The church stood on the foundations of the former guesthouse (or *xenon*): this was probably built to accommodate the athletes who took part in the Games and also, perhaps visiting dignitaries and officials who supervised the Games. The model in Figure 56 illustrates the basilica, with its baptistery to the left. In the foreground, a

FIGURE 56. Model of Nemea's basilica, viewed from the south-west, Nemea Museum. Photo by Stephen Miller.

domestic building that could have provided accommodation can be seen to the right. Three smaller units attached to it may have been a later addition, but all were in use at the same time. In the foreground to the left, rows of graves can be seen, and there were many more beyond them, further to the west.

The nave of the church was separated from its north and south aisles by a row of columns, probably five or six on each side, made of drums recycled from the interior Corinthian colonnade of the temple of Zeus that dominates the site. Inside the church, the recycled columns rested on a raised stylobate, or flat pavement; between the columns, a low parapet prevented movement between the nave through which the clergy walked in procession and the aisles where the congregation stood. There are smaller rooms on either side of the *narthex*, or corridor at the basilica's western end; there is also slight evidence of an *atrium*, or assembly room.[29]

At the eastern end is the sanctuary: it contained the altar and, against the back wall, a *synthronon*, a row of semi-circular seating for officiating clergy. The altar may have been a plain rectangular marble table, supported on four legs or small columns. The sanctuary was separated from the nave by a low screen, or *templon*. This was a parapet decorated with patterns incorporating the cross and other Christian motifs, executed in relief or perforated latticework: many of its fragments have survived.[30] In later centuries this was to develop into the *iconostasis*, a screen decorated with icons that prevented the congregation from seeing into the sanctuary. As was normal in early Greek basilicas, the roof was made of wood and has therefore perished, but hundreds of terracotta tiles that once covered it have survived. There may have been a clerestory above the nave to provide more light (see Fig. 56), but it is more likely that lighting was limited to windows in the north and south walls, and possibly the apse.[31]

A row of small square rooms that adjoin the basilica's south wall may have served as a *diakónikon*, or sacristy, to house the community's offerings. In the fifth and sixth centuries, members of the congregation might bring offerings of grain, olive oil and wool, as well as bread and wine for the eucharist. As we have seen, the domestic building south-west of the church may have provided accommodation for its clergy; the eucharistic bread stamp was found here.[32]

About 3.3 m south-east of the basilica's apse are the foundations of a circular structure, over 1 m high, It appears to have been erected at the same time as the church since one early grave adjoins it and another is very close – it could have been a bell tower. No other bell towers survive from this early date, but in the third quarter of the fifth century, when relating events in the life of Sidonius Apollinaris, Gregory of Tours mentions church bells. St Paulinus of Nola (*c.* 354– 431) is associated with the construction of the first church bells in Campania, in south-west Italy, although this tradition has not been verified.[33]

The baptistery

The rectangular baptistery was built on the basilica's north side, with a circular pool at the centre of its inner chamber; this small room was named the *photisterion* or 'place of enlightenment'. There was a corridor round three sides of the chamber, a pattern found in similar baptisteries in Greece, Asia Minor and elsewhere. The baptismal pool is a shallow stepped concrete basin, sunk into the ground (Fig. 57, Plate 16). It was originally paved with white marble from a recycled ritual dining table: the broken pieces of the *agape* table had been turned upside-down. The candidate stood in the pool, while the bishop poured water over his or her head from a small vessel.[34]

Like the basilica, the baptistery had a wooden roof. Glass fragments suggest glazed windows, and its walls were stuccoed and painted in bright colours. The baptistery was separated from the corridor by a screen wall, whose inner face was decorated with green marble. Later, as Christianity spread and the baptism of adults became less frequent, this type of large independent baptistery became obsolete throughout Christendom, and was replaced by a small font inside the church, more suitable for infant baptism.[35]

A narrow room between the baptistery and the church may have been a *chrismarion* or *consignatorium*.[36] As these names suggest, here the candidates might be chrismated, or anointed with blessed olive oil, and signed with the cross, for in baptism they symbolically died and rose again with Christ. The word *Christos* means 'the Anointed One': at baptism, the bishop anointed each candidate as a sign that they were now united with Christ. In the fourth century, Bishop Cyril of Jerusalem described how these new converts were anointed on the forehead, ears, nose and breast. He told them: 'Having been counted worthy of this holy chrism, you are called Christians; the name also belongs to you through your new birth [in baptism]'.[37]

FIGURE 57. Baptismal pool when first re-excavated, fifty years after its first discovery. Photo by Stephen Miller.

Nemea's community declines

In the sixth century the water supply dried up, and the community declined. In the 580s, the defences of the Corinthian isthmus were breached, and life grew more unstable for local residents. It appears that a single person began to live in the partially silted-up tunnel that led to the ancient stadium (Fig. 58). Archaeological evidence suggests that he lit the darkness with lamps, and cooked his meals in coarse pots. He buried several bronze coins, and two thirds of the way through the tunnel from the stadium entrance, on the right wall at shoulder height, he scratched a faith-filled inscription, which has been read as 'ethereal life' (ΑΙΘΕΡΙ ΖΩΗΣ), on top of older graffiti carved by athletes of long ago (Fig. 59).[38]

His skeletal remains were discovered scattered over an area 5 m wide; his skull lay against the south wall of the tunnel. It bore the remains of a head wound, inflicted by a straight-edged instrument, that had partially healed before his death. He may have survived an attack by the Slavs, only to be later discovered in his refuge inside the tunnel.[39] Perhaps the community had already disbanded, and he was a squatter, killed by robbers. The scratched inscription suggests that his faith sustained him in the tunnel's darkness. Although life in this rural Christian community had come to an end, maybe this man's faith taught him that if he wrestled with the lion of death, he would enter heaven, to live the ethereal life.

Left: FIGURE 58. Tunnel leading to Nemea's stadium (with modern scaffolding at its entrance).

Below: FIGURE 59. Inscription scratched on the tunnel wall of the stadium at Nemea (GRAF 15G). It reads: ΑΙΘΕΡΙ ΖΩΗΣ ('ethereal life').

A basilica on Evangelistria Hill

Above the watershed of the Nemea river valley, at the summit of Evangelistria Hill, a second basilica overlooks the sanctuary at Nemea,[40] as we have seen. It is named after Our Lady of the Annunciation: 'Evangelistria' refers to the 'good news' of her agreement to become the mother of God. It can be reached by a dirt track leading to an adjacent transmission station.[41] The road was constructed some thirty years earlier, however, in the 1950s, to provide access to a modern church and a house for a nun, both built by the villagers themselves.

Local people recall that in the late 1940s or early 1950s a young teenage girl from Nemea, Vasiliki Gkotsi, had a dream in which the Evangelistria appeared to her and told her that if she climbed to the top of the stadium hill and excavated, she would find gold. She told her family and soon the whole village assembled, with picks and shovels; they uncovered the remains of the basilica. On the northern side of the nave, just at the start of the apse, a grave was discovered, in which skeletal remains were found, with a pair of gold earrings. Since the dream had been fulfilled, Vasiliki decided to devote her life to the Evangelistria. A small *iconostasis* was constructed in the apse next to the tomb, and the skeletal remains were placed within it. Vasiliki later died and was buried in the church that she had discovered.[42]

There are magnificent views over distant mountains from the basilica on Evangelistria Hill. If it was a pilgrimage church, perhaps it was not visited during the winter, when driving winds cut across the hilltop. At the eastern end of the basilica, the apse appears to have contained two large windows: they would have enabled light to shine on the altar. There is a nave, separated from the north and south aisles by a raised stylobate that would have supported columns. A small room extending from the north aisle, at the eastern end of the nave, may have been a sacristy; it could have housed offerings made by the faithful. At the west end are remains of the *narthex*, or entrance corridor. Flat red tiles are built into the basilica's walls, which survive to a metre in height.[43]

Since the church dates from the same period as the basilica below, perhaps this was a pilgrimage site, rather than a church in regular use; it would have been a steep climb from the valley. Professor Rebecca Sweetman observes of such churches:

> *The action of making a pilgrimage to a church, particularly if it involved a long journey and arduous conditions, induced a great sense of well-being and achievement on arrival. If undertaken with other members of the community, the shared effort made would have emphasised the commonality of identity among participants ... The establishing of churches on edges of communities or in difficult-to-reach locations symbolically defined a region, and gave a community a shared identity tied to ownership of the landscape, particularly as they moved across the space.*[44]

Sikyon

Another location associated with the Games was the city of Sikyon, twelve miles north of Nemea and seven miles north-west of Corinth. As we saw in Chapter 3, the Isthmian Games were administered by the residents of Sikyon for a while, until the sanctuary at Isthmia could be repaired. By that time, the Games held at Nemea had already been transferred to Argos, further to the south. The city of Sikyon was formerly in the coastal plain between the Rivers Asopos and Helisson, with direct access to the Gulf of Corinth. The name Sikyon means 'gourd' – this useful source of food grows plentifully in the area. When dried, gourds can be fashioned into utensils: cups and bottles, scoops and ladles, pipes and whistles.

Unlike Nemea, which was not inhabited until the early fifth century AD, Sikyon was an ancient city that subsequently dwindled in size. In the seventh century BC, the local Ortha-gorid family assumed control of the town. One of its members, Kleisthenes, who ruled from 590 to 560 BC, developed the city as a centre for scholarship, sculpture and painting; its schools remained famous until the third century BC. Sikyon experienced various political vicissitudes; eventually, after the death of Alexander the Great, a Macedonian nobleman and military leader named Demetrios Poliorketes (or 'the Beseiger'), captured Sikyon in 303 BC. He was later to become

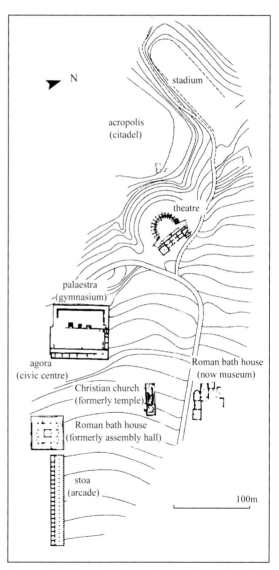

FIGURE 60. Roman Sikyon, after a plan at the site.

124

King Demetrius I of Macedon, from 294–288. Poliorketes persuaded Sikyon's inhabitants to abandon their city in the plain and to build a new one on the flat hill above, on the site of the former acropolis.[45]

When the Romans conquered Greece in 146 BC and Sikyon's neighbour, Corinth, was destroyed by the Roman general Mummius, Sikyon became the administrative centre of the region. There was a long, straight Roman road leading from Corinth to Sikyon.[46] The city organised the Isthmian Games until the second half of the first century BC, when Corinth was re-founded by Julius Caesar as a Roman colony. Sikyon occupied a large area, much of which has not yet been excavated. The ancient theatre near the site's western end was partially uncovered at the end of the nineteenth century by the American School of Classical Studies at Athens, and later by the Archaeological Society of Athens. The theatre was cut into a slope of the acropolis; temples would have dominated the skyline above. Further to the west, the city's stadium has not been excavated, but its outline can be seen (Fig. 60).[47]

Public buildings

A number of monuments further to the east were excavated by Professor Anastasios Orlandos in the 1930s. He uncovered public buildings in the *agora*, or civic centre, including a *bouleuterion*, or assembly hall where the citizens' council met. In the south-west part of the city centre, Orlandos identified a monumental *palaestra*, or gymnasium, which was built on two terraces, connected by three staircases; it contained two fountain houses.[48] West of the assembly hall, he excavated a *stoa*, or long, roofed walkway, with columns on one side and a wall on the other. It was used as a public meeting place or promenade.

The Roman inhabitants of Sikyon converted the assembly hall into a public bath house, and built a second bath house to the north

FIGURE 61. Roman bath house, Sikyon, now an archaeological museum.

(Fig. 61). Since this brick building was in good condition, with walls surviving to a height of 4 m, Orlandos excavated the monumental complex, and restored four of its rooms to serve as an archaeological museum. The Roman traveller Pausanias visited Sikyon after AD 150. He informs us that in the second century AD it was destroyed by an earthquake that ruined the city: 'When they had lost their power there came upon them an earthquake, which almost depopulated the city and took from them many of their famous sites'.[49]

A Christian church

The town was restored by the sixth century AD, and was then known as New Sikyon. Orlandos had excavated a temple that appears to have been converted into a Christian basilica in the sixth century.[50] Pausanias states that the temple had been dedicated to Aphrodite, and was tended by two celibate women:

> From here is a way to a sanctuary of Asclepius ... and opposite is another enclosure, sacred to Aphrodite ... into which enter only a female verger, who after her appointment may not have intercourse with a man, and a virgin, called the Bath-bearer, holding her sacred office for a year. All others are wont to behold the goddess from the entrance, and to pray from that place.[51]

FIGURE 62. Christian basilica, Sikyon.

The sanctuary of the Christian basilica (Fig. 62) faces east; in the sanctuary, which was occupied by the clergy, the foundations of the apse wall behind the altar are visible. To the right of the sanctuary is a smaller apsed room that may have been a chapel: part of its mosaic floor survives, decorated with geometric designs in pink and white *tesserae*, or small square stones. Christian tombs were found beside the church.[52] An inscription from Sikyon names the martyr Kodratus, who is honoured at one of the Corinthian basilicas (see Chapter 4): the inscription may have formed part of a list of locally honoured saints.[53]

Later, a new town was built a mile to the east, on the south-eastern portion of the hill that was formerly occupied by the ancient town of Sikyon. The new settlement was named Vasiliko (Greek for 'basilica'), after its new church; it became the cathedral of the surrounding area (Fig. 63). There are also remains of a sixth-century church in Vasiliko, in the ruins of a temple dedicated to Apollo, from which mosaic fragments, architectural sculpture and some tombs survive.[54] The present cathedral dates from the thirteenth century. Much of its stone comes from ancient Sikyon; a seat outside the small cathedral rests on drums from two of Classical Sikyon's former columns (Fig. 64).

Closer to the sea, two miles north-east of Vasiliko, a sixth-century basilica has been excavated at the coastal port of Kiato. It has long north and south aisles

FIGURE 63. The thirteenth-century cathedral, Vasiliko.

FIGURE 64. Drums from two of Sikyon's ancient columns form a seat outside the cathedral, Vasiliko.

separated from the central nave by a raised stylobate on which columns stood.[55] There are indications of a horse-shoe shaped *synthronon* for officiating clergy who surrounded the bishop's throne in the central apse, and remains of a central pathway or *solea*, for the bishop to walk down before preaching to the people who stood in the aisles.[56] The church may have contained a *martyrium*, or saint's shrine, and there were ancillary rooms to the north, south and west. A baptistery leads directly into its south aisle, and there is a large *atrium* that could have provided ample space for baptismal candidates to be instructed.[57]

At Zemeno, seven miles north-west of Sikyon, a tenth-century hermit lived on a pillar for many years: monks who adopted this form of asceticism were known as *stylites* (meaning 'pillar dwellers'). This extreme expression of the monastic vocation symbolised a holy man's calling to live in the world, yet also in the heavenly realm. Fresh water and gifts of food might be hauled up to the hermit on a rope and pulley. These men visibly gave their life to prayer, and were not afraid to witness to their unceasing quest for God; they were sought out for their holiness. This vocation was practised in the Eastern Churches (though not in the West) from the fifth to the twelfth centuries. The pillar might have a square platform at the top: a square turreted tower near an early monastic complex in the semi-desert at Um-ar-Rasas in central Jordan has been interpreted as a stylite tower. It stands 13 m tall and is considered to be the last surviving example of its kind in the Middle East.[58]

The hermit on his pillar at Zemeno was visited by pilgrims from far away. At the age of twenty-one, Osios Loukas (or 'St Luke') was invited by the hermit to become his disciple, and served him for ten years; eventually Osios Loukas retired to a monastery at the foot of Mount Helikon, some thirty miles east of Delphi. In his Life, written a generation later, we are told that the young Luke 'ceaselessly carried wood and water and tended to the cooking and table preparations, mending nets and looking after the catch'.[59] Luke's work suggests that he acted as guest master for the pilgrims and visitors who came to consult his revered teacher. Osios Loukas was widely venerated for his gift of healing; his life will be discussed more fully towards the end of Chapter 8.

Thus during the early Christian and medieval period, a wide variety of Christian lifestyles could be encountered in Nemea and its surrounding region. Much of the surviving archaeological evidence relates to the early community at Nemea itself but whereas that group died out, leaving no trace, the Christians of Sikyon survived and flourished in their new hilltop location of Vasiliko. The settlement grew, its church became the administrative and spiritual centre of the region, and there are indications of other early basilicas and medieval monks in the surrounding settlements.

Notes

1   J.C. Marchand, 'Kleonai, the Corinth-Argos road, and the "Axis of History"', in *Hesperia*, vol. 78 (2009), pp. 107–63, at pp. 97–8, 161.

2   Pindar, Nemean Victory Ode no. 4. 27, in F.J. Nisetich, *Pindar's Victory Songs* (Baltimore: Johns Hopkins University Press, 1980).

3   Marchand, 'Kleonai, the Corinth-Argos road', pp. 140–45.

4   A. Avramea, *Le Péloponnèse du IVe au VIIIe siècle* (Paris: Publications de la Sorbonne, 1997), p. 169.

5   Pausanius, 'Description of Greece', Bk. 5. 5 ff., in *Pausanius, Description of Greece*, transl. W.H.S. Jones, Loeb Classical Library (Cambridge, MAS: Harvard University Press, 2005).

6   Diodorus Siculus, 'Bibliotheca historica', Bk. 4. 33, in *Diodorus Siculus, The Library of History*, vol. 2, transl. C.H. Oldfather, Loeb Classical Library (Cambridge, MAS: Harvard University Press, 1933).

7   N. Karela, *Greek Mythology* (Athens: Michalis Toubis, 1998), pp. 62–3.

8   R.M. Jensen, *Understanding Christian Art* (London, New York: Routledge, 2000), pp. 90–91, 119–20. A fuller exploration of this theme is presented by M. Simon in *Hercule et le Christianisme* (Paris: Les Belles Lettres, 1955).

9   For Daniel and the lions in early Christian sculpture at Meigle and at Braddan on the Isle of Man, see E. Rees, *Celtic Saints of Scotland, Northumbria and the Isle of Man* (Stroud: Fonthill, 2017), pp. 107, 160–61.

10 Quotations from the psalms are taken from *The Psalms: A New Translation* (London: The Grail, 1963).

11 See also Ps. 9/10. 9–10; Ps. 16. 9–12; Ps. 21. 22; Ps. 34. 17.

12 S.G. Miller, 'Theodosius II and the Temple of Nemean Zeus', in *ΗΡΩΣ ΚΤΙΣΤΗΣ II, Memory of Charalambos Bouras*, ed. M. Korres, S. Mamaloukos, C. Zambas and F. Malloukou-Tufano (Athens: Melissa, 2018), p. 185.

13 O. Broneer, 'The Isthmian victory crown', in *American Journal of Archaeology*, vol. 66 (1962), pp. 261–3.

14 Miller, 'Theodosius II', p. 185.

15 For a full account of the excavated stadium, see S.G. Miller, *Excavations at Nemea II: The Early Hellenistic Stadium* (Berkeley: California University Press, 2001).

16 The discoveries form the entire contents of J.J. Bravo III's book, *Excavations at Nemea IV* (Berkeley: California University Press, 2018).

17 Greek News Agenda, 20 February 2019, https://www.greeknewsagenda.gr/index.php/ interviews/arts-in-greece/6931-stephen-miller. Dr Stephen Miller on uncovering the Sanctuary of Zeus and the revival of the Nemean Games. Accessed 30.06.2020.

18 Information about the revival can be found at https://nemeangames.org/nemean-games-revival/ancient-basis.html. Accessed 30.06.2020.

19 S.G. Miller, *Nemea: A Guide to the Site and Museum* (Athens: Ministry of Culture Archaeological Receipts Fund, 2004), pp. 106, 108.

20 E. Honigmann, *Le Synekdèmos d'Hiéroklès et l'opuscule géographique de Georges de Chypre* (Brussels: Éditions de l'Institut de philologie et d'histoire orientales et slaves, 1939), 646. 8, quoted in S.G. Miller, *Into Darkness – The End of Antiquity*, forthcoming.

21 Miller, *Into Darkness – the End of Antiquity*.

22 *Ibid.*

23 Miller, 'Theodosius II', pp. 187, 189.

24 Theodosian Code 16. 10. 25; 14 November 435.

25 November 435, no. 16. 10. 25. Miller, 'Theodosius II', p. 190.

26 U. Becker, *The Continuum Encyclopedia of Symbols* (New York, London: Continuum, 1994, 2005), p. 225.

27 I am grateful to Sr Christine Owen for this suggestion.

28 Derwas J. Chitty, *The Desert a City: An Introduction to the Study of Egyptian and Palestinian Monasticism Under the Christian Empire* (Oxford: Blackwell, 1966).

29 L.H. Kraynack, in S.G. Miller, *Nemea I: Excavations at Nemea, Topographical and Architectural Studies* (Berkeley: University of California Press, 1992), pp. 99–187.

30 *Ibid.*

31 Miller, *Nemea, A Guide*, pp. 101–2.

32 Information at Nemea Museum.

33 Miller, 'Theodosius II', pp. 190, 192.

34 *Ibid*, pp. 102, 104.

35 Kraynack, in S. Miller, *Nemea I*, pp. 99–187.

36 Miller, *Nemea, A Guide*, p. 104.

37 St Cyril of Jerusalem, *Catechesis Mystagogia*, 3. 5, in J.-P. Migne, *Patrologia Graeca* (Paris: Imprimerie Catholique, 1857-66), vol. 33; English translation in J.W. Drijvers, *The Works of Saint Cyril of Jerusalem* (Washington: Catholic University of America Press, 2004), vol. 1.

38 Miller, *Excavations at Nemea II*, pp. 332–5.

39 *Ibid.*

40 See Miller, *Nemea, A Guide*, p. 98 and fig. 68.

41 To reach the basilica on Evangelistria Hill, leave the E65 Tripolis road at the Mycenae / Nemea intersection, turning right. After 100 m turn right again. After 500 m turn left at the Nemea / Cleonae road. Continue for 200 m past the watershed of the Nemea valley, and turn left onto a steep unsigned dirt track. There is parking at the summit.

42 I am grateful to Professor Stephen Miller for providing this information via email on 07.07.2020.

43 A.K. Orlandos, *Atti del III Congresso Internazionale di Archaeologia Cristiana* (ACIAC), Paris, 1957, p. 112; W. Caraher, *Church, Society and the Sacred in Early Christian Greece*, PhD diss., Ohio State University, 2003, p. 466; plan 32, p. 296.

44 R. Sweetman, 'The Christianization of the Peloponnese: the topography and function of late antique churches', in *Journal of Late Antiquity*, vol. 3, no. 2, Fall 2010, pp. 227–8.

45 Information at Sikyon Museum.

46 D.G. Romano, 'Urban and rural planning in Roman Corinth', in *Urban Religion in Roman Corinth: Interdisciplinary Approaches*, ed. D. Schowalter and S. Friesen, Harvard Theological Studies, vol. 53 (Cambridge, MAS: Harvard University Press, 2005), ch. 2, p. 50.

47 Information at Sikyon Museum.

48 *Ibid.*

49 Pausanias, *Description of Greece*, Classical Texts Library, transl. W. H. S. Jones, Bk. 2. 1–4, 2. 6. 7, in https://www.theoi.com/Text/Pausanias2A.html, accessed 30.06.2020.

50 For the religious sites at Sikyon, see Y. Lolos, *Land of Sikyon: Archaeology and History of a Greek City State*, Hesperia supplement no. 39 (Princeton, NJ: American School of Classical Studies at Athens, 2011), ch. 6, 'Sacra Sicyonia', pp. 377–414.

51 Pausanias, *Description of Greece*, Bk. 2. 10. 2, 10. 4.

52 Caraher, *Church, Society and the Sacred*, Appendix, p. 467.

53 A.R. Brown, 'Medieval pilgrimage to Corinth and Southern Greece', in *Journal on Hellenistic and Roman Material Culture* (HEROM), vol. 1 (2012), p. 216.

54 Caraher, *Church, Society and the Sacred*, Appendix, p. 468.

55 Sweetman, 'The Christianization of the Peloponnese', pp. 220–21, 237.

56   *Ibid*, pp. 238–9.
57   *Ibid*, pp. 248, 234–6.
58   It can be viewed at https://en.wikipedia.org/wiki/Umm_ar-Rasas, accessed 30.06.20.
59   C. and R. Connor, *The Life and Miracles of Saint Luke of Steiris: Text, Translation and Commentary* (Brookline, MAS: Hellenic College Press, 1994), ch. 35, p. 57.

Chapter 7

ATHENS: A DAUGHTER CHURCH OF CORINTH

Athens is well to the east of the Peloponnese, on the opposite side of the Corinth canal. However, by the second century AD, Athens lay under the ecclesiastical jurisdiction of Corinth, when it is recorded that Dionysius, Bishop of Corinth, reprimanded the Christians of Athens for their lack of faith.[1] In this chapter we shall begin with Luke's brief account of Paul's activities in Athens, and then consider the growth of Christianity in the city. Basilicas began to be constructed from the late fifth century, a number of them on the sites of pagan temples. Many sculptures and other artefacts survive from the early Christian basilicas of Athens: they can be viewed in the Byzantine and Christian Museum on Vasilissis Sofias Avenue. Other finds were discovered unexpectedly during recent excavations to extend the Athens Metro.

Towards the end of the first century AD, Luke, the author of the Acts of the Apostles, described St Paul's oration to the Athenians who formed the Council of the Areopagus, which had authority over the religious life of the city. Paul observed an altar dedicated 'to an unknown god', and seized this as an opportunity to preach about Christ, who was to them an unknown divinity (Acts 17. 22–34). Luke depicts Paul as another Socrates, whose beliefs were held in high regard by Athenian philosophers.[2] To them, the strangest part of Paul's speech was his belief in resurrection:

> At the mention of rising from the dead, some of them burst out laughing; others said, 'We would like to hear you talk about this again.' So Paul went out from among them. But some joined him and believed, among them Dionysius the Areopagite and a woman named Damaris and others with them (Acts. 17. 32–4).

133

It seems, therefore, that a small Christian community was established in Athens, perhaps as a result of Paul's preaching. Dionysius was a member of the Council of the Areopagus; he is said to have become the first bishop of Athens, and is its patron saint.

Athenian martyrs and bishops

Although during the first five centuries AD Christianity was spreading throughout the Roman empire, there is little evidence of Christians in Athens before the fourth century. Yet there must have been a small, fervent community in the city, for three Athenian bishops, Narcissus, Quadratus and Publius are recorded as being martyred in the second century. Leonidas, martyred at Lechaion in the third century, was also claimed as an Athenian bishop, but this is considered to be unlikely.[3] Eusebius, the fourth-century bishop of Vercelli, praised the Athenian martyr bishop, Quadratus, for having revived the faith of the Christian community in Athens. He also relates that Origen visited Athens in 240, where he completed his *Commentary on the Prophet Ezekiel*, and began another on the Song of Songs.[4] Origen declared that he disliked the unruly pagan people's assembly of Athens, while he considered the Christian community in the city to be 'gentle and orderly'.[5]

The Christian population of Athens increased during the first half of the fifth century, but the only indications of this are inscriptions on semi-literate gravestones and Christian symbols on lamps and pottery. Shops sold artefacts that offered a choice of Christian symbols and pagan scenes, while pagans and Christians were buried in the same cemeteries. Three fifth-century Athenian bishops are recorded attending Church councils: Modestus was present in 431 at a council in Ephesus, Athanasius I attended one in Corinth in 458, and Anatolius travelled to another held in Constantinople the following year.[6]

The tombstone survives of another fifth-century bishop, Klematios: it was found at the entrance to a church now named after him. The basilica was discovered in the late nineteenth century at the foot of Mount Lykabettos, beyond the north-east portion of the city wall (see Fig. 65). The faithful poured offerings of oil into the bishop's tombstone through a hole at the centre; the large monument can be seen in the Byzantine and Christian Museum.[7] The church lay beyond the city walls, since burials within the city were forbidden at this time. Clergy and distinguished lay people including officials and donors were buried in such churches, which were usually dedicated to the memory of martyrs. Later, churches were built within the town walls. Some were erected in the *agora*, the civic centre of the city, and churches were also built inside ruined temples on the Acropolis. Both pagans and Christians liked to worship on holy mountains: these were visibly nearer to the heavens, where divine beings were considered to dwell.

Christian burial

Christians considered death to be the passage 'from this corruptible material world to a place of light, in green pastures, in a place of refreshment', in the words of the Orthodox Burial Service. According to this theology, death is a time of sleep, in anticipation of the resurrection, which will take place when Christ will appear in glory to judge the world. St John Chrysostom (*c.* 349–404), bishop of Constantinople, comments: 'Before the coming of Christ, death was called death ... but since Christ has come ... it is no longer called death, but rest and sleep'.[8]

During the first three centuries AD, Christians usually buried their dead in pre-existing cemeteries that were used by pagans as well, as we have seen. The first exclusively Christian cemeteries were built in the late second century. The various types of Christian tombs – vaulted, cist (or slab-lined) graves and simple pits – differed little from earlier Greek or Roman types, and many Christian burial practices, such as placing grave goods around their owner, performing rites in their memory, or placing offerings on top of graves, indicate how pagan customs passed into Christian tradition.

Paganism and Christianity

After the legalisation of Christianity in AD 313, pagan practices were increasingly repressed, as we have seen in earlier chapters. In 435, the emperor Theodosius decreed the destruction of all pagan temples.[9] After the mid-fourth century, pagan sacrifices and other rites were strictly forbidden, but this appears to have been disregarded in Athens, where perhaps temples were officially closed, but remained quietly in use. With its rhetorical and philosophical schools, Athens was still a centre of classical culture and a stronghold of paganism for at least two hundred years after the official recognition of Christianity. Gradually, however, Christianity spread among the wealthy, and in the sixth to the seventh centuries, the major Athenian temples were converted into churches, both on the sacred mountain of the Acropolis, and in the city spreading out beneath it (see Fig. 65).

Perhaps the first of these was the *Agoranomeion* (Fig. 66), at the south-east corner of the Roman *agora*, or civic centre. The original function of this building is unknown; it might have been the office of the magistrates. An inscription on its white marble architrave (the beam resting upon its marble columns) states that it was dedicated to the goddess Athena and the imperial deities (*Sebastoi Theoi*); this probably refers to the emperor Claudius and his wife, who were deified around AD 60. The *Agoranomeion* was built on a slope, and designed as a broad columned stairway leading to a façade;[10] it was converted into a church without internal or external alteration. As it rises towards the east, this would

135

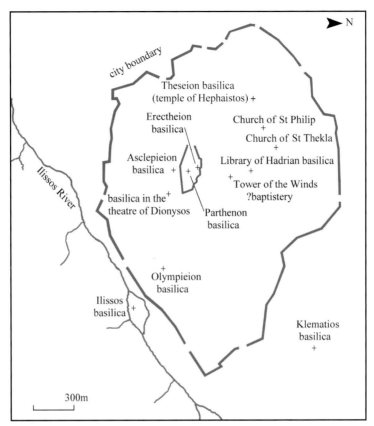

FIGURE 65. Athens basilicas in the mid-sixth century, after Ioannis Travos.

FIGURE 66. The *Agoranomeion*, Athens; the Tower of the Winds is just visible to the left.

form a natural setting for a church: Christian altars normally face the rising sun, which was considered to represent Christ rising from the dead. A few Christian symbols are carved on the walls of the *Agoranomeion*.

The Tower of the Winds

Adjacent to the *Agoranomeion* is the Tower of the Winds, or *Horologium of Kyrrhestes*, named after the astronomer who designed it. It was built in the second or first century BC, and is mentioned by Horace and Vitruvius; the tower has been described as an early meteorological station. There are two entrances with porches, and a cylindrical annexe to the south. Personifications of the eight winds were carved at the top of each of the tower's eight sides, and beneath each figure, curved rays created a sundial. The Tower of the Winds is described as a church in a fifteenth-century description by a pilgrim known as 'the Anonymous of the Ambrosian Library': 'Until now it is a church of the Greeks, and a most worthy building, all of marble'.[11]

Although this is a late text, two Maltese crosses carved inside circles on the door jambs of the north-west porch suggest that the Tower of the Winds had become a Christian building by the fifth century. On one column are graffiti of a dove (representing the Christian soul), a fish (whose letters form the initials of a Greek title for Christ) and a cross monogram: these date from the fifth to the seventh centuries. Some of the stone blocks scattered on the ground around the Tower of the Winds also date from early Christian times, including a column capital decorated with foliage and a cross within a circle (Fig. 67).

FIGURE 67. Early Christian column capital beside the Tower of the Winds, Athens.

An early baptistery

The octagonal plan of the Tower of the Winds (Fig. 68), together with its position alongside the *Agoranomeion*, indicate that it could have served as a baptistery for the adjacent church (Fig. 69). The Tower of the Winds contained an elaborate water system in order to power its clockwork, and since both were secular buildings, Christians might have claimed them more easily than pagan temples, at a time when paganism was still quite strong in Athens.[12] Baptisteries were designed as octagonal buildings for both architectural and theological reasons. The earth was considered to be square and flat, while the heavens formed a dome above them. An octagonal building, basically a square with its angles flattened, is easily roofed with a dome. As the candidate approached the baptismal pool at the centre of the building, he or she symbolically approached the centre of the cosmos, where heaven joined earth.

Early baptisteries were often eight-sided: the octagonal baptismal font used by St Ambrose (*c.* 339–97) in Milan cathedral, constructed in 387, can still be seen. An octagonal baptistery symbolised the seven days of creation (Gen. 2. 3), followed by the 'eighth day' (Sunday) on which Christ rose from the dead, into which the new Christian entered on Easter night: the Church Fathers thought of this eighth day as the start of eternity.[13] On the final page of *The City of God*, written between 413 and 426, St Augustine wrote poetically:

> *The seventh day shall be our Sabbath, which shall be brought to a close, not by an evening, but by the Lord's Day as an eighth and eternal day, consecrated by the resurrection of Christ, and prefiguring the eternal repose, not only of the spirit, but also of the body. There we shall rest and see, see and love, love and praise.*[14]

Pope Gregory the Great (540–604) explained more succinctly:

> *Seven days represent the present time, the eighth day designates eternal life, which the Lord revealed to us through the resurrection.*[15]

At night and on cloudy days, a water clock inside the Tower of the Winds was used to calculate the time, instead of the sundials; it was powered by water flowing down from the Acropolis. There was a bronze weather vane at the top of the tower's pyramidal roof, since it was important for merchants to know the direction of the wind, in order to estimate the arrival time of goods coming by sea.[16] At first sight, the original function of the Tower of the Winds appears very different from its subsequent Christian use. However, many churches throughout Europe had sundials on their exterior walls, in order for worship to take place at the appropriate time, particularly if there was a resident community who would

Left: FIGURE 68. The Tower of the Winds, detail. Each 'wind' casts a shadow, as a sundial.

Below: FIGURE 69. Location of the Tower of the Winds and *Agoranomeion*, at the foot of the Acropolis.

be called to prayer several times a day. Again, many churches had a weather vane attached to their tower: in an agricultural society, it was helpful to know if there was a warm wind from the south-west or a cold wind from the north-east, while offshore winds affected the currents, and shipping.

Mosque of the Conqueror

As Christianity grew stronger, the *Agoranomeion* may no longer have served as a church, since a new purpose-built basilica was constructed a little to the north-west. Much later, in 1456, the *Fetiye Djama* Mosque (or 'Mosque of the Conqueror') was

FIGURE 70. Eastern end of the basilica beneath the *Fetiye Djama* Mosque, Athens.

built over the three-aisled basilica. The church was partially excavated in 1963: fortunately, its sanctuary extended beyond the later mosque, and was preserved beneath its courtyard. The masonry of the basilica is of poor quality, much of it recycled; this suggests that it was built comparatively late, in the seventh century.[17] The photograph (Fig. 70) shows the eastern end of the sanctuary, where the altar would have been. One can see the marble floor, and an elaborate carved capital that once stood on top of a column (centre, left), but the church was damaged when the mosque was constructed above it.

Church of Dionysius

According to tradition, there was a church dedicated to St Dionysius on the northern slope of the Areopagus, at the foot of the Acropolis, but despite intensive excavation, no remains of an early basilica have been found. The ruins of a sixteenth-century church of St Dionysius are still visible on the Areopagus; it was surrounded on two sides by an archbishop's palace. Both were short-lived, for they were destroyed by an earthquake in 1601. A fragment of a fifth-century lamp, depicting the head of St Paul as a bearded patriarch, was found below the terrace of the upper north slope of the Areopagus, where the early church of St Dionysius is likely to have been.[18]

A gravestone from the Areopagus area which can now be seen in the Byzantine and Christian Museum may also have been associated with the church of St Dionysius. Its touching inscription informs us that it was erected in memory of 'little Andreas and his mother Theodora'; it dates from the fifth or sixth century.[19] A decorated column capital and the stone door from the screen that separated the nave from the sanctuary, both dating from about the eighth century, were found close to each other on the Areopagus; they are also likely to have been associated with the church of Dionysius.[20]

The church at Hadrian's Library

The first Christians in Athens probably met together for worship in their own homes, and perhaps continued to do so as late as the fourth century, but by the mid-fifth century, the Christian population was growing, and a number of new churches were built in the fifth and sixth centuries. Some of these churches were imperial foundations, magnificently built and lavishly decorated with sculptures and paintings. While some were further expanded in the seventh century, others were destroyed in the Slavic invasions that took place from the late sixth century onwards; their ruins became convenient quarries for building stone, which was used in construction across the town. Many examples of carved decoration survive from these early churches, but not in their original locations.[21]

The earliest of the new churches in Athens is likely to have been that built in the courtyard of Hadrian's Library in the mid-fifth century. It is the most complex and sophisticated of the early Athenian basilicas, and was perhaps commissioned by the empress Eudocia, wife of the emperor of Byzantium, Theodosius II. Known as the *tetraconch* (or 'four-apsed') church, its four semi-circular apses surrounded the sanctuary in the shape of an elaborate cross. It was burnt down, and a large three-aisled basilica with smaller apses was built over its ruins, perhaps for the visit of the emperor Constantine II in 662/3. It incorporated what was left of the first church (Fig. 71).[22]

This church, too, was burnt down in the eleventh century, and replaced in the twelfth by a simpler basilica; it became known as the first metropolis, or cathedral, of Athens. In the photograph (Fig. 72), the apses of the first two churches on the site are visible, and four of the columns that separated the aisles of the seventh-century church. Part of the mosaic floor, not of outstanding quality, can also be seen to the right of the photograph. A second church, dedicated to the archangel Michael, was built nearby in the twelfth century, incorporating the ruins of the monumental *propylon* (or entrance) to Hadrian's Library. An engraving etched in 1833 (Fig. 73) shows the entrance to the church, alongside the giant columns of the *propylon*. The solid column bases of the *propylon* can be seen in Figure 74:

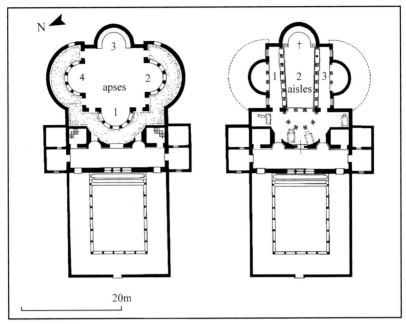

FIGURE 71. Church in Hadrian's Library in the fifth century (L) and the seventh century (R). Courtesy of the American School of Classical Studies, Athens.

FIGURE 72. View looking north across the sanctuary of the church in Hadrian's Library, Athens.

Above: FIGURE 73. Engraving of St Michael's church, Hadrian's Library, Athens. K.W. Heideck, 1833.

Left: FIGURE 74. Decorated stone panel from the early church in Hadrian's Library, Athens.

in front of the columns is a long decorated panel from the early church in Hadrian's Library. The carvings include crosses, rosettes and other geometric designs, inside interlinked circles.

Church on the Ilissos

Perhaps the basilica on the Ilissos was the next to be built, after the church in Hadrian's Library. It occupied a small island between two branches of the River Ilissos, in the south-east quarter of the city. There were a number of early churches in this area, well away from the town centre: perhaps there was still plenty of available land to build large monuments at this distance from the city centre. The Ilissos basilica probably dates from the fifth century; it appears to have been dedicated to the martyr Leonidas, who was murdered at Lechaion in the mid-third century.

This was a three-aisled basilica, with a transept designed with projecting wings, a *narthex*, and probably an *atrium*. Outside, on its northern side, an underground burial chamber formed the so-called *martyrium* (or 'saint's shrine') of Leonidas and his followers. However, it is more likely that Leonidas was buried at Lechaion, as we saw in Chapter 5. Significant portions of the Ilissos basilica can be seen in the Byzantine and Christian Museum of Athens, including much of its fine mosaic floor, decorated with tendrils, grapes and vine leaves. These symbolise Christ and his followers: Jesus declared 'I am the vine; you are the branches; whoever remains in me bears fruit in plenty' (Jn. 15. 5); grapes symbolise his blood, poured out in love for the world. Other panels depict natural scenes, including a stork pecking a flower, and a snake devoured by a second stork.[23] A marble slab from the fifth-century *ambo* (or pulpit) survives, decorated with stylised floral ornaments carved in relief.[24]

Baptistery at the Temple of Zeus

To the west of the basilica on the Ilissos, there was another large three-aisled church, situated between the outer wall of the enormous Temple of the Olympian Zeus and an elaborate second-century bath complex. The temple, one of the largest in the ancient world, was eventually completed in AD 131 by the Roman emperor Hadrian. The baths were built at the same time, in AD 124–31, and continued to be used until the seventh century, by which time they probably formed the baptistery of the nearby church. The floors of the northern building in the bath complex were elaborately decorated with mosaics, while the shape of the bathing pools to the south followed complex geometrical designs: this is the best preserved Roman bath house in Athens.

The bathers passed through the entrance, and venerated the water nymphs in the *nympheum*, or shrine dedicated to them. They proceeded through a vestibule into a large dressing room (or *apodyterium*) at the western end of the northern building. The *apodyterium*, found at the entrance to public baths, was a large changing room with cubicles or shelves around its walls, where citizens could store their clothing and other belongings while they bathed. They then enjoyed bathing in a series of pools which are seen in the foreground of Plate 17. Since Christianity was a relatively new religion, a baptistery in which newcomers could be initiated, in this case, through emerging from water 'newborn', was almost as important as a basilica. A building already available that might suit the purpose, such as the water clock in the Tower of the Winds, or the ritual baths of the disused Temple of the Olympian Zeus, were readily employed by Christians.

Basilica beneath the Russian Church

There may have been another baptistery beneath the Church of the Saviour of Lykodemos in Philhellene Street: it now serves the Russian Orthodox Christians of Athens. This is the biggest medieval building in the city; it was erected in 1031, as part of a Roman Catholic monastery. The monastic church is built over the large apsed *caldarium* (or heated room) of a Roman public bath. Below present ground level, an early Christian basilica was built upon the floor of the *caldarium*; it is not aligned with the great Russian Church that stands above it (Fig. 75).

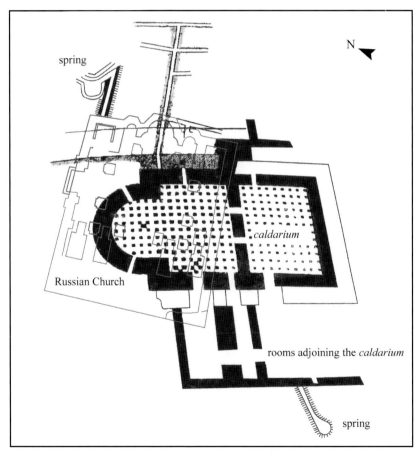

FIGURE 75. Christian basilica built within the Roman baths beneath the Russian Church, Athens, after a plan at the site.

FIGURE 76. An entrance to the *caldarium* beneath the Russian Church, with its *hypocaust* visible beyond the iron gate.

FIGURE 77. A small Roman pillar in the bath complex beneath the Russian Church, Athens.

The *caldarium* was warmed by rows of symmetrical blocks which formed the hypocaust, or under floor heating system: hot air circulated between the short pillars. Figure 76 depicts one of several entrances to the *caldarium,* which is largely constructed of brick. The hypocaust is just visible, beyond the iron gate. A Roman column has been positioned to form the base of an altar for a small modern underground chapel. In periods of prolonged rain, the volume of water flowing from underground springs increases so much that the chapel floor is submerged. A number of Roman pillars were recycled in the early church (see Fig. 77), and some of its mosaic floor survives, including a portion decorated with a cross (Plate 18).

The Roman baths

The *caldarium* beneath the Russian Church is part of a much larger complex of buildings that were gradually uncovered in 1992–4 during excavations to extend the Athens Metro. Two rivers flowed through the area, the Ilissos to the south and the Eridanos to the north. The excavations revealed the river bed of a tributary of the Eridanos, which was later canalised through a conduit; cemeteries were also uncovered, dating from the early fourth century BC to the early third century AD, in which there were Christian graves. There was a Roman aqueduct with a dense network of pipes, and the full extent of the late Roman complex of bath installations was gradually revealed.[25]

The bath complex was built between the late third and the early fourth century AD. It was damaged in the late fourth century, perhaps during an invasion by Alarich, the first king of the Visigoths, in 396, and was rebuilt in the mid-fifth century. It was very large, with many ancillary rooms around the main bath facilities, and was therefore a public, civic bath (or *balaneum*). The central nucleus included two hearths for heating the water in tanks, four chambers for hot and warm baths (*caldaria* and *tepidaria*) and pools for cold plunges (*frigidaria*).[26]

The river bed was subsequently filled in, and in the fifth or sixth century, a cluster of seventeen early Christian graves was constructed in the former water course, with walls and vaulted roofs; they often contained two or three bodies. The joint graves were probably ossuaries, intended to contain the bones of several people, perhaps from the same family; they remained in use until the eleventh or twelfth century. A few grave goods had been buried with their owners, mainly bronze jewellery, crosses and coins.[27]

A possible saint's shrine

Further downhill on Amalia Street, where a ventilation shaft was sunk for the Athens Metro, another Roman bath was found, dating from the third to the fourth century AD, with remains of its *tepidarium* and *caldarium*. Some recycled marble grave columns had been used to form its hypocaust. In the fifth and sixth centuries these rooms were repaired, and given tiled floors. In one underground room with a vaulted roof, a well was dug to draw up water; its interior was nicely furnished with a tile and mortar floor. On its northern wall are traces of a rather crude scene with human figures, fish, birds and crosses. These rough wall paintings suggest that the underground room was later used by Christians as a refuge, or as a saint's shrine. The small room can be seen in the centre of Figure 78, with traces of coloured paint on its white plastered wall. At the upper right-hand corner of the photo, an assortment of columns taken from graves is visible: they formed the hypocaust of the earlier Roman bath.

FIGURE 78. Possible saint's shrine (centre) inside the Roman baths on Amalia Street, Athens.

The *Asclepeion* basilica

The *Asclepieion*, or temple of Asclepius, was situated to the south of the Acropolis; it was probably converted into a church towards the end of the reign of the emperor Justinian (527–65); there is a spring beside it. A funerary inscription found nearby can be seen in the Byzantine and Christian Museum.[28] It dates from the fifth or sixth century, around the time of the temple's conversion into a church, and alongside the inscription is a pair of peacocks facing each other, separated by a large leaf. The peacock, with many eyes in its tail, symbolised the loving gaze of God; it was also a symbol of happiness in paradise.[29]

The *Asclepieion* basilica was evidently reordered in the late tenth and early eleventh centuries; a large section of the *templon*, or screen separating the sanctuary from the nave, which dates from this time, can also be seen in the Byzantine and Christian Museum.[30] Its central door is decorated with a cross growing from the tree of life. At its base perch two doves eating grape clusters: they symbolise faithful Christian souls, feeding on the wine that represents the blood of Christ. A large border is filled with geometric carpet designs. At some point the church appears to have been dedicated to St Andrew.[31]

Church at the *Hephaisteion*

On a hill at the north-west corner of the *agora* stood the *Hephaisteion* (Fig. 79); it is the best preserved ancient temple of antiquity, built in 460–415 BC, and was dedicated to Hephaistos and Athena, whose statues adorned the temple. It retains some of its original friezes, which depict the Labours of Hercules and the adventures of the Athenian hero, Theseus: for this reason the temple is also known as the *Theseion*. The temple subsequently became a church dedicated to St George; its eastern entrance was replaced by one at its west end, so that a sanctuary with its apse could be constructed at its eastern end. The piers supporting the apse

FIGURE 79. The *Hephaisteion*, viewed from the Acropolis, Athens.

were crowned with new capitals carved with a cross surrounded by foliage, to represent the tree of life.[32] The temple appears to have been converted into a church in the sixth century; it was altered further in the early seventh century, perhaps during the reign of Heraclius, a Byzantine emperor who reigned from 610 to 641. The basilica's apse was reconstructed in the later medieval period.

The Parthenon becomes a church of the Virgin Mary

The Parthenon, which crowned the Acropolis, was constructed and decorated from 447 to 432 BC; it stands on the site of an earlier temple that was built in the late sixth century BC to honour the goddess Athena. Inside, in front of a pool of water, stood a magnificent statue of the goddess, 12 m high, carved by Phidias around a wooden core; her flesh was made of ivory, while her removable robe and her helmet were coated in gold. In the late sixth century AD, the Parthenon was transformed into a Christian basilica: it became known as the Church of the Parthenos Maria (the Virgin Mary), or the Church of the Theotokos (the Mother of God). The orientation of the building was changed to face east; the main entrance was placed at the building's western end, and the altar was placed at the east end, close to an apse built on the site of the temple's antechamber.[33]

The three-aisled basilica included a gallery, two porches and a baptistery. An impressive marble door from the foot of the staircase leading up to its *ambo*, or pulpit, can be seen in the Byzantine and Christian Museum.[34] It stands 2 m tall, and is decorated with a large cross, carved in relief. The chancel screen survives, and a raised stylobate was built: a low screened barrier supporting columns.[35] This enabled the people to watch the processions of the clergy down the nave for the proclamation of the gospel and the offertory, and at the beginning and the end of the liturgy. There were burials outside the church. It was considered appropriate that Mary, 'the Athenian Virgin' or 'Virgin Atheniotissa', should be honoured at the site where her predecessor Athena was formerly venerated. Icons were painted on the walls and many pilgrims carved inscriptions on the Parthenon's columns.[36]

As a shrine of the Virgin Mary, it attracted pilgrims from far afield. In 1018, the emperor Basil II made a pilgrimage to the basilica and gave precious offerings in gratitude for his victory over the Bulgars. In the twelfth century, the church underwent further repairs, additions and adornment; pilgrims who visited the church wrote in admiration of an 'ever-burning lamp', a golden dove donated by Basil II and the basilica's gates, brought from Troy.[37] Four large, slightly concave stone slabs from the cathedral can be seen in the Byzantine and Christian Museum. They are segments of a decorative marble cornice, or horizontal moulding in relief, along the top of its internal wall; they form part of an inscription referring to the reconstruction carried out in the twelfth century.[38]

A few pilgrims from the West visited southern Greece. In the summer of 1102, an English pilgrim named Sæwulf travelled from Apulia, in southern Italy, through Greece to the Holy Land, as we learn from a manuscript preserved in Cambridge.[39] The pilgrim party experienced difficulties in Corinth, although Sæwulf does not go into detail:

> From Patras we came to Corinth on the vigil of St Laurence (9 August) where blessed Paul the apostle preached the word of God and to those people he wrote a letter. Here we endured many hardships (multa passi sumus contraria).[40]

In Athens, Sæwulf described the church in the Parthenon thus: 'A church is there of the Blessed Virgin Maria in which is oil in a lamp always burning but never running out'.[41] Michael Choniates, who was bishop of Athens from 1182 to 1205, described local benefactions to the cathedral and its many foreign visitors; he observed that the building was a source of honour both for its bishop and for the city.[42]

Church at the *Erechtheion*

The *Erechtheion* (Fig. 80) was built close to the Parthenon in 420–406 BC, over the site where the goddess Athena was said to have planted a sacred olive tree. Pausanias wrote that the architect and sculptor Callimachus (*c.* 432–*c.* 408 BC)

FIGURE 80. The *Erechtheion*, with Caryatids supporting its balcony roof, Athens.

installed a lamp dedicated to Athena in the *Erechtheion*: the magnificent lamp contained sufficient oil to burn for a year without being re-filled.[43] The *Erechtheion* is built on two levels; six beautiful figures of maidens, the Caryatids, support the roof of its southern balcony. They were said to have been modelled upon women of Caryes, an ancient city of Arcadia in the Peloponnese. The *Erechtheion* was probably converted into a church in the seventh century. One might question the appropriateness to a Christian church of the six maidens who serve as columns, yet the clergy within the basilica would have chanted Psalm 143 with its description of a similar scene:

> *Let our sons then flourish like saplings*
> *grown tall and strong from their youth;*
> *our daughters graceful as columns,*
> *adorned as though for a palace* (Ps. 143. 12).

A door from the Christian basilica survives, as does the marble *templon*, or screen that separated the sanctuary from the nave.[44] The stylobate can also be seen, decorated with a low screen like that in the Parthenon. Architectural sculpture survives from other basilicas on the Acropolis: in the Byzantine and Christian Museum, four large concave slabs probably formed part of the apse of one of them;[45] they are decorated with stylised reliefs inspired by classical antiquity. When wandering round the Acropolis, one can find smaller remains from Christian basilicas, such as the two large carved stone segments photographed beside the path leading up to the grand entrance, or *propylaea* of the Acropolis (Fig. 81). The upper slab is decorated with a cross and stylised trees of life.

FIGURE 81. Slabs from a Christian basilica on the Acropolis, Athens.

Simpler churches

The turbulent historical and economic circumstances of the seventh and eighth centuries in Byzantium led to a reduction of building activity, especially in the provinces. The new churches were generally smaller, with simpler decoration; they have been largely destroyed. Fragments of their carvings have survived, showing an artistic decline and more schematisation. The only Christian symbol to appear is the cross; geometric and foliage designs, birds and animals are common.[46] In Athens in the following centuries, a new type of church came into being: small, with harmonious proportions, an elegant eight-sided dome, and carefully executed stonework with elaborate brickwork decoration. Examples of this are the Church of the Saviour of Lykodemos (the Russian Church) and the Church of St Theodore in Klafthmonos Square (Fig. 82). This, the church of *Agioi Theodoroi*, was built in the ninth century, and reconstructed in the eleventh. Like many Athenian churches, it now nestles beneath modern apartment blocks.

Other Byzantine churches include that of the Holy Apostles, built early in the eleventh century over a fountain house or *nymphaion*, dating from the second century BC, and the church of Karnikarea, named after the official who was charged with collecting tax on tobacco.[47] The Karnikarea church (Figs 83 and 84) is dedicated to the

FIGURE 82. Church of St Theodore, Athens.

FIGURE 83. Church of the Karnikarea, Athens.

153

FIGURE 84. Karnikarea Church, Athens: detail of its exterior wall, showing stylised trees (L) and Kufic script (R).

Virgin Mary; it is built just below ground level at the intersection of Ermou and Kalamrotou Streets, above the ruins of a temple to a female goddess, probably Athene or Demeter. It was not completed until the thirteenth century, and is a cruciform, domed church. An interesting feature of this church is a frieze of terracotta tiles with Moslem Kufic motifs adorning the north, south and west sides of its exterior walls. Kufic writing was an ornamental form of Arabic script said to have been developed in the city of Kufa, in Iraq. It was often copied and adapted in eleventh-century Greece.[48]

Most of the significant Athenian churches dating from this time were built as part of a programme of reconstruction following the campaigns of emperor Basil II in the Balkans: during his lengthy reign of almost fifty years (976–1025) he amassed vast wealth from the regions he had conquered. Basil was not an intellectual but he was a religious man, who constructed monasteries, churches and, to some extent, cities.[49] The re-ordering of the basilica inside the Parthenon also took place at this time. The Athenian churches dating from the eleventh and twelfth centuries are considered to represent the golden age of Byzantine architecture. Whereas in Corinth, most of its early temples and Byzantine basilicas no longer survive, Athens still preserves outstanding buildings from both eras, and also provides valuable evidence of the utilisation of pagan buildings by the later Christian inhabitants of the city.

Notes

1   Dionysius is known to us through the bishop and historian Eusebius (AD 260/65–339/40), who described a collection of seven *Catholic Letters to the Churches* written by Dionysius. Eusebius mentions a letter to the Athenians, in which Dionysius exhorted them to live according to the gospel, since they were close to abandoning their faith.

2   L. Willis, 'The depiction of the Jews in Acts', in *Journal of Biblical Literature*, vol. 110, no. 4, 1991, p. 651.

3   A. Frantz, *The Athenian Agora: Results of Excavations Conducted by the American School of Classical Studies at Athens, vol. 24. Late Antiquity: AD 267–700* (Princeton, NJ: The American School of Classical Studies at Athens, 1988), pp. 18–19.

4   Eusebius, *The Ecclesiastical History*, Bk. 6. See J.W. Trigg, *Origen: The Bible and Philosophy in the Third-Century Church* (Atlanta: John Knox Press, 1983), p. 9.

5   Origen, *Contra Celsum* 3. 30, J.-P. Migne, *Patrologiae cursus completus, series graeca* (Paris: Imprimerie Catholique, 1857–66).

6   Frantz, *The Athenian Agora*, pp. 68–9.

7   Exhibit no. BXM 410, Byzantine and Christian Museum, Athens. The site of this discovery is at no. 22, Odos Kalof.

8   John Chrysostom, in Migne, *Patrologiae graeca*, vol. 49, cols. 393–4.

9   Theodosian Code, November 435, no. 16. 10. 25. See S.G. Miller, 'Theodosius II and the Temple of Nemean Zeus', in *ΗΡΩΣ ΚΤΙΣΤΗΣ II, Memory of Charalambos Bouras*, ed. M. Korres, S. Mamaloukos, C. Zambas and F. Malloukou-Tufano (Athens: Melissa, 2018), p. 190.

10   A. Choremi-Spetsieri, ed., *Archaeological Promenades Around the Acropolis, no. 6. Roman Agora – Library of Hadrian* (Athens: Hellenistic Ministry of Culture, 2004), p. 13.

11   Quoted in Frantz, *The Athenian Agora*, p. 71: *al presente è una chiesa dei greci et è opera molta degna, tutta di marmoro.*

12   Frantz, *The Athenian Agora*, p. 71.

13   E. Rees, *Early Christianity in South-west Britain* (Oxford: Windgather Press, 2020), p. 10.

14   St Augustine, *The City of God*, transl. Marcus Dodds (Peabody, MAS: Hendrickson, 2009).

15   St Gregory the Great, *Moralium libri* 25. 8, J.-P. Migne, *Patrologia Latina* (Paris: Imprimerie Catholique, 1841-49), vol. 76, col. 759.

16   Choremi-Spetsieri, *Archaeological promenades*, pp. 14–15.

17   Frantz, *The Athenian Agora*, p. 73.

18   J. Perlsweig, *Lamps from the Athenian Agora* (Princeton, NJ: American School of Classical Studies at Athens, 1963), nos. 59, 60.

19   Exhibit no. BXM 398.

20   A. Frantz, *The Middle Ages in the Athenian Agora*, (Princeton, NJ: American School of Classical Studies at Athens, 1961), illus. 16, 17.

21   Frantz, *The Athenian Agora*, p. 73.

22   Choremi-Spetsieri, *Archaeological promenades*, pp. 22–4.

23 Exhibit nos. BXM 17, 53, 55, 56, 58–67.

24 Exhibit no. BXM 290.

25 Information in the display at the Athens Metro.

26 *Ibid.*

27 *Ibid.*

28 Exhibit no. BXM 400.

29 U. Becker, *The Continuum Encyclopedia of Symbols* (New York, London: Continuum, 1994), p. 229.

30 Exhibit no. BXM 976.

31 A.R. Brown, 'Medieval pilgrimage to Corinth and Southern Greece', in *Journal on Hellenistic and Roman Material Culture* (HEROM), vol. 1 (2012), p. 203.

32 Frantz, *The Middle Ages in the Athenian Agora*, illus. 5, 6, 7.

33 J. Hurwit, *The Athenian Acropolis: History, Mythology and Archaeology from the Neolithic Era to the Present* (Cambridge: Cambridge University Press, 2000), p. 293.

34 Exhibit no. BXM 393.

35 W. Caraher, *Church, Society and the Sacred in Early Christian Greece*, PhD diss., Ohio State University, 2003, appendix, p. 404.

36 Acropolis Restoration Service, 28 August, 2012.

37 Brown, 'Medieval pilgrimage to Corinth and Southern Greece', p. 203.

38 Exhibit no. BXM 395.

39 Cambridge, Corpus Christi College, MS 111.

40 R.B.C. Huygens, ed., *Peregrinationes Tres: Saewulf, John of Würzburg, Theodericus* (Turnhout: Brepols, 1994), pp. 59–60.

41 Brown, 'Medieval pilgrimage to Corinth and Southern Greece', p. 200–1.

42 *Ibid*, p. 203.

43 Pausanias 1. 26. 7, in *Pausanius, Description of Greece*, transl. W.H.S. Jones, Loeb Classical Library (Cambridge, MAS: Harvard University Press, 2005).

44 Caraher, *Church, Society and the Sacred*, appendix, p. 396.

45 Exhibit nos. BXM 394, a–d.

46 Information at the Byzantine and Christian Museum, Athens.

47 *Ibid.*

48 Frantz, *The Middle Ages in the Athenian Agora*, illus. 19.

49 C. Holmes, *Basil II and the Governance of the Empire (976–1025)* (Oxford: Oxford University Press, 2005), p. 280.

Chapter 8

HEALING GODS: ASCLEPIUS AND CHRIST

In this chapter, we will explore the interrelationship between Asclepius, the Greek god of healing and Christ who, particularly in the early Church, was revered as the great physician of humankind. We shall begin our exploration at Bethesda in Jerusalem where, perhaps deliberately, Jesus healed a lame man close to a shrine of Asclepius. For much of the chapter we will focus on Epidaurus in the Peloponnese: this was revered as the birthplace of Asclepius, and was the most important healing sanctuary of ancient Greece. Christian monks studied the techniques of healing employed at Epidaurus, and we shall trace their use in two widely separated monasteries at Whithorn in south-west Scotland and at the monastery of Hosios Loukas, between Athens and Delphi.

In chapter five of St John's gospel, the author describes Jesus healing a lame man at Bethesda. By the time the gospel came to be written, in the late first century AD, devotees of Asclepius had been coming for healing to the shrine at Bethesda for decades, and it is possible, though not certain, that it was a healing sanctuary of Asclepius at the time when the miracle of Jesus took place. The gospel text is as follows:

> There was a Jewish festival, and Jesus went up to Jerusalem. Now at the Sheep Pool in Jerusalem there is a building, called Bethzatha in Hebrew, consisting of five porticoes, and under these were crowds of sick people – blind, lame, paralysed – waiting for the water to move, for at intervals the angel of the Lord came down into the pool, and the water was disturbed, and the first person to enter the water after this disturbance was cured of any ailment they suffered from.
> One man there had an illness which had lasted thirty-eight years, and when Jesus saw him lying there and knew he had been in this condition for a long time,

*he said, 'Do you want to be well again?' 'Sir,' replied the sick man, 'I have no one
to put me into the pool when the water is disturbed; and while I am still on the
way, someone else gets there before me.' Jesus said, 'Get up, pick up your sleeping
mat and walk.' The man was cured at once, and he picked up his mat and walked
away* (Jn. 5. 1–9).

The Aramaic name *Bethzatha* suggests two pools within which water welled up.
Perhaps, as at the nearby Gihon spring, the water welled up intermittently, 'when
the angel of the Lord came down and moved the water', as the gospel puts it.[1]
The gospel depicts the crowd pushing the sick man aside in their haste to reach
the pool before the water, with its curative properties, subsided. In AD 333, the
Pilgrim of Bordeaux described the twin pools of Bethesda whose 'glowing' waters
were renowned for their medical value.[2]

Bethesda, a healing shrine

The site forms a deep complex of excavations north of St Anne's church,
belonging to the White Fathers (Plate 19) inside the Old City of Jerusalem, not
far from its eastern wall. Mary's birthplace was traditionally located in this area,
and a fine Crusader church commemorates this. Its crypt is part of a network of
caves that once formed part of the sanctuary of Asclepius, the god of healing.[3]
The site was excavated under the direction of the Dominicans at the *École Biblique*.
In Old Testament times, Bethesda was a valley through which flowing rainwater
was dammed to create two artificial pools. Isaiah appears to refer to the northern
pool (Is. 7. 3), which can be dated by archaeological evidence to the late Bronze
Age (Fig. 85). The southern pool was constructed later, in the third century BC,
under the high priest Simon (220–195 BC), son of Onias. The Book of Sirach
(50. 3) comments on its extraordinary size: 'in his day the pool was excavated,
a reservoir as huge as the sea'.[4]

Between 150 BC and AD 70, a popular healing centre developed to the east of
the pools. It contained a water cistern, baths and grottos dedicated to Asclepius,
designed for religious and healing purposes. After bathing in one of the pools,
patients slept in a darkened room; their drug-induced dreams provided a basis
for the priest at the shrine to diagnose the patient's illness and prescribe a cure.[5]
Offerings to Asclepius were found at the site: one represents a bandaged foot; it
was given by a lame person in thanksgiving for their healing (see inset, Fig. 85).

There were at least five grottos, partly or completely hollowed out of the rock.
In one of the best preserved, about a dozen steps lead down to a small room,
at an angle of 90 degrees from the entrance. The room would have been out
of direct light, invisible from the grotto's entrance: it ends in a small pool that
was deep enough for a person to stand in upright.[6] At these grottos, a crowd

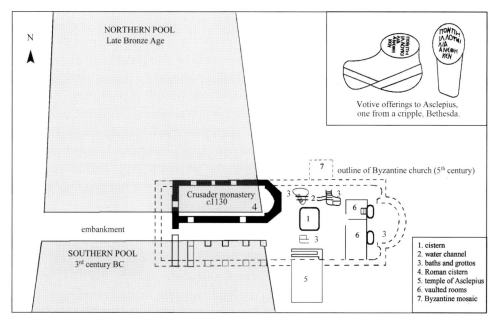

FIGURE 85. Excavations at Bethesda in Jerusalem, after a plan at the site.

of invalids, who were barred from the nearby temple because they were legally unclean, would wait to be cured. Jesus not only preached to the ritually clean in the temple precincts, but he also mingled with the unclean sick at the pagan sanctuary outside the temple. There may be a hint of irony in John's gospel when the author points out that in thirty-eight years, Asclepius had been unable to heal a lame man whom Jesus cures in an encounter that perhaps lasted only a few moments.

In the first century AD, the construction of a larger pool nearer to the Jewish Temple made the pools of Bethesda redundant, and in AD 44, Herod Agrippa built a new city wall to the north, which prevented water from flowing down into the pools. The Romans built a water cistern, before filling in the pools; small channels conveyed the water to the baths. Between AD 200 and 400, fine new buildings were constructed, including a temple dedicated to Asclepius, or his Egyptian counterpart, Serapis; vaulted rooms were also added in front of some of the baths. Some mosaic floors, frescos, votive offerings and coins were found, dating from this period.[7] When Juvenal was patriarch of Jerusalem (422–58), a large Byzantine basilica was built over the healing complex, supported by seven arches. The sanctuary of the basilica was built over the healing baths and grottos; its apse is visible today, together with four column bases, and the mosaic of its *martyrium*, or saint's shrine.[8] The site demonstrates a remarkable interweaving of pagan and Christian traditions of healing.

Asclepius the healer

In early Christianity, the gospel (or 'good news') was preached as medicine for wounded humanity, and Christ was understood to be the great healer of diseases of body and soul. To pagans, Christ seemed to be another Asclepius. For centuries, a parallel was drawn between the miracles of Christ and the glorious deeds of Asclepius by both pagan and Christian writers. When we compare Christianity with any of the Greek and Roman cults, Asclepius comes nearest to the model presented by Jesus. Asclepius had become patron of physicians, he was held to be divine, and was considered foremost among the gods in his kindness to humanity and through the efficacy of the healing that was carried out in his name. He was reverenced longer than all the other Greek gods.

Initially, Asclepius was held to be human, not divine. Homer describes him as a king who lived in Thessaly during the Trojan War. He had immense medical knowledge, which he taught his sons; both sons became doctors and also commanders in the Trojan War. Later myths describe Asclepius as a demigod, born of a mortal woman and the god Apollo. Later still, he was considered to be divine. He was attributed with prophetic powers, and was believed to raise the dead. His mother died while giving birth to him, which was why he was believed to know death's secrets, with power to resurrect the dead.[9]

Asclepius and Christ

By early Christian times, Asclepius was worshipped throughout the known world. Most gods of late antiquity were hailed as saviours, but Asclepius fulfilled this role more fully, since he healed people. His deeds resembled those of Jesus, the healer, more closely than the deeds of any other pagan god. Jesus healed the lame and the paralysed and raised the dead, as Asclepius had done. The heroic deeds of Asclepius and his mission to help people were well known. John's gospel describes the *philanthropia* of the Father, in sending his Son: 'God loved the world so much that he gave his only Son' (3. 16). As Christ came in the name of his Father, so Asclepius was believed to have been sent into the world by his father, Apollo, in his love for the world.[10]

There was a difference between Christ and Asclepius, however: Jesus not only healed the sick of body and soul, he also helped 'the tax collectors and sinners', while Asclepius rejected the impure, those who did not think 'holy thoughts'. But it was difficult for Christians to find fault with Asclepius. Unlike others in the Classical pantheon, he did not claim to be one of the cosmic elements; he was mortal, not immortal. Like Jesus, he performed no heroic or worldly exploits, he fought no battles, but only helped those in need. Like Christ, his life was blameless.[11]

'Come to me'

In his love, Asclepius invited his patients to come to him, or else he wandered about in search of them. Matthew has Jesus proclaim: 'Come to me, all you who labour and are overburdened, and I will give you rest' (Mt. 11. 28). In the same way, Asclepius is quoted by Epictetus as saying 'Come together, all you who are suffering from gout, headaches, fever, who are lame and blind, and look at me, who is free from every suffering'.[12] Jesus said 'Let the little children come to me, and do not stop them' (Lk. 18. 16). Asclepius, too, had compassion on the young, and showed great love for them.

Both Asclepius and Jesus were understood to be at once human and divine: the son of God, yet born of a mortal woman. Their birth stories were similar in some details, and both rose to heaven through the power of God. However, Jesus was killed by people, while Greeks held that Asclepius was killed by Zeus with a thunderbolt, because he dared to raise people from the dead. As the protector of cosmic harmony, Zeus could not accept this challenge to natural law: mortals could not become immortal.

Jesus acted on behalf of his Father. In John's gospel he says:

> *The Son can do nothing by himself;*
> *he can only do what he sees the Father doing:*
> *and whatever the Father does, the Son does too* (Jn. 5. 19).

Similarly, Asclepius acted as the son of Apollo. Even in Epidaurus, which was considered his birthplace, he acted together with his father. The famous miracles that took place at Epidaurus are recorded on carved columns in the names of both Apollo and Asclepius. As Christ came in the name of his Father, prayers were made to Asclepius 'in the name of your father'. For example, a prayer offered in the second century AD by Diophantus of Sphettus runs: '...So I, Diophantus, pray you, save me, most powerful and blessed one, by healing my painful gout: in the name of your father, to whom I offer earnest prayer...'.[13]

Asclepius the teacher

Like Jesus, Asclepius was not only a healer but also a teacher. Jesus told his followers: 'You must be perfect, just as your heavenly Father is perfect' (Mt. 5. 48). Asclepius, too, followed the highest moral standards, and expected those who came to him to strive for perfection. People washed themselves clean and prepared themselves through rites and ceremonies in order to attain inner purity of heart. St Clement of Alexandria (*c.* 150–*c.* 215) tells us that inscribed above the entrance to the temple of Asclepius at Epidaurus were the words: 'Pure must

161

be those who enter the fragrant temple: purity means to think nothing but holy thoughts'.[14]

After curing the lame man at Bethesda, Jesus told him: 'Now you are well again, be sure not to sin any more, or something worse may happen to you' (Jn. 5. 14). Similarly, after his patients were healed, Asclepius expected them to lead a better life in the future: an inscription in the sanctuary of Asclepius at Lambaesis in north Africa reads: 'Enter a good person, depart a better one' (*Bonus intra, melior exi*).[15] For Asclepius, health and healing were the means to some higher attainment. One of the finest Greek physicians in the Roman empire, Galenus (AD 129–200/216), informs us that older patients were encouraged not only to do physical exercises, but also to stretch their minds through reading and study, through writing poetry and songs. The Greek orator Aelius Aristides (AD 117–81) considered disease to be almost an advantage, because it enabled him to know the greater happiness of being healed.[16]

Christian attitudes to Asclepius

The Greek god of medicine was perhaps the clearest pagan precursor of Christ.[17] When Christianity became the state religion, Christians noted that Asclepius was still revered in secret corners, and libations were still offered to him. Early Christian theologians were divided over whether Asclepius was good or bad. To the purists among them, Asclepius came from the devil; to other theologians, like Clement of Alexandria, Asclepius was a forerunner of Christ, sent to the pagans to prepare them for Christianity. Writing in about AD 150, Justin Martyr, who came from Samaria and worked in Rome, considered Asclepius to come from the devil. In his *Dialogue* he writes: 'And when he [the devil] brings forward Asclepius as the raiser of the dead and healer of other diseases, may I not say that in this matter likewise he has imitated the prophecies about Christ?'[18] St Ambrose (340–97) accepts that Asclepius raised the dead, but reminds his hearers that, unlike Christ, he could not raise himself. He writes: 'To Asclepius let them grant that he revived the dead, provided only that they admit that he himself did not escape being struck dead by lightning'.[19]

Asclepius and Christ in early Christian art

In the early Church, Christ was depicted as another Asclepius, as we find, for example on a third-century Christian sarcophagus in Rome. Indeed, it is difficult to tell which of the two are being represented in early reliefs. Joan Taylor observes:

There are then three types of Jesus: one clad ordinarily, one clad as a philosopher only in a mantle, and one clad as a seated god. Jesus is presented as a seated philosopher in terms of his Gospel activities, but also as Asclepius enthroned; thus Jesus is a kind of incarnated Asclepius. The differences are slight, and ultimately the message of the sarcophagus is one of blending: Christ gloriously enthroned as a divinity is the philosopher-healer Christ, however you want to see him, and all is revealed by reading the Gospels advertised by the scrolls held in the hands.[20]

Taylor addresses the question of the difference between the two mighty figures. A statue of Asclepius at Paneas (later known as Caesarea Philippi, in Upper Galilee) was mistakenly thought to depict Jesus:

The sarcophagus might even beg the question: how would one tell the difference between Christ and Asclepius? ... The likely mistaken identification of the Paneas relief of Asclepius as being Jesus indicates at the very least that people in the early fourth century could imagine Asclepius and Jesus as looking identical.[21]

Healing serpent

Asclepius is often depicted with a serpent, to symbolise his healing power. A marble statuette from Corinth, dating from the third or fourth century AD, portrays Asclepius enthroned, probably feeding his serpent with an egg (Plate 20). It is one of nine statuettes (two of which depict Asclepius) found in a late Roman house, 900 m south of Corinth's *Asclepieion*, in 1999. Traces of red pigment can be seen, decorating the hem of the god's white toga; this served not only as decorative colouring but also as an adhesive for gold leaf.[22] The statue's late date suggests that worship of Asclepius survived well into the Christian era.

In other depictions, Asclepius stands majestically, holding a staff around which a serpent is coiled (Fig. 86). Symbolically, the snake represents pure energy, perhaps because of its sinuous movement. In our culture, we tend to dislike snakes, but ancient peoples saw and used them more than we do. In Egypt, people kept house-snakes to kill rats and mice, much as we keep cats today. The two intertwined snakes of the god Mercury represent integration and healing. This symbol, the *caduceus*, is used by doctors to this day.[23]

A snake coiled around a tree trunk features in various ancient Near Eastern cultures: the tree was a symbol of growth whilst the snake signified fertility. In Israelite mythology, a snake encircled the tree of life in the Garden of Eden. The Book of Genesis depicts the snake coiled round the tree in upright posture, its energy directed towards God. When God cursed the snake in the words 'You shall crawl on your belly and eat dust all the days of your life' (Gen. 3. 14), it became a symbol of negative energy as it crawled in horizontal position, its energy diffused along the ground, no longer focused on God.[24]

FIGURE 86. Asclepius with his healing snake, Epidaurus Museum.

Good and bad serpents reappear in the story of the Israelite runaway slaves trekking through the desert towards their promised land. They became hungry and thirsty and complained to God, who punished them with poisonous snake bites. Moses intervened, and God instructed him to make a bronze serpent coiled round a pole, the symbol of life and healing familiar to ancient Near Eastern peoples. The sick gazed on it and were healed. The story is recounted in the Book of Numbers:

> *The people came and said to Moses, 'We have sinned by speaking against the Lord and against you. Intercede for us with the Lord to save us from these serpents.' Moses interceded for the people, and the Lord answered him, 'Make a metal serpent*

and put it on a pole; if anyone is bitten and looks at it, he shall live.' So Moses
fashioned a bronze serpent and put it on a pole, and if anyone was bitten by a
serpent, they looked at the bronze serpent and lived (Num. 24. 4–9).

Medieval and renaissance artists depicted this dramatic scene.

Christ, the healing serpent

In John's gospel, Jesus used this powerful symbol to describe his own healing death
that would render powerless the poison of sin. Raised high on the tree of the
cross, he would bring life to all who gazed on him. Jesus explains to Nicodemus:

The Son of Man must be lifted up
as Moses lifted up the serpent in the desert,
so that everyone who believes
may have eternal life in him (Jn. 3. 13–15).

According to the gospel, Jesus longed for this to happen, and nearer to his
death, he repeated:

When I am lifted up from the earth
I shall draw all people to myself (Jn. 12. 32–33)

John adds: 'By these words he indicated the kind of death he would die'. In
medieval paintings of the crucifixion, especially those of the Sienese school,
which flourished between the thirteenth and fifteenth centuries, Jesus hangs
in snake-like posture on the cross. In a redemptive movement he absorbs the
negative energy of the world, raising it towards God as positive energy. His action
reverses that of the serpent in the Garden of Eden.[25]

Asclepius heals through his followers

After his death, Jesus continued to heal through the acts of his followers and the
faith of his devotees, and Asclepius was believed to act in a similar way. According
to Greek mythology, like many other heroes, he was taught by the wise centaur,
Cheiron, from whom he learned his healing skills. When Asclepius tried to
restore the dead Hippolytus and other humans to life, Zeus killed him with a
thunderbolt, and he went to the underworld, from where he continued to heal
people. Another myth relates that after his death, Zeus set Asclepius among the
stars, with his healing serpent.

His cult at Epidaurus, some 25 miles south of Corinth, began in the sixth
century BC. In the following century, a series of plagues swept through the cities

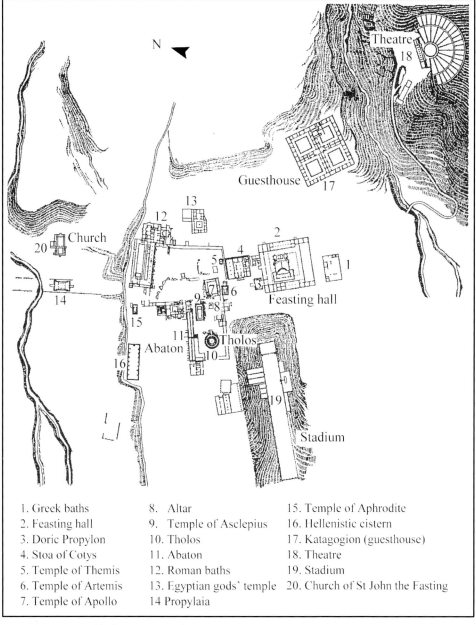

FIGURE 87. Sanctuary of Asclepius at Epidaurus, after a plan at the site.

1. Greek baths
2. Feasting hall
3. Doric Propylon
4. Stoa of Cotys
5. Temple of Themis
6. Temple of Artemis
7. Temple of Apollo

8. Altar
9. Temple of Asclepius
10. Tholos
11. Abaton
12. Roman baths
13. Egyptian gods' temple
14 Propylaia

15. Temple of Aphrodite
16. Hellenistic cistern
17. Katagogion (guesthouse)
18. Theatre
19. Stadium
20. Church of St John the Fasting

of Greece, and it became vital to pray to the god of healing. The sanctuary at Epidaurus expanded and grew in fame, and other great *asclepieia* were built in Athens, Corinth, Sikyon, Cos and Rhodes. It was traditional to hold competitive contests at great sanctuaries; the throngs of pilgrims and spectators brought economic prosperity to Epidaurus, and a lavish building programme was carried out in the fourth and third centuries BC (Fig. 87).[26]

The treatment

The god's cure was based on the faith of the person undergoing treatment. The patient was purified, offered sacrifice, and slept in the precinct of the god, who appeared in a vision or a dream, and gave instructions for the patient's treatment. He might appear in the form of one of the creatures sacred to him: a serpent or a dog. The patient was put on a special diet, and instructed to do physical exercises. Inscriptions with medical prescriptions and accounts of cures are preserved in the museum at Epidaurus; large numbers of surgical instruments were also found; patients paid fees for their treatment.[27]

In ancient times, pilgrims approached the sanctuary from the north; today, however visitors enter the site from the south (Fig. 87). To the right, a path leads up to the theatre, built into the hillside. By the second century BC it could seat over 12,000 people; its perfect acoustic enabled every spectator to enter fully into the therapeutic dramas performed there. Because they enacted the ancient myths, Greek tragedies highlighted perennial problems in family dynamics, and the tensions that patients might experience in their own family life. Returning down the hill from the theatre, one can visit the luxurious guest house or hospice (the *katagogion*) for patients and their companions, built on a smaller rise at the end of the fourth century BC. It is divided into four quadrants, each with forty rooms arranged around a colonnaded court. Sections could be sealed off, perhaps in epidemics, or during the winter season, when there were fewer pilgrims.

The feasting hall

Next, visitors pass an enormous feasting hall (or *hestiatorion*), which former archaeologists mistook for a gymnasium. This was a banquet hall in which ritual meals were eaten in honour of Asclepius. The remains of couches were found at its eastern end, where pilgrims reclined to eat in comfort. There were traces of fires with food residues in the courtyard. Devotees believed that Asclepius was summoned to, and present at, the holy meal. As they ate the sacred food offered in sacrifice to Asclepius, they received his divine power. This was an experience similar, perhaps, to the sacred meal of the Christian eucharist.

167

FIGURE 88. Fountain (right) adjoining the eastern wall of the feasting hall, Epidaurus.

The feasting hall had a monumental entrance which, in the second century AD, was converted into a temple to honour Hygeia, goddess of healing, who was held to be a daughter of Asclepius. A white marble fountain adjoins the eastern wall of the banquet hall (Fig. 88); it dates from the third to the second centuries BC. As we have seen, washing was an important prelude to the meal, for physical cleanliness was seen as an expression of ritual purity.

In a valley to the west of the banquet hall at Epidaurus is the stadium, built in the fifth century BC. Here, games were performed in honour of the god. Nearby are what is thought to have been a wrestling school and accommodation for athletes.

FIGURE 89. Reconstruction of the sanctuary of Asclepius, Epidaurus, after E. Spatharis.

One next enters the spacious sanctuary area (Fig. 89), with a magnificent temple of Asclepius at its centre. It was built in 380–375 BC by the architect Theodotus, and housed a statue of the god constructed of gold and ivory. To the south, a paved way led to a great open-air altar.

The tomb of Asclepius

To the west was the *Tholos*, whose name means 'circular building' – it is the largest such building from early times. It was constructed a little earlier than the temple, in 365–335 BC, and is designed as three concentric circular courts separated by colonnades. Beneath was an underground crypt, following the same plan, which may be 200 years earlier than the rest of the building. Here, pilgrims walked from one circle to another, as in a labyrinth: beside the low doors between the circles, stone blocks are so positioned that in order to travel from the outside to the centre, one must complete the whole circuit three times. At the centre may have been what was believed to be the tomb of Asclepius. A single white stone block at the centre of the building could be removed to allow entry to the crypt.[28] The crypt was intended to imitate the dark corridors of the underworld, where pilgrims could encounter Asclepius, who now lived in Hades, from where he continued to heal the sick. Above, on the ground floor, there was an altar, and the roof was beautifully decorated with elegant floral designs. These lovely carvings make the *Tholos* one of the most important buildings of the late Classical period.

The sacred dormitory

Along the northern perimeter of the sanctuary was a long, covered portico named the *Abaton* (Fig. 90). Its name means 'Forbidden': no one was allowed to enter it except the sick and those who healed them. It served as the hospital's sacred dormitory; nearby was a bath suite and a library. The *Abaton* was the place in which patients were cured: they encountered Asclepius during the night, often through a dream. Other gods healed the sick in a similar way: in the sanctuary at Oropos, 25 miles north-north-east of Athens, in the hills above the sea, a relief depicts the god Amphiaraos appearing in a dream to a youth with an injured shoulder, while an attendant observes a snake healing the young man (Fig. 91).

Angeliki Charitonidou has reconstructed what happened at Epidauros:

The priests led the invalid to the Abaton ... This was the building in which he would spend the night of great expectation. Within its hallowed halls, illuminated initially with the subdued mysterious light emitted by the sacred oil lamps, overcome with religious desire, with an inflamed imagination and anxiety over the outcome,

Above: FIGURE 90. The *Abaton*, where patients were cured, Epidaurus.

Left: FIGURE 91. In Oropos sanctuary, a snake heals the shoulder of a youth (L), who dreams that the god Amphiaraos cures him (R).

the invalid surrendered his body to sleep. The priests withdrew, leaving the halls in darkness. The god appeared in a dream and performed the miracle. The next morning the sick person awoke, cured.[29]

The *Abaton* was a long, narrow building, constructed in two phases, in response to the sanctuary's growing fame. In the early fourth century BC, the first architect designed it as a single storey building; in the late fourth century, the architect of the second phase took advantage of the gradient of the hillside, and added a two-storey wing onto its western end, thus doubling its length. Because of the difference in height between the two sections, a monumental staircase was built, to link the two (Fig. 90).

The sacred well of Asclepius was incorporated into the north-east corner of the *Abaton*; behind the building was a great wall. On the ground floor of the two-storey west wing there were stone couches where patients slept, in order to encounter the god. High stone screens prevented outsiders from observing the patients. First the sick purified themselves with water from the holy well. They might read accounts of other cures, inscribed on pillars inside the building. Their sleep symbolised the death of the sick body. Recent excavations have shown that the same procedure was followed close to the well in smaller and lighter buildings, as early as the sixth century BC.[30]

Types of cures

An offering survives, donated perhaps in 9 or 8 BC by Cutius, King of the Alpine Gauls, in gratitude for the cure of his deafness (Fig. 92). This is a plaster copy of a marble plaque that was once gilded; the original can be seen in the National Museum, Athens.[31] The sculptor has depicted the royal pair of ears, above the grateful king's inscription; the tablet was found in the early *Abaton*. People with a wide range of illnesses came to the sanctuary, including the blind and the dumb, the lame and the paralysed, soldiers with war wounds and sterile women. About seventy written accounts of cures survive on the *stelai*,

FIGURE 92. Tablet erected by the king of the Alpine Gauls, in gratitude for the cure of his deafness, Epidaurus Museum.

or columns containing votive inscriptions: these provide valuable information about how early peoples understood healing. In one example, a dumb child is given speech:

> *A small dumb child came to the sanctuary to beseech the god to give him a voice. After performing all the preliminary sacrifices and rites, the pyrphoros, the servant of the temple, turned to the father of the child and asked him 'Do you promise to pay the medical fees within one year if your child is cured?' 'I promise', replied the child suddenly.*[32]

Most invalids were cured while they slept:

> *Pandharos of Thessaly had blemishes on his forehead. While sleeping in the* Abaton
> *he had a vision. The god wound a band around his brow. He ordered him to come*
> *out of the* Abaton, *to remove the band and dedicate it in the temple. At daybreak*
> *he arose from his bed and removed the band. His forehead was completely clear.*
> *The blemishes were stuck to the band. Then he offered it to the temple.*[33]

The sanctuary suffered a number of disasters during the early years of Roman
rule, but revived under the emperors, especially in the third and fourth centuries
AD. The *Abaton* was incorporated into the late Roman sanctuary, which included
the most important buildings. By this time, accounts of cures are more detailed,
and include advice about diet and exercise, which the priests and doctors
offered on the god's behalf. In the second century AD, a man named Apellas,
who suffered from indigestion and chronic anxiety about his health, recorded
his cure on a votive plaque. He describes his treatment; he might have received
similar advice today.

> *...When I reached the sanctuary, [the god, through the person of the doctor]*
> *instructed me to cover my head because it was raining; to eat bread, cheese, celery*
> *and lettuce; to bathe unaided by a servant, to exercise in the gymnasium, to drink*
> *lemon juice, to go for walks. Finally the god ordered me to write all this on a stone.*
> *I left the sanctuary healthy, thankful to the god.*[34]

A Christian church

In AD 395 the sanctuary was destroyed by incursions of Goths, and in AD 426,
the Christian emperor Theodosius II gave orders for the ceremonial entrance
gates of the *propylaia* to be closed. A Christian basilica was built on the edge of
the sanctuary, with material taken from earlier ruined buildings (Plate 21, Figs
93 and 94). The church was dedicated to St John Nestikos (which means 'the
Fasting'); it has an apse, with a *synthronon*, or raised seats for the clergy round the
altar. Most apses are semi-circular but this one, unusually, is horseshoe-shaped.[35]
One of the small side chambers close to the sanctuary may have been a *diakónikon*,
in which vestments or liturgical books could be stored.[36] A room with a richly
patterned mosaic floor on the north side of the sanctuary is considered to have
been a baptistery. There is a *solea*, or central paved walkway, extending down the
nave of the church, and a *narthex* at the west end, where the people could gather
before entering the church.[37]

An *atrium*, or courtyard surrounded by a covered colonnade, adjoins its
western wall at a slight angle; a small hollow at its centre suggests a fountain.[38]

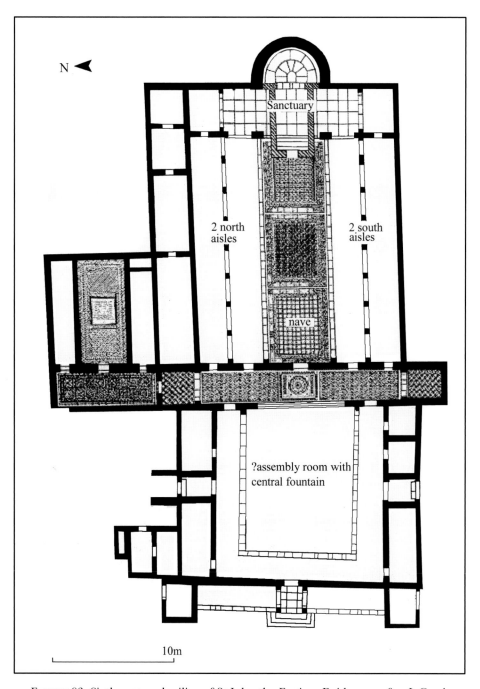

N ◀

Sanctuary

2 north
aisles

2 south
aisles

nave

?assembly room with
central fountain

10m

FIGURE 93. Sixth-century basilica of St John the Fasting, Epidaurus, after J. Cami.

FIGURE 94. View from the altar of the basilica, looking into the nave, Epidaurus.

It could have provided an assembly space for baptismal candidates. Among the 130 basilicas known in the Peloponnese, that of Epidaurus is one of only eleven that appears to have a baptistery inside its church.[39] However there is no evidence of a baptismal pool, like that at the Kraneion basilica (Fig. 28, Chapter 4) in Corinth. The church was lavishly decorated with mosaics featuring a range of geometric patterns in the nave, the *narthex* and the *atrium*, as well as the possible baptistery. Parapet screens survive from the church, and considerable architectural fragments.[40] Behind the apse of the church, the land rises steeply towards the hills that surround the area. As Christians approached Epidaurus along the old sacred way, the church now lay to the left of the impressive ruined *propylaia*. The position of the new basilica conveyed that it was no longer necessary to visit the pagan sanctuary, for the Christian one rendered it obsolete.

Monks learn from Asclepius

The healing cult of Asclepius embodied a profound and highly developed approach to healing, which Christians could not ignore. Monks were familiar with classical authors, and the teachings of Asclepius were not forgotten. A number of early monasteries developed healing shrines, sometimes connected with the cult of their own founding saint. Since monasteries were centres of learning, monks also studied pre-Christian medical texts, and were able to combine surgical skills with a detailed knowledge of herbal medicine. The tradition and techniques developed at Epidaurus influenced Christian practice at monasteries as far apart as that of Whithorn in south-west Scotland and, later, at that of Hosios Loukas, east of Delphi.

Whithorn's healing shrine

Perhaps as early as the sixth century, the monastery of St Martin at Whithorn in Galloway developed as a healing shrine that employed significant elements of the healing methods practised at Epidaurus. The early bishop, Ninian, was at the centre of the shrine's healing cult, and miracles were worked through his intercession. The name Ninian is now thought to be a scribal error for Uinniau; it is likely to refer to St Finnian of Movilla (d. 579), a Briton who also worked in Ireland, where Columba was his disciple. While Finnian may have been sent as a bishop to the church of Whithorn, he is unlikely to have founded it. Whithorn was a secular settlement which had developed from a late Roman trading station, where some people may already have been Christians.[41]

A monastery was established at Whithorn around AD 500. A group of grave stones dating from this time, found at the nearby monastic settlements of Kirkmadrine and Curghie appear to commemorate a group of immigrant clerics from Gaul, who introduced the cult of St Martin to Galloway. Excavations of the monastery at Whithorn during the same period show continental influence through the presence of imported artefacts, new technologies, exotic plants and a therapeutic regime originating in the classical world.[42]

From the sixth century, Whithorn's monks grew a sophisticated range of medicinal herbs for curing a wide range of diseases: human faeces in an early sixth-century latrine contained seeds, including a large quantity of coriander, together with dill, neither species being native to Britain. They are of Mediterranean origin, and were found together with a sherd of an amphora of Bi type pottery, which would have been imported from mainland Europe. The coriander and dill may have been used to flavour food, but both were also used medicinally. Seeds of other healing herbs were found in the faeces: black mustard, chickweed and dog rose seeds.[43]

Another early pit contained elder seeds, woundwort, hemlock and nettle, all valued for their healing properties. Elder was used for colds, influenza and rheumatism; woundwort was made into ointments and compresses for wounds, and was also taken internally as an infusion for cramps, joint pains, diarrhoea and dysentery. Hemlock is a powerful sedative, while nettles have astringent, diuretic and tonic properties, and are also prescribed for eczema and haemorrhage. The herbs in this second pit, found together with fragments of wood bark, roots and stems, may be the remains of compresses for wounds or inflammations.[44]

The Life of Ninian

Two early texts were written at Whithorn: a Latin Life of Ninian in verse, *Miracula Nynie Episcopi*, probably written in the late eighth century, and an acrostic poem, *Hymnus Sancti Nynie Episcopi*. Both of these were sent to the Northumbrian scholar Alcuin (735–804) at Charlemagne's court in Aachen. Alcuin thanked the community, and sent back a silk veil for the shrine at Whithorn. He referred to its reputation for healing, with a sideways stab at Asclepius: '... And is the blessed Martin himself, worshipper of the true God, to be worshipped less in the kingdom of Christ than the false Asclepius has power for the pagans?'[45]

The two poems are preserved at Bamberg, in Germany. They are among the sources for a Latin prose Life, *Vita Niniani*, probably written by Aelred, abbot of Rievaulx, between 1154 and 1160. At this time, Whithorn belonged to Aelred's own diocese of York. The two *Lives* record miracles worked by Ninian for those who came to his shrine. Often Ninian appeared to them during the night, as Asclepius had done at Epidaurus. There are other points of similarity: in *The miracle of the presbyter accused of unchastity* (*Miracula* 6; *Vita* 5), a young child suddenly speaks, as did the dumb child in the cure at Epidaurus described earlier.

A priest was wrongfully accused of fathering a child. In Aelred's version of the story, we read:

> ... *The bold woman, casting aside all shame, thrust the child in the face of the presbyter, and shouted in the ears of all the congregation that he was the father of the child ... But the saint, commanding the people to keep quiet, ordered the newborn child to be brought to him... He said: 'Hear, O child, in the name of Jesus Christ, say out before this people if this presbyter begot you.'... Accordingly, from the infant body a manly voice was heard... Stretching out his hand, and pointing out his real father among the people: 'This,' said he, 'is my father'...*[46]

Cures at the shrine

Both the *Miracula* and the *Vita* describe cures at Ninian's shrine. The earlier work focuses on Ninian's tomb, and gives clear descriptions of the symptoms of infantile paralysis, elephantiasic leprosy and blindness, suggesting that the stories are based on case histories prepared by a trained observer, perhaps a doctor. They appear to be factual accounts of a healing centre. The cure of the boy Pethgils involved a night vigil, like those at Epidaurus. The boy was brought to the church by his parents after a long illness and carried to the 'sacred tomb in the chapel'. His parents prayed for a cure and then, as night fell, left the boy lying at the tomb. Bishop Ninian entered at midnight and touched the boy's head, releasing a stream of healing energy that corrected his misaligned feet and removed the numbness from his body.[47]

A blind woman named Desuit was cured in a similar way. She was brought to the church by her parents after prolonged suffering. She arrived,

> *... weighed down by her long sleep at the place where the saint's body is held prisoner by the hollowed out interior of the rock, prostrated herself... and prayed that the long night should be brightened, and then ... with her whole body flung down, she pressed against the earth with her forehead and lay in the hollowed out cave. She jumped up and dazzling light filled her eyes as darkness fled away... [and began] to cross on foot the famous shrine.*[48]

Promotion of the monastery's healing cult is a primary aim of the *Miracula*. In chapter 4 the author writes with enthusiasm:

> *This is the house of the Lord, which many are eager to visit, for many who have been afflicted with a longstanding disease hurry there. They eagerly accept the ready gift of health-bringing healing, and they grow strong in all their limbs by the power of the saint.*[49]

Medical care

Divine intervention was probably supported by appropriate medical care. By the time the *Miracula* came to be written, the monastery buildings may have included an infirmary for the sick and accommodation for their families and servants. In one Northumbrian deposit, a possible surgeon's knife was found. The presence of more than sixty eighth- and ninth-century coins suggest offerings for healing from visitors used to cash transactions, who had the means to pay.[50] Some fine sculptured crosses survive from the early monastery. The photograph (Fig. 95) shows the site of the wooden Northumbrian church, dating from around AD 750. Beyond, wooden posts indicate the position of two timber halls, which

FIGURE 95. Site of the Northumbrian monastery church, Whithorn, Galloway.

would have had bowed walls and curved, ridged roofs. They were part of a large monastic complex.

Sleeping at Ninian's tomb

The miraculous cures are focused on Ninian's tomb, particularly when visited at night, unlike most cures at saints' shrines during this period, which were effected through contact with a saint's bones, or through touching his or her clothes, or dust from the grave, or water in which the bones had been washed. The miracles at Whithorn reflect a different therapeutic tradition, rooted in classical medicine, and especially in the cult of Asclepius, which was adapted by the early Church and used in the Mediterranean world. This appears to have been introduced to Whithorn as early as the sixth century and to have continued for some three hundred years.

The custom of sleeping at a holy place in order to receive a divine revelation was not, of course, a phenomenon unique to Epidaurus and Whithorn, but was practised widely in the ancient world. In the Old Testament, the child Samuel slept in the temple and was woken three times by the voice of God, who then gave him his prophetic call (1 Sam. 3. 1–9). In Christian Britain, Whithorn was not alone in its encouragement of the sick to spend the night at the saint's shrine in order to receive healing. At hundreds of holy wells across Ireland and mainland Britain, the sick came to wash in the healing water and sleep beside the well or within its adjacent chapel, in order to be cured. This pre-Christian practice continued into the late medieval period and well beyond. The tradition was rooted in a widespread and very ancient layer of belief, of which Epidaurus was, perhaps, the most highly developed expression.

Ligourio

We are fortunate to be able to trace the development of Whithorn's monastic healing cult in Celtic and, later, Northumbrian times; there is no evidence of similar developments at Epidaurus. The earliest complete Byzantine building in the district is the church of St John the Almoner, in the small town of Ligourio, a few miles west of Epidaurus. Since there is a deep well in the adjoining courtyard, east of the church, this was probably a monastic site. The present building (Plate 22) was perhaps the main church, or *katholikon*, of the monastery: it dates from the eleventh and twelfth centuries, and was largely constructed from recycled columns and other stone taken from the *Asclepieion* and from other buildings at Epidaurus.[51] This gives it an unusual appearance, as if it were built of spare parts.

Its dedicatory inscription survives on the pillar to the right of the original entrance, which faces north. It reads in translation:

> *Lord, help your servant Theophylactos, a builder from the island of Kes.*[52]

It is rare to find an architect's name recorded. This entrance was later blocked up, and replaced by one facing west. The inner walls of the church are richly decorated with murals. Perhaps the power of the cult of Asclepius was so strong in this region that no local monastic community would have dared to employ the healing skills which had been exercised for so long in the name of Asclepius.

Osios Loukas

Some thirty miles north of Corinth on the Greek mainland, Osios Loukas (896–953), or 'the venerable Luke', whom we encountered briefly at the end of Chapter 6, was regarded as a powerful healer in the tradition of Asclepius. A *Life of Osios Loukas* was written a generation after his death by a monk using information from Luke's sister, Kale, and from monks who had known him. Luke is described as another Christ, healing the blind and the lame, the paralysed and the possessed. He is presented as 'the new Luke',[53] who imitates Luke, the evangelist and physician. As we find in Luke's compassionate gospel, many women were healed by the new Luke, who was 'exceedingly inclined to sympathy'.[54] His biography is followed by fifteen detailed accounts of cures at his shrine in Hosios Loukas, where Luke's *Life* was read aloud each year on his feast day.

Luke became a monk at fourteen; he ran away from home, first to Thessaly and then to a monastery in Athens. As we have seen, when he was twenty-one, a stylite in Zemena (or Gimenes), west of Sikyon, invited Luke to become his disciple; this suggests that they had already met, and that the stylite recognised the young man's aptitude as a monk. Luke served the pilgrims who visited the stylite on his pillar for ten years. During the Bulgarian invasions, Luke lived as a hermit in various places, and became known for his gifts of wisdom and healing. The author of Luke's *Life* valued both pagan and Christian wisdom, and alludes to various ancient Greek writers including Homer and Plutarch;[55] he employs Aristotle's lofty and complex literary style. He recounts how Luke consults a pagan, 'Theophylaktos the Wise, a teacher of pagan wisdom, who nevertheless transmitted virtue by his deeds to lovers of the good. [Luke] sent to him seeking to learn what he should do …' With equal respect, the pagan advised Luke to follow the teaching of Arsenios, a Christian Desert Father: 'Flee, keep silence, be tranquil'.[56]

For the last seven years of his life, Luke lived in the monastery that is now named after him, at the foot of Mt Helikon, thirty miles east of Delphi, where his tomb became the focus of his healing cult, in a manner resembling the supposed tomb of Asclepius. Luke's tenth-century walled monastery is situated near the town of Distomo, in Boeotia, central Greece. The Hosios Loukas church is the oldest at the site, dating from the tenth century; a larger church, or *Katholikon*, dates from the early eleventh century. The *Katholikon* is the earliest extant domed octagonal church in Greece, with eight piers, or upright supports, arranged around the perimeter of the nave.

Its main shrine is the tomb of St Luke: this was originally in the crypt beneath the dome of the *Katholikon*, but was later placed at the juncture of the two churches. The monastery was famed throughout Byzantium for its lavish decoration. The burial crypt beneath the *Katholikon* includes a sanctuary with an altar and a chancel barrier – these suggest that the liturgy may have been celebrated here as part of the burial services of abbots, or of ceremonies relating to the healing cult of Saint Luke.[57] Here, local Christians celebrate the springtime feast of St Osios Loukas (Plates 23 and 24) on the date of his death, or birthday into heaven, 7 February 953.

Luke's healing ministry

Luke's monastery is portrayed as a new Epidaurus: when the sick visit his shrine, he often comes to them in a dream. He appears in a vision to a possessed man and inserts a hook, a medical instrument, into his throat to draw out the evil spirit.[58] The title of the shrine attendant, *neokoros*, is a term also used for servants at the sanctuary of Asclepius.[59] As the sick approached the tomb of Asclepius in the *Tholos* at Epidaurus, so they sat beside Luke's tomb or prostrated before it.[60] They slept all night at his tomb,[61] as pilgrims slept in the *Abaton* at Epidaurus, where the god might appear to them in a dream as a handsome youth. In a manner similar to practices at Epidaurus, when the young Luke struggles against sexual temptation, 'in a dream he saw an angel dressed as a young man. In his hand was the hook which he let down inside Luke through his mouth'.[62]

After his death, the sick were anointed with a perfumed liquid 'like myrrh' (*myron*) that flowed from Luke's tomb, or with oil from the lamp hanging above it, or they might drink either liquid.[63] Pilgrims hoping for a cure slept in both the *Katholikon* and the crypt, close to Luke's tomb; after his death, all the miracles associated with him involved the healing power of his tomb. Some of those who sought healing stayed for periods of up to six days beside the tomb or in nearby rooms. A cure could be immediate, or it might require several visits to the tomb, or even take up to six months.[64] Luke healed a monk named Gregorios in the guise of a physician: 'He appeared in a dream in the garb of a doctor and seemed to put cauterizers upon his stomach and said, "Go away, humble Gregorios, in health, for no longer will you suffer pain in your stomach when you eat!" And this actually happened, as he [Gregorios] who is still alive attests'.[65] It is remarkable that both Luke and his biographer should situate his *therapeia*, or ministry of healing, not only in a gospel context but also within pre-Christian healing practice. With his unique blend of wisdom and sympathy, Luke achieved a fusion of the healing traditions of both Asclepius and Christ; his shrine became a new Epidaurus, translated into Christian terms.

What were early churches like?

Although the foundations of a number of churches in southern Greece still survive, there are few sites where the walls or interior furnishings of an early basilica can still be seen. In order to imagine standing inside an early Greek church, one must travel north to the plain of Thessaly, where the rocky pinnacles of the Meteora were colonised by monks and hermits. This was where Osios Loukas first learned holiness as a teenager. At the foot of the Meteora, on the edge of the town of Kalambaka, one can visit the church of the Dormition, or 'Falling Asleep' of the Virgin Mary, which commemorates her death and her assumption into heaven. From the ninth century, it was a cathedral, and the surviving church dates from the eleventh century. It is, however, an early Christian site: 25 cm below the present sanctuary, part of a mosaic floor depicting peacocks and pomegranates can be seen; it has been dated to the fifth century.[66]

Around the eastern wall of the sanctuary, one can still see the seventh-century *synthronon*: four semi-circular tiers of seats, with the bishop's throne at their centre. Since the throne is built on the highest tier, the bishop could see the entire congregation, for at this time, there would have been no *iconostasis*, or screen decorated with icons, to impede his view. The altar in the sanctuary is a stone slab supported by a pillar, above which a *kiborion*, or canopy, is supported on four columns. Their simple capitals are decorated with four vine leaves, one on each side, and a grape cluster at each corner; these motifs are commonly found in seventh-century churches.[67]

Even more impressive is the

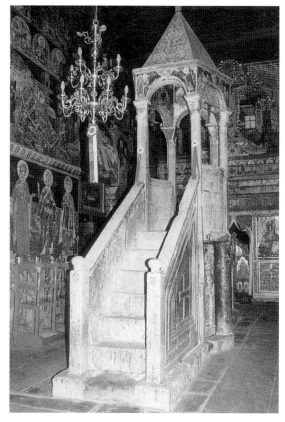

FIGURE 96. The *ambo*, or pulpit, Church of the Dormition, Kalambaka, Thessaly.

large seventh-century *ambo*, or pulpit, at the centre of the nave (Fig. 96), also supported by pillars. The bishop could mount and descend the pulpit by two flights of stairs, facing east and west. The *ambo* has been restored, and a painted canopy was added in 1669.[68] In the eleventh century, such a pulpit would have been anachronistic, since by then, a much smaller lectern was commonly in use. The seventh-century basilica was evidently larger and wealthier than its eleventh-century successor on the same site. The interior of the church today is reminiscent of a doll's house, whose furniture is twice the size required for the space. Sitting in the church at Kalambaka, it is possible to imagine these impressive church furnishings adorning a basilica in Corinth or Kenchreai.

We have now examined what archaeology can tell us about the early Church in southern Greece. This has been a very selective account, because there are a great number of early Christian sites in such an extensive region. Only a small proportion of them have so far been thoroughly investigated. The study of archaeology and the early Church in Greece is a relatively young discipline, and it is developing year by year. It is to be hoped that as archaeologists increasingly focus on post-Classical Greece, there will be many more exciting early Christian discoveries in southern Greece.

Notes

1   'A pool called Beth-zatha: archaeological evidence and the New Testament', in *Holy Land* (Jerusalem: Franciscan Printing Press, Summer 1993), p. 81.

2   *Ibid*, p. 80.

3   J. Murphy-O'Connor, *The Holy Land: An Archaeological Guide from Earliest Times to 1700* (Oxford: Oxford University Press, 1980), p. 31.

4   'A pool called Beth-zatha', p. 82.

5   *Ibid.*

6   The White Fathers, *Bethesda: St Anne* (St Anne's Church, Jerusalem: the White Fathers. n.d.).

7   D. Pringle, *The Churches of the Crusader Kingdom of Jerusalem. A Corpus*, vol. 3, *The city of Jerusalem* (Cambridge: Cambridge University Press, 2007), pp. 142–56.

8   *Ibid.*

9   A. Charitonidou, *Epidauros: The Sanctuary of Asclepius and the Museum* (Athens: Clio Editions, 1978), pp. 9, 10.

10   E. and L. Edelstein, *Asclepius: A Collation and Interpretation of the Testimonies*, vol. 2 (Baltimore: Johns Hopkins Press, 1945), pp. 133–5.

11   *Ibid*, pp. 134–6.

12   Epictetus, *Dissertationes* 4. 8, 28–9, in E. and L. Edelstein, *Asclepius: A Collation and Interpretation of the Testimonies,* vol. 1, (Baltimore: Johns Hopkins Press, 1945), p. 136.

13   Edelstein, *Asclepius*, vol. 1, Testimony 428, p. 242.

14   Clement of Alexandria, *Stromateis* 5. 13, in Edelstein, *Asclepius*, vol. 1, Testimony 336, p. 177.

15   Edelstein, *Asclepius*, vol. 1, Testimony 319, p. 164.

16   Galenus, *De Sanitate Tuenda* 1. 8. 19–21, in Edelstein, *Asclepius*, vol. 1, Testimony 413; Aristides, *Oratio* 23. 15–18, in Edelstein, *Asclepius*, vol. 1, Testimony 402, pp. 202–3.

17   Parallel figures include Apollonius of Tyana (AD *c.* 15–*c.* 100), a philosopher born in Cappadocia, who also worked miracles.

18   Justin, *Dialogus* 69. 3, in Edelstein, *Asclepius*, vol. 1, Testimony 95, p. 49.

19   Ambrose, *De Virginibus* 3. 176–7, in Edelstein, *Asclepius*, vol. 1, Testimony 113, p. 56.

20   J. Taylor, *What Did Jesus Look Like?* (London/New York: Bloomsbury, T & T Clark, 2018), pp. 38–42, 132–136, at p. 136.

21   *Ibid.*

22   L.M. Stirling, 'Pagan statuettes in late antique Corinth: sculpture from the Panayia Domus', in *Hesperia*, vol. 77 (2008), pp. 89–161, at pp. 91, 97–101.

23   E. Rees, *Christian Symbols, Ancient Roots* (London: Jessica Kingsley, 1992), p. 52.

24   *Ibid*, p. 54.

25   J.E. Cirlot, *A Dictionary of Symbols* (London: Routledge, 1990), pp. 288–9.

26   E. Apatharis and K. Petropoulou, transl. W. Phelps, *Ancient Corinth, Nauplion, Tiryns, Mycenae, Epidaurus* (Athens: Olympic Color, n.d.), ch. 5 'The Cult of Asclepius at Epidaurus'.

27   *Ibid.*

28   Charitonidou, *Epidauros*, p. 34.
29   Charitonidou, *Epidauros*, p. 13.
30   Information at the site.
31   The National Museum of Athens, exhibit no. 1428.
32   Charitonidou, *Epidauros*, p. 14.
33   *Ibid.*
34   *Ibid*, p. 15.
35   R. Sweetman, 'The Christianization of the Peloponnese: the topography and function of late antique churches', in *Journal of Late Antiquity*, vol. 3, no. 2, Fall 2010, p. 217.
36   *Ibid*, p. 233.
37   W. Caraher, *Church, Society and the Sacred in Early Christian Greece*, PhD diss., Ohio State University (2003), appendix, p. 381; plan on p. 296.
38   *Ibid.*
39   Sweetman, 'The Christianization of the Peloponnese', pp. 235–6.
40   Caraher, *Church, Society and the Sacred*, appendix, p. 381
41   E. Rees, *Celtic Saints of Scotland* (Stroud: Fonthill, 2017) p. 51.
42   P. Hill, *Whithorn and St Ninian: The Excavation of a Monastic Town 1984-91* (Stroud: Sutton Publishing, 1997), p. 12.
43   *Ibid*, p. 124
44   *Ibid*, p. 128.
45   *Aut ipse beatus Martinus, verus Dei cultor, in Christiano imperio minus venerari fas est, quam Scolapius falsator in paganorum potestate habuit?* Alcuin, *Epistolae*, 245.
46   Aelred, Abbot of Rievaulx, *Saint Ninian*, ed. I. MacDonald (Edinburgh: Floris Books, 1993), pp. 34–7.
47   P. Hill, *Whithorn and St Ninian*, p. 19.
48   *Ibid.*
49   J. and W. MacQueen, *St Nynia. With a translation of the* Miracula Nynie episcope *and the* Vita Niniani (Edinburgh: Birlinn, 2005), *Miracula*, ch. 4.
50   P. Hill, *Whithorn and St Ninian*, pp. 20, 47.
51   Information at the site.
52   *Ibid.* 'Kes' is Kos, to the north of Rhodes, near the Turkish mainland.
53   C. and R. Connor, *The Life and Miracles of Saint Luke of Steiris: text, translation and commentary* (Brookline, MAS: Hellenic College Press, 1994), 'Life of Osios Loukas', ch. 66, p. 111.
54   *Ibid*, ch. 59, p. 97.
55   *Ibid*, ch. 8. p. 17; ch. 17. p. 27.
56   *Ibid*, ch. 47, p. 79.
57   C.L. Connor, *Art and miracles in medieval Byzantium: The crypt at Hosios Loukas and its frescoes* (Princeton, NJ: Princeton University Press, 1991), pp. 3–9, 93–7.
58   Connor, *The Life and Miracles of Saint Luke of Steiris*, ch. 76, p. 127.
59   *Ibid*, ch. 69, p. 115.
60   *Ibid*, ch. 70, p. 117; ch. 72, p. 121.
61   *Ibid*, ch. 82, p. 135.
62   *Ibid*, ch. 29, p. 45.
63   *Ibid*, ch. 69, pp. 113–7.
64   *Ibid*, ch. 81, p. 135.
65   *Ibid*, ch. 57, p. 91.
66   I.S. Pispa, *The Church of the Dormition in Kalambaka* (Kalambaka: Pispa, 1992), pp. 9, 12.
67   *Ibid*, p. 25.
68   *Ibid*, p. 22.

INDEX

References in *italics* are pages with illustrations

PLATE 1. West wall of tomb 4, decorated with murals, Kenchreai cemetery.

PLATE 2. View looking north across the submerged ruins of Kenchreai harbour. The rising sun is reflected on the hull of an upturned boat.

PLATE 3. Detail from a glass panel found at Kenchreai, depicting a colonnaded building (Panel VI, 4B, Isthmia Museum). Courtesy of Joseph L. Rife.

PLATE 4. View from Kenchreai basilica, looking east across the possible *atrium* or assembly room, formerly considered a temple of Isis.

PLATE 5. Kenchreai basilica facing south: the nave (left) and southern aisles (right).

PLATE 6. Northern end of the paved road beside the Corinth Canal.

PLATE 7. Temple of Poseidon, Isthmia, with the sea in the background.

PLATE 8. Feasting cave for worshippers, outside the theatre, Isthmia, fifth century BC.

PLATE 9. Red marble *agape* table from the Lechaion Road, in the Archaeological Museum, Corinth (MF-13302).

PLATE 10. The Peirene Fountain, Corinth, its façade dating from the second century AD.

PLATE 11. View looking east towards the sanctuary of Lechaion basilica; fallen columns once flanked the nave.

PLATE 12. Baptistery complex, Lechaion basilica, viewed from the west.

PLATE 13. Temple of Hercules, among vineyards below the ancient town of Kleonai.

PLATE 14. Model of Nemea's basilica in about AD 500 (Nemea Museum).

PLATE 15. Semi-circular apse of Nemea's basilica, facing east.

PLATE 16. Circular baptismal pool (foreground), with the ruined temple of Zeus behind, Nemea.

PLATE 17. View over the baths towards the Temple of the Olympian Zeus, Athens.

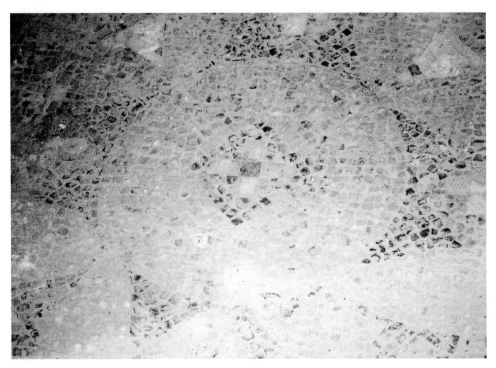

PLATE 18. Part of the mosaic floor of the basilica beneath the Russian Church: concentric patterns surround a cross.

PLATE 19. View across the grottos and pools to the Crusader church of St Anne, Bethesda, Jerusalem.

PLATE 20. Statuette of Asclepius, Archaeological Museum, Corinth (S-1999-8). Photo by Petros Dellatolas. Courtesy of the American School of Classical Studies at Athens, Corinth Excavations.

PLATE 21. Altar in the sanctuary of the basilica, Epidaurus.

PLATE 22. Monastery church, Ligourio, near Epidaurus.

PLATE 23. Christians come to pray at the monastery of Hosios Loukas on his feast day.

PLATE 24. A young Orthodox woman prays at the hermit's shrine, Hosios Loukas.